Also by John Grant Ross

FORMOSAN ODYSSEY: TAIWAN, PAST AND PRESENT

YOU DON'T KNOW CHINA

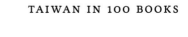

TAIWAN IN 100 BOOKS

Taiwan in 100 Books

John Grant Ross

A Camphor Press book

Published by Camphor Press Ltd
83 Ducie Street, Manchester, M1 2JQ
United Kingdom

www.camphorpress.com

ISBN   978-1-78869-199-4 (paperback)
          978-1-78869-200-7 (hardcover)

The moral right of the author has been asserted.

Set in 11 pt Linux Libertine

Contents

9. Taiwan after Dark   191

10. Rich and Free   211

The Food of Taiwan: Recipes from the Beautiful Island, by Cathy Erway

A Culinary History of Taipei: Beyond Pork and Ponlai, by Steven Crook & Katy Hui-wen Hung

Taiwan: A Travel Guide for Vegans, by Jessie Duffield

An American Teacher in Taiwan, by Ken Berglund

A Taipei Mutt, by Eric Mader

A Far Corner: Life and Art with the Open Circle Tribe, by Scott Ezell

Welcome Home, Master: Covering East Asia in the Twilight of Old Media, by J.D. Adams

Black Island, by J. Michael Cole

Convergence or Conflict in the Taiwan Strait: The Illusion of Peace?, by J. Michael Cole

The Chinese Invasion Threat: Taiwan's Defense and American Strategy in Asia, by Ian Easton

Taiwanese Feet: My Walk Around Taiwan, by John Groot

Formosa Moon, by Joshua Samuel Brown & Stephanie Huffman

Bibliography

Introduction

TAIWAN'S cultural diversity, natural riches, and its complicated history and continuing geopolitical importance make it a gold-mine of potential book material. Sadly, the country's obscurity – both as a travel destination and as a success story of a poor, authoritarian state becoming a modern, prosperous democracy – is matched by a dearth of English-language books. Although relatively few have been written about Taiwan, the bigger problem is availability: works that should be must-read classics are all too often out of print and long forgotten; numerous others – self-published ones chief among them – die silent deaths upon publication; meanwhile, expensive academic tomes gather dust in a handful of specialist libraries; and even the best selling of Taiwan books written for the general reader are usually considered too niche to be stocked in bookstores.

It was these twin frustrations – the relative lack of books, and the fact too many were going unread – that sparked the creation of *Taiwan in 100 Books*. My hope is not only to encourage people to read more but also to inspire some readers to join the brotherhood of writers and help fill the large gaps in the Taiwan bookshelf.

Any list is contentious, and I'm sure there will be questions about inclusions and omissions. I aimed for what I think are the best, the most important, and the most influential books; but I've also included some quirky forgotten gems and others that have flown under the radar. If you feel strongly about a book I have not included, feel free to write to me (john at camphorpress dot com) and make a case for it being included in the next edition.

Are there really one hundred books featured as per the title? Yes, more or less, though some are described only briefly. The number of books covered in depth (whose titles are given in bold when they are first introduced) will grow as I add titles to future editions.

The majority of the entries in *Taiwan in 100 Books* are non-fiction, reflecting my own preferences. With two exceptions, I've not included English translations of Chinese-language books because Camphor Press is going to publish a separate collection on these.

Rather than just summarize the contents and outline the merits of the selected books, I've often included backstories about the works and authors. And it's worth noting that a few of the titles are not focused primarily on Taiwan; rather, they earned their place by containing unique, fascinating stories largely unknown to even the most diehard Taiwan bibliophiles. Such is the title with which this book opens. Although *Taiwan in 100 Books* follows a generally chronological approach from the seventeenth century through to the present, we begin our journey to Taiwan in the 1950s, with *Secret Fighting Arts of the World*.

In the interests of disclosure, I should note that I'm one of the three bibliophiles behind Camphor Press, an independent publishing house focused on East Asia. Many of Camphor Press' Taiwan titles are featured or mentioned in *Taiwan in 100 Books*, not only because I like and have an intimate knowledge of them, including background information on the works and authors, but also from the simple fact that Camphor is now the leading English-language publisher of books on Taiwan.

TAIWAN IN 100 BOOKS

MAP OF TAIWAN

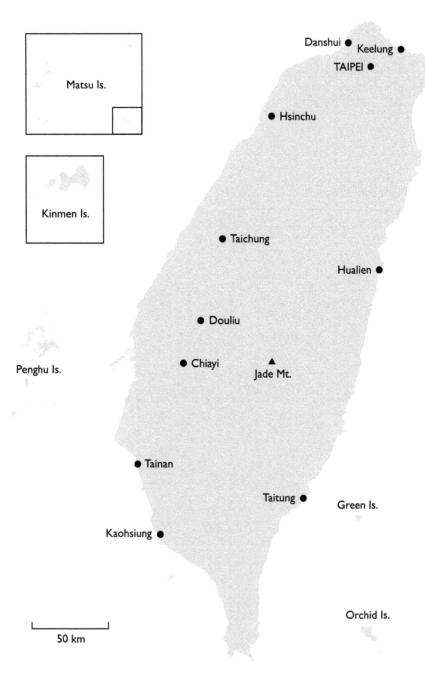

Danshui ●
Keelung ●
TAIPEI ●

Matsu Is.

Kinmen Is.

Hsinchu ●

Taichung ●

Hualien ●

Penghu Is.

Douliu ●

Chiayi ●
▲
Jade Mt.

Tainan ●

Taitung ●

Green Is.

Kaohsiung ●

Orchid Is.

50 km

1

Mysterious Taiwan

TAIPEI in 1957. A poor, bustling city of shopkeepers and soldiers, the once orderly Japanese colonial city now a sprawling settlement accommodating the tsunami of Chinese refugees who had fled to the island after the Communist victory in China. The exodus had brought to Taiwan the wheat and the chaff: the artists and academics, engineers, master chefs, gangsters, warlords, whores, battle-hardened officers, and more often press-ganged village boys. In the shacks that sprung up, in the appropriated Japanese-style houses, in the military villages could be heard the tongues from every corner of China. The exiles carried with them the smoldering embers of Chinese culture in all its diversity – its literature, religions, languages and dialects, cuisines, and martial arts.

And into this concentration of culture came American millionaire John F. Gilbey, a world-renowned martial arts expert and practitioner. He had been to Taiwan in 1955 and seen gifted fighters of every description, some capable of amazing feats; "men who could lightly touch your body and bring a bright red blood line immediately to the surface," and others who "could support over a two-hundred-pound weight attached to their genitalia."

One art, however, eluded Gilbey. He had heard for years of "the delayed death touch." Intrigued yet doubtful that it existed, he would see it firsthand on his 1957 trip to Taiwan and describe this experience in his bestselling *Secret Fighting Arts of the World* (1963), which he wrote at the insistence of Tuttle, Japan's leading English-language publisher.

Gilbey was conversing (in Mandarin) with a renowned Shaolin teacher in Taipei called Oh Hsinyang, when the topic turned to the correlation between vulnerable body points and the time of day. Oh explained "that *shaolin* masters for centuries had been guided in their *atemi* (strike) by the time of day." The theory was that blood came close to the surface at different times of the day. "A boxer had only to be aware of the course of this circulation and to attack the appropriate part at the time the blood was near the surface. Injury was certain and death probable then." But did it really work? Gilbey asked for proof. Oh obliged, demonstrating a light but rapid touch on a student, who immediately collapsed into an incapacitated heap. No need to worry, Oh assured, as fellow students administered some medicine to revive the student.

Before taking his leave, Gilbey raised the topic of the delayed death touch, asking if it was a variation on what he had seen. Could the impact be delayed? Had Oh heard of it? The Shaolin master remained silent for a moment. A few words to his students and all except a teenage boy vacated the dojo room. Yes, he said, the time strike and delayed death touch were indeed related, though the ability to perform such a feat was beyond all but the very best masters. In Taiwan he alone possessed the skill and he almost never performed it because of the obvious danger, and there were, of course, not many volunteers stepping forward to have it demonstrated on them.

Oh asked Gilbey if he would be willing to submit. The American stammered out a series of excuses. Oh summoned the boy who had remained behind; his son had never experienced it and, his father said, was badly in need of the education. With his right index finger, Oh touched a point just below the boy's navel. Turning to Gilbey, Oh explained:

"That is all, just a touch, the *ch'i* transmitted very smoothly. Since you leave in a week I have timed the effect of this touch for three days hence. About noon on that day Ah-lin will begin to vomit and must go to bed. So that your Western cohorts will not accuse me of chicanery I make you a present of Ah-lin until that time. I shall meet you in Taipei three days hence at the Union Hotel. Until then, farewell."

Gilbey spent the next three days with the boy, who helped him with various chores and errands. When Mr. Oh came to the hotel on the morning of the third day, Gilbey confirmed that Ah-lin had not left his sight, and reported that the boy was in good health. The three of them took a walk around "the disordered, squalid downtown area of the city" then returned to the hotel room. A short time later, the boy suddenly lost consciousness. Gilbey could hardly feel a pulse, and Ah-lin appeared dazed and pale. The father administered medicine and massage treatment. Ah-lin revived but was still weak. From the father there was no hint of triumphant pride or theatrical showmanship, but instead a somberness as if regretting the display and now feeling irked that he had been pushed into proving his martial arts prowess. Oh said it would take three months for the boy to recover, but that there would be no lasting aftereffects. And there was no lasting ill will – when Gilbey departed Taiwan a few days later, Oh Hsin-yang and his son were at the port to see him off.

"The Delayed Death Touch" was the first chapter of Gilbey's *Secret Fighting Arts of the World*, and perhaps the most memorable, though there was plenty of competition. Other chapter titles included "The Ganges Groin Gouge," "The Macedonian Buttock," and "The Parisian Halitotic Attack." Yes, if the insane content was not enough, the very chapter titles themselves should have alerted readers to the fact the book was a hoax.

The man behind the deception was Robert W. Smith (1926–2011), a real-life Gilbey of sorts: as a teenager he had begun his martial arts odyssey with Western boxing and wrestling, and then moved on to judo, and finally in his mid-thirties, while stationed in Taiwan (1959–1962) as an intelligence officer for the CIA, found his home in the Chinese martial arts training under celebrated masters. On his return to the United States, writing about and teaching what he had learned, he was an important pioneer responsible for bringing East Asian martial arts to the West.

"Gilbey was a joke, an exaggeration, a fantasy," Smith says in his 1999 memoir, *Martial Musings: A Portrayal of Martial Arts in the 20th Century*. "We were sure that readers would be smart enough to realize this. We were wrong." When Smith wrote "we," he was referring to the hoax being a joint inspiration: "John Gilbey was born in Donn Draeger's house in Tokyo in 1961." Draeger was a World War II and Korean War Marine vet who became an influential practitioner of martial arts. Among his many books, the most important was *Asian Fighting Arts* (1969), which he co-authored with Smith. To the general public, Draeger was best known as the martial arts coordinator (and actor Sean Connery's stunt double) for the 1967 James Bond film *You Only Live Twice*.

Smith and Draeger's wild inventions were aimed at lampooning the oft-told legendary feats of superhuman fighters. You have to admire the publisher for being willing to go along with the joke. Charles E. Tuttle Co. (now called Tuttle Publishing) was a respectable publisher, established by American Charles E. Tuttle in 1948. After working on General MacArthur's staff during the post-war reconstruction of Japan, Tuttle, who was from a publishing family, stayed on and set up his company. Among the wide range of titles published by Tuttle were numerous books on martial arts, especially on Japanese forms; these books would play a significant role in introducing East Asian martial arts to the West.

Smith wrote a sequel to his bestselling hoax, called *The Way of a Warrior*, which contained even more outrageous tall tales – though there were some straight stories thrown in; part of the fun is in trying to distinguish them, though you don't need to speculate too long to decide which category held Mama Su's deadly art of spitting betel nuts, and Fotan, an Icelandic martial art drawing on energy from black holes. A third Gilbey book, *Western Boxing and World Wrestling* (1986), was almost entirely factual. Unlike the earlier titles, it didn't sell well and was seldom quoted.

Robert W. Smith's greatest written contribution was his **Chinese Boxing: Masters and Methods** (1974). Covering his time in Taiwan training with martial arts masters, it's a magnificent book; the rich variety of fighting forms then concentrated on the island was exceptional. As Smith wrote, "No national form of fighting approaches Chinese boxing in the diversity and profundity of its forms."

In *Chinese Boxing*, Smith wanted, on top of educating readers about Chinese fighting arts, to offset the sensational way kung fu was portrayed in the media, especially in films. Notice the use of "boxing" in the title rather than the more exotic "kung fu." Although *Chinese Boxing* is seemingly matter-of-fact – Smith relays fantastic tales and then dismisses them – this remains the book of a romantic who was a firm believer in that magical life force called *qi*.

Smith was based in Taipei, a city he describes as having been built for 250,000 but accommodating six times that population. He counted himself lucky to have a house on "beautiful Yang Ming Mountain," a short distance to the north. Smith met and trained with an incredible array of masters, packing more into his three-year stay in Taiwan than most expats manage in a decade or two. It was the kind of immersive exploration we like to imagine ourselves doing but don't get around to. Studying with several teachers concurrently, with hours of practice every day and then hours digesting it all, was mentally and physically grueling: exhaustion and pain were constant companions. Smith's perseverance was admirable, yet it also reveals a certain selfishness; he was a married father at the time, so his deep dive into martial arts in Taiwan meant ignoring the family.

Among the masters Smith describes was Liao Wu-ch'ang, known as "the Monkey Boxer" because of his low, crouching style. Nimble and energetic despite his advanced years and four wives, Liao credited his impressive health to getting up at three in the morning for a daily cold bath (which consisted of simply pouring a basin of cold water over himself). Liao was a traditional Chinese medicine doctor and taught Smith about "the esoteric art of attacking vital points," as well as introducing him to a native Taiwanese boxer, Ch'en Ching-chang, near Keelung, who possessed "one-finger skill." Ch'en gave a minor demonstration hinting at his power but would not show the one finger fighting application, having sworn not to use it since killing a man with it fifteen years previously.

Chinese Boxing includes fascinating sections on elite masters Wang Shujin and Hung I-Hsiang; both men were devastating fighters, famed practitioners of the internal martial arts of *xingyi* (*hsing-i*) and *bagua*, which rely on the subtle channeling of qi rather than brute physical force.

It was the third main internal art, tai chi (*taiji*), however, that captivated Smith. And the man who won him over to this was Cheng Man-ch'ing – known as the "Master of the Five Excellences" for his skill in painting, calligraphy, poetry, medicine, and tai chi. Smith describes Cheng's teaching as "the most profound" he encountered and writes of the man with reverence, in many ways taking on the Chinese model of disciple to master. Whereas Smith would increasingly move toward the artistic and spiritual aspects of martial arts – asking what tai chi could do for character – his old friend Draeger disagreed about Cheng's approach, favoring a more scientific focus on effective violence.

Shortly after moving to Washington, D.C., in 1962, Smith began teaching tai chi to a Saturday-morning YMCA class, which was to continue for twenty-seven years. In 1964 Cheng Man-ch'ing moved with his family to New York, where he taught tai chi. Cheng and Smith collaborated on a book *T'ai Chi, the Supreme Ultimate Exercise for Health, Sport, and Self-defense* (1967).

* * *

As audacious and successful a hoax as Smith's *Secret Fighting Arts of the World* was, it pales in comparison to a 1704 work on Taiwan called **An Historical and Geographical Description of Formosa, an Island Subject to the Emperor of Japan**.

The book, one of the most outrageous literary hoaxes ever perpetrated, was authored by a young Frenchman calling himself George Psalmanazar. He claimed to be a native of Formosa who was abducted by Jesuits and carried off to France, where despite being threatened with the tortures of the Inquisition, had bravely refused to become a Roman Catholic, instead finding the true faith of Protestantism.

"Viceroy's Lady" from Psalmanazar's
An Historical and Geographical Description of Formosa

Although Psalmanazar wrote *Memoirs of ****: Commonly Known as George Psalmanazar: A Reputed Native of Formosa* (1764), a confessional memoir published a year after his death at the age of about eighty-four, he was a close-mouthed man, and many of the details of his life remain a mystery. We do not know his real name (his fake one, Psalmanazar, was inspired by an Assyrian king "Shalmaneser" in the Bible). Psalmanazar was born about 1679 and is believed to have come from southern France. According to his memoir, he attended a Jesuit school, but finding theology too dull, dropped out; a little later, he took to the road in the guise of a pilgrim, first as an Irishman and then as a Japanese converted to Christianity. Discovering that soliciting alms was easier the more exotic his disguise, he decided to pass himself off as a Japanese heathen. He made a little "bible" filled with figures of the sun, moon, and stars, and verses in a language of his own invention that he would chant to the rising and setting sun.

In 1702 Psalmanazar's deceit was uncovered by Alexander Innes, an Anglican chaplain stationed with a Scottish regiment then in Holland. Innes had asked Psalmanazar to write a passage in Japanese, and then, pretending to have lost the piece, had him rewrite it. The two samples were different and Psalmanazar confessed. Innes, a greedy opportunist, thought to take advantage of Psalmanazar's talents and invited him to England, though instead of a fake Japanese identity, the imposter was now to be a native of the even more obscure Formosa.

Psalmanazar was warmly received in England and soon became a minor celebrity. People were, however, surprised by his appearance, in particular by his fair complexion. This, he explained was because Formosans went to such great lengths to avoid the sun, living underground in the summer and in the shade of thickly wooded gardens and groves at other times.

Not only was Psalmanazar fair-skinned, but he had blond, shoulder-length hair and the facial features of a quintessential northern European. He tried to compensate by putting on a good show, which he seems to have enjoyed doing. As well as his existing habit of chanting gibberish to the skies in prayer, he came up with the ruse of eating raw meat. In his memoir, Psalmanazar writes:

> I fell upon one of the most whimsical expedients that could come into a crazed brain, viz. that of living upon raw flesh, roots and herbs; and it is surprising how soon I habituated myself to this new, and, till now, strange food, without receiving the least prejudice in my health; but I was blessed with a good constitution, and I took care to use a good deal of pepper, and other spices, for a concocter, whilst my vanity, and the people's surprize at my diet, served me for a relishing sauce.

Two months after arriving in London, Psalmanazar was persuaded to translate some religious texts into the supposed Formosan language. These translations were so well received that Innes prompted him to write a complete history of Formosa. And so Psalmanazar went to work, creating an untidy mix of Oriental exoticism, fevered imagination, and religious philosophy. In his memoirs he says it was written in great haste: "the booksellers were so earnest for my dispatching it out of hand, whilst the town was hot in expectation of it."

Psalmanazar wrote the draft in Latin; this was immediately translated into English, perhaps by Innes. But just two months before it was ready to hit the printing press, every writer's pre-publication nightmare was realized. Another account on Formosa appeared in the bookshops, and from someone who had actually been there. The book was the second edition of *A Collection of Voyages and Travels* (1704), edited by brothers Awnsham and John Churchill, which included *A Short Account of the Island of Formosa in the Indies* by Reverend Georgius Candidius, translated from the original Dutch.

Candidius, the first Dutch missionary on Formosa, had arrived there in 1627 at the age of thirty and spent the better part of a decade on the island. The Dutch East India Company (VOC) had, in 1624, established a colony in southwest Taiwan in what is now the city of Tainan, built two forts, developed agriculture and trade, and tried to convert the local aborigines to Christianity. It was a profitable colony for the Dutch. Trade consisted of exports of venison, sugar, and rattan to China, and sugar and deerskins (around fifty thousand a year) to Japan. Porcelain was shipped from China through Taiwan on to Europe.

A Short Account of the Island of Formosa describes the life and customs of the Siraya lowland aborigines. Headhunters and heathens they might have been, but Candidius considered them, all in all, "very friendly, faithful and good-natured."

They were, however, certainly a challenge for a missionary: "drunkenness is not considered to be a sin; for they are very fond of drinking, women as well as men; looking upon drunkenness as being but harmless joviality. Nor do they regard fornication and adultery as sins, if committed in secret; for they are a very lewd and licentious people."

And a missionary faced stiff competition in the form of the local priestesses, who presided over religious ceremonies with a considerable amount of flair. Candidius describes heavily intoxicated priestesses climbing atop a temple roof, making long orations to their gods, and beseeching them for rain: "At last they take off their garments, and appear to their gods in their nakedness."

Rain and nakedness seemed to go together. "At certain times of the year the natives go about for three months in a state of perfect nudity. They declare that, if they did not go about without any covering whatever, their gods would not send them any rain, and consequently there would be no rice harvest."

The strangest of the Siraya customs described by Candidius relate to marriage and mandatory abortion. He says husbands and wives lived separately until middle age, and women were not allowed to bear children till they were over thirty-five, and any pregnancies before that were terminated. The reason according to Candidius related to superstitions that a pregnant woman brought bad luck to a man when he was hunting or raiding.

You can imagine Psalmanazar staring at his desk, the Candidius account alongside his own completed manuscript, and wondering what to do. In the end, he seems to have not altered his text; but he did call out Candidius in the preface, disputing the Dutchman's claim that Formosa had no central government. And with that, the manuscript was sent to the printer, the Black Swan – in fact, the same printer as had produced Candidius' account. The Black Swan, (formerly a pub, I assume, converted into a printer at the back and a bookshop at the front, which was a typical set-up at the time) was in Paternoster Row, a publishing street in central London near St. Paul's Cathedral. The bookshop, along with the others on Paternoster Row, was destroyed during the blitz in 1940. Incidentally, next door to the Black Swan was the Swan, where in 1719, *Robinson Crusoe*, the greatest publishing sensation of the age, was printed.

In the sequel that was released later that same year, *The Farther Adventures of Robinson Crusoe*, the hero of the novel briefly stops in Taiwan.

And then we steered north, till we came to the latitude of 22 degrees 30 seconds, by which means we made the island of Formosa directly, where we came to an anchor, in order to get water and fresh provisions, which the people there, who are very courteous in their manners, supplied us with willingly, and dealt very fairly and punctually with us in all their agreements and bargains. This is what we did not find among other people, and may be owing to the remains of Christianity which was once planted here by a Dutch missionary of Protestants, and it is a testimony of what I have often observed, viz. that the Christian religion always civilises the people, and reforms their manners, where it is received, whether it works saving effects upon them or no.

Publication of the first edition of *An Historical and Geographical Description of Formosa* was announced in the *London Gazette* of April 17–20, 1704, with the highlighted aspect being the author's conversion from paganism. This emphasis was reflected in the book too, with the conversion story and related attacks against the Jesuits accounting for a good third of the text. In the Formosa sections Psalmanazar described a rich land of good government, prosperous towns, and grisly customs. The inhabitants were wealthy enough to eat with utensils and dishes "made of Gold and China Earth." The typical breakfast doesn't sound too appetizing though: "first they smoke a pipe of tobacco, then they drink *bohea*, green or sage tea; afterward they cut off the head of a viper, and suck the blood out of the body; this, in my humble opinion, is the most wholsom breakfast a man can make."

The most shocking claim in Psalmanazar's book was that eighteen thousand young boys were sacrificed to the gods each year; and in the second edition, published in 1705, cannibalism was added to the mix.

A few individuals came forward to challenge Psalmanazar – even before his book was published – but their critiques were ignored.

Psalmanazar benefited enormously by being such a champion of the Protestant church and by doubling down on the fraud. He did a good job of refuting the charges. Psalmanazar appeared before the Royal Society to address doubts about his outlandish description of Formosa. It's hard not to admire the pluck needed to do this. Here was a young foreign man going head to head with heavyweight intellectuals and men of standing — the likes of astronomer and mathematician Edmond Halley and French Jesuit priest Father Jean de Fontenay, who had lived in China (and had spoken with priests who had been in Formosa). In a later enquiry (1707) into the veracity of Psalmanazar's claims, the blond Formosan produced a surprise witness by the name of John Albert Lubomirski, a supposed Polish prince and former missionary of decades to China and Formosa, who corroborated the tales of child sacrifice, the natives' fair appearance, and other details. Not unexpectedly, Lubomirski had never been seen or heard of before his testimony and disappeared after the enquiry.

Psalmanazar addressed criticisms of his book in the preface to the second edition. He dismissed differences between Dutch accounts of Formosa with his own as them describing different regions. The Dutch had possessed a colony in southwestern Taiwan; however, Psalmanazar said, this had been on remote islands, a wild region unlike the more civilized Formosan heartland. In the preface to the French edition (September 1704) he gives the analogy of Japanese coming to Europe and thinking the Scottish Hebrides were representative of England. In a remarkable piece of boldfaced jujitsu, he tried turning the differences between the Formosa of his imagination and the real one to his advantage; a fraudulent account, he explained with some logic, would surely have been more wisely based upon the existing materials. Psalmanazar also attacked the veracity of Candidius' account, joining others in ridiculing the

Dutchman's claim that women not yet in their late thirties were forced to have abortions.

Looking back upon the fraud during his later years, Psalamanzar would write that his critics erred in not targeting his weakest point: the fake language he had invented. A simple test along the lines of the one Innes had originally used would surely have exposed the hoax.

Though not conclusively exposed, Psalmanazar was losing his novelty and credibility, which he countered by taking his Formosan show further down-market; he added excessive drug taking to the repertoire, consuming huge amounts of laudanum (opium in liquid form) and tobacco. After all, Formosans were hearty smokers, and, as he told people, even the women on the island smoked pounds of tobacco in a day.

By 1711, the impostor's credibility largely gone, we see him being ridiculed for the sensational gore in his stories. That year, in the very first edition of the *Spectator*, the newspaper ran a fake advertisement for an upcoming play featuring Psalmanazar:

> On the first of April will be performed at the Play-house in the **Hay-market**, an Opera call'd **The Cruelty of Atreus**. N. B. The Scene wherein **Thyestes** eats his own Children, is to be performed by the famous Mr Psalmanazar, lately arrived from Formosa; The whole Supper being set to Kettle-drums.

The tales of child sacrifice and cannibalism in Psalmanazar's account made an impression on *Gulliver's Travels* author Jonathan Swift, who references the Formosan imposter in his satirical essay *A Modest Proposal* (1729). Swift writes in the proposal – which suggests that the Irish poor could ameliorate their economic woes by selling their children as food to the rich – had been inspired by a conversation with "the famous Salmanaazor, a native of the island Formosa, who came from thence to London, above twenty years ago."

A lesson of the Psalmanazar fraud is in that the truth was out there for those who wanted to find it; some people chose to believe the lies for their own reasons, either through unenquiring, gullible ignorance or from alignments of prejudice. It's important to stress that Formosa was obscure but hardly unknown. There was English-language material on the Dutch settlement (1624–1662), such as Candidius' account mentioned earlier. Originally published in Dutch in 1666, and in English in 1704, the book also became a source for *Atlas Japannensis* (1670) and *Atlas Chinensis* (1671), both English-language works.

Closer to home, there was **Notes on Formosa**, by Scotsman David Wright, a former employee of the Dutch colony in Formosa. When we refer to the Dutch presence in Asia, it's actually a shorthand way of saying the Dutch East India Company (or VOC). Arguably the world's first international corporation, the VOC was strikingly multinational – with Dutch nationals accounting for only half the staff; the last VOC governor in Taiwan, for example, was a Swede, and the traitor who helped ensure the governor had no successor was a German. Wright spent more than twenty years in Formosa; around 1655 (the timing is based on a plague of locusts he describes) he wrote a detailed, wide-ranging account of the island. Wright's description was superior to Candidius', in part because the Dutch had greatly expanded their control and knowledge of the island at this later time. Although Wright's *Notes on Formosa* is a lost work, we have significant quoted material from it in *Atlas Chinensis* (which was available in England in Psalmanazar's day).

Wright's account describes a wide range of topics, from Formosa's eleven political dominions, to agriculture, fishing, hunting, brewing, taboos, and religious ceremonies. Of the latter, like Candidius, he expressed his disapproval at the rampant and unbridled fornication during religious festival days.

And, if Wright's account wasn't enough proof of Psalmanazar's hoax – and surely there were oral ones from other former VOC employees – remarkably, there had even been a direct English presence on Taiwan; from 1670 to 1685 – well within living memory at the time – the British East India Company had a trading post (called a "factory") at the old Dutch settlement. This was during the short-lived Kingdom of Dongning (1661–1683), established by Ming loyalist Koxinga just a year before his death. It was Koxinga's son who extended an invitation to the British East India Company's regional headquarters in Bantam, an English enclave on the island of Java. The first English ship arrived in Taiwan in 1670, hopes high that the British could fill the vacuum created by the expulsion of the Dutch. The post, however, was a failure. The rulers' monopolies on sugar and deer-hide exports kept competitors out, and English expectations of trade with China rested largely on the unreasonable hope of Koxinga's heirs retaking the mainland. The company sought to establish trade in the region, especially with Japan, whose cooler climate was seen as making it a better market than southern China for the woolen goods they were selling. One ship was dispatched to Japan; but it was sent away and the English didn't try again – Japan was then off-limits to Europeans, except for the Dutch in Nagasaki.

The Englishmen at the factory had a lot of free time for writing letters outlining their plans and frustrations. These can be read in *The English Factory in Taiwan: 1670–1685*, an 808-page behemoth by Chang Hsiu-jung et al., published by National Taiwan University in 1995.

2

Early Formosa

BUT we have skipped over the story of the Dutch in Taiwan much too quickly. We should return to the early 1620s. The VOC, having failed to take Macau from the Portuguese, denied permission to establish a post on the Chinese coast, and having been told by the Ming authorities to move from the Penghu Islands to Taiwan, founded a settlement in southwestern Taiwan.

Although there were only about two thousand VOC employees – about half of whom were soldiers – the Dutch radically altered the course of the island's history by opening it to the outside world and bringing in Chinese settlers (mostly males) to work the land. By the end of Dutch rule, between forty and fifty thousand Chinese lived in Taiwan.

Dutch rule was both harsh and exploitative, with onerous taxes on almost everything: growing rice, trading, fishing, butchering pigs, and even hunting deer. A poll tax provided the catalyst for an uprising of Chinese settlers in 1652, which was brutally suppressed.

Over a period of two weeks Dutch troops and two thousand aboriginal allies slaughtered about five thousand poorly armed peasants. These Chinese immigrants would have their chance to extract revenge a decade later.

On the morning of April 30, 1661, a massive fleet of Chinese war junks and transport ships carrying about twenty-five thousand men appeared off the coast. It was Koxinga, son of a Chinese merchant pirate and a Japanese mother, a Ming loyalist who came to Taiwan to establish a base from which to keep resisting the Manchus and their newly established Qing dynasty.

Koxinga landed his troops a little to the north of Fort Zeelandia in Anping, and was welcomed by the Chinese inhabitants as a liberator. The Dutch, trying to prevent the invaders from grabbing a strong foothold, threw a force of 240 men against an advance party of four thousand Chinese troops. The Europeans soon found they had underestimated Koxinga's men. This time the Dutch weren't fighting lightly armed farmers. Musket fire was answered with a rain of arrows and such a ferocious attack that the Dutch fled in terror, some flinging their weapons aside in haste to escape. Only half the force made it back to the fort.

Koxinga gave the Dutch an ultimatum: leave now with all their goods or stay and perish. The situation for the Dutch was hopeless; there were only about twelve hundred men and limited ammunition. Nonetheless, they decided to stay and fight. The Chinese attacked several times but were driven back with heavy loss of life. Koxinga, deciding to give priority to housing and feeding his troops and followers, chose to lay siege to the stronghold and wait. A terrible fate befell the Dutch who were caught outside the fort. Charged with inciting the locals to revolt, the men were killed, some crucified or impaled; and the women were killed, divided among the commanders, or sold off.

The Dutch held out in Fort Zeelandia for nine months before a traitor provided valuable advice on overcoming the defenses, which, combined with new, persistent attacks, made their position untenable. The stubborn defenders, now reduced by fighting and especially disease to just four hundred, had earned the grudging respect of Koxinga, who let them surrender on generous terms: they could leave on their ships, and even take some of their cash and possessions with them. Furthermore, they were given the honor of being allowed to leave their fort marching, fully armed, bearing banners, and with drums beating.

The deadly fight for Taiwan centered on Fort Zeelandia is Taiwan's single greatest story. Other events in Taiwan's history are missing some narrative ingredients and a certain X factor. For example, the Japanese takeover in 1895, which was the result of Peking ceding the island as war reparations for events in Manchuria and Korea; although some Taiwanese resisted the Japanese fiercely, the sporadic, drawn-out, one-sided fighting doesn't lend itself to a gripping storyline. Likewise, the end of the Japanese colonial period was determined by events elsewhere (e.g., the dropping of the atomic bombs in 1945); and the Chinese Nationalists didn't arrive in Taiwan as liberating heroes. Furthermore, the Cold War defiance against Communist China was a prolonged standoff with relatively few hot flare-ups.

The best account of the clash between Koxinga and the Dutch is history professor Tonio Andrade's masterpiece **Lost Colony: The Untold Story of China's First Great Victory over the West** (2011). It's gripping from start to finish, filled with fascinating details, explanations, and cliffhanger chapter endings. Even in the sections covering the middle of the long siege, where you'd expect a lull in the tension, there are incredible side stories, such as an epic long-distance sailing feat that almost turned the battle, or an amusing, equally "what if" accidental encounter, that could have led to Manchu–Dutch cooperation in defeating Koxinga.

Lost Colony has a profile of "characters" at the start of the book. This dramatis personae is useful and funny, though at times slightly jarring in its flippancy. For the Chinese general "Chen Ze" we get: "Brilliant commander on Koxinga's side. Defeated Thomas Pedel with clever ruse. Defeated Dutch bay attack with clever ruse. Was defeated by Taiwanese aborigines in clever ruse." For traitor Hans Radis we get: "German sergeant who defected from Dutch to Koxinga with vital military advice. Liked rice wine." Entries for three of the Dutch leaders end with a suggestive observation about the last governor, Frederick Coyet: "Coyet hated him. He hated Coyet." History has treated Coyet kindly, portraying him as a courageous, dogged, and intelligent leader, a hero who was badly let down by incompetent Dutch leaders in Batavia and then unfairly made a scapegoat. This picture was partly of Coyet's own making; he wrote an influential memoir blaming the loss of the colony on Dutch political and military leaders. Historians through the centuries have accepted and repeated his accusations. Near the end of the book Andrade suggests the fault for the personal animosity and feuds – and the negative consequences that resulted from them – lay with Coyet. Though there's no doubt what Coyet achieved was remarkable, Andrade says the last governor seems to have been "a difficult man, indignant, quick to avenge perceived slights."

Lost Colony has the overreaching subtitle: The Untold Story of China's First Great Victory over the West. While the story of the battle for Fort Zeelandia in 1661–1662 is little known to those unfamiliar with Chinese or Taiwanese history, it's hardly untold. Nor can it be called a "great victory over the West," seeing as it involved a small Dutch outpost holding off a numerically superior force of battle-hardened Chinese troops for nine long months. In the acknowledgements, author Tonio Andrade, a professor of history at Emory College, explains that the title was the publishing team's idea and he agreed to it only after their insistence that it would give the book wider appeal.

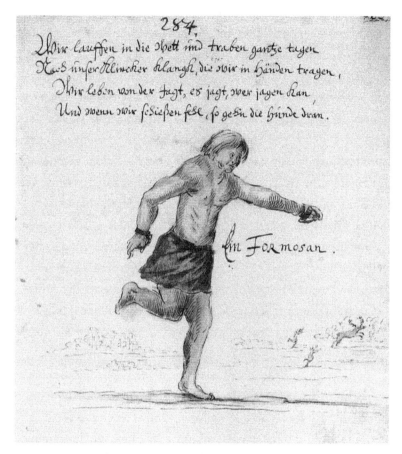

A painting of a Formosan native by the German East Asia traveller
Caspar Schmalkalden (c. 1650)

At the end of the day, the title and cover of a book are the publisher's call, so I can't fault Andrade for backing down. The overreach in the title, however, does extend a little into the book itself. The problem for Andrade is that he is interested in comparing the military technology and techniques of Europe and China; but before the First Opium War of 1839–1842 there were very few conflicts to gauge the relative strengths. This lack of Chinese–European military clashes raises the importance of the Zeelandia episode for comparative purposes. Andrade's conclusions are that Dutch technology proved superior in several important areas. Although Chinese cannons and muskets were just as good as the Dutch ones, and Koxinga's soldiers were well trained, disciplined, and experienced, the Renaissance fortress and the broadside sailing ship gave the Dutch an advantage. Koxinga had lain siege to Chinese cities with walls that dwarfed those of Fort Zeelandia, but he was thwarted by the Dutch fort's ability to deliver deadly crossfire, and "it wasn't until he got help from a defector from the Dutch side … that he finally managed to overcome it."

Andrade says that "Coyet, with his twelve hundred troops, might well have won the war." Koxinga prevailed because of superior leadership and men: "His troops were better trained, better disciplined, and most important, better led than the Dutch. Bolstered by a rich military tradition, a Chinese 'way of war,' Koxinga and his generals outfought Dutch commanders at every turn."

Though this is a reasonable assessment, it's important to remember we're not comparing like with like; Koxinga was the experienced military leader of a large force, while Coyet was a colonial administrator for what was essentially a trading company. Though the VOC had pseudo-governmental powers, the bottom line was profits. The Dutch were in Taiwan first and foremost to trade with China and Japan, not to conquer territory, and this fundamental point affected their willingness to spend blood and treasure in defense of the colony.

* * *

At times *Lost Colony* reads like a novel, which raises the mystery over the long absence of fictional works about Koxinga and his fight with the Dutch. That it was only in 2018 with Joyce Bergvelt's **Lord of Formosa** that we saw a novelized examination of the conflict is a reminder that there are still big stories out there awaiting a willing writer. Dutch-born Bergvelt gives us a complete story of Koxinga from his birth in Japan in 1624 – conveniently the very same year the Dutch founded their settlement in Taiwan – to his battle of wills with Governor Coyet. She also cleverly gives the VOC interpreter He Ting-bin an important role in the novel. Not only does He Ting-bin provide the spice of treachery and intrigue, but as a character moving between the worlds of the Dutch and the Chinese, he helps weave the two streams of the novel together. And he truly was one of the most important figures in the real historical drama.

He Ting-bin was a middle-man playing multiple sides, telling both Koxinga and the Dutch what they wanted to hear, and whatever would work best for his own private squeezes. When his Dutch employers discovered that he had been secretly extracting heavy tolls from Chinese merchants, he was arrested, tried, and found guilty. He was fired and fined. We next find him in Xiamen with a map and dishonest sales pitch for Koxinga: that Taiwan was an Eden of vast fertile fields and enormous potential – perfect as a new base. Weakly guarded by the Dutch, it could be taken "without lifting a finger." Had it not been for He Ting-bin's assurances of riches and easy victory, Koxinga may well never have attempted to oust the Dutch.

Of all the Taiwan novels I've read, *Lord of Formosa* stands out for its great cinematic potential. As yet, no English-language work set in Taiwan has made it to the big screen, though several big-budget American film adaptations of novels set elsewhere have been shot on the island; in *Sand Pebbles* (1966), from the 1962 novel by Richard

McKenna, locations near Keelung stood in for the Yangtze River in the 1920s, and in Martin Scorsese's *Silence* (2017), based on Shusaku Endo's 1966 novel of the same name, Taiwan was transformed into seventeenth-century Kyushu. Taiwanese director Ang Lee won the Academy Award for Best Director for his 2012 film adaptation of Yann Martel's *Life of Pi*. Much of the film was shot in Taiwan, though this was largely done in a specially built giant wave tank.

* * *

For history buffs looking to track down the vestiges of the Dutch period, there's a guidebook dedicated to the task: **The Real Taiwan and the Dutch: Traveling Notes from the Netherlands Representative** (2010), by Menno Goedhart and Cheryl Robbins.

My first impressions of this Dutch-flavored guidebook were decidedly mixed. Beautifully printed and lavishly illustrated, it looked, however, with its multitude of pictures of the author and local food specialties, like a cross between a Tourism Bureau publication and a typical Taiwanese Facebook feed.

I admit I've always had a curmudgeonly attitude toward Taiwanese food-tourism culture and especially its elevated reverence for traditional local dishes. In our hyper-interconnected world there's a reason a food is only a local specialty: it's probably not good enough to spread beyond that particular place. If a dish is sufficiently tasty (beef noodles, for example) or even middling (the likes of Chiayi turkey rice), then it will spread. As a result of this natural sorting, the "famous" local specialties you encounter are usually worse than normal, everyday fare. Although the nondescript cookies, noodles, sticky rice balls, and other offerings provide nostalgia value for Taiwanese customers, for Johnnie foreigner they are consistently underwhelming. And it's not because the modern versions are inferior to the originals. Let's face it: most of these dishes were never that great; what constituted a treat for an impoverished peasant in the 1950s and before – when even white rice was something of a luxury – is going to struggle to impress in our current age of 24/7, all-you-can-eat overabundance.

Happily, *The Real Taiwan and the Dutch* proved more substantial than I thought it would be. It's a delightful resource for travelers, residents, and history enthusiasts, a 270-page guide focused on getting off the beaten path to explore Taiwan's contemporary aboriginal cultures and the old Dutch heritage. The book contains hundreds of photographs, some maps, lots of practical travel information (complete with addresses, phone numbers, accommodation recommendations), and, as I mentioned earlier, a Taiwanese-level dedication to eating; restaurants and signature regional dishes are given a lot of space.

The book's main author, Menno Goedhart, was, from 2002 until his retirement in 2010, the Netherlands' representative at their Trade and Investment Office (i.e., the de facto embassy) in Taipei. Goedhart stayed on after his retirement, settling in Xinhua, Tainan, to further his investigations into Taiwan's Dutch heritage and continue his work promoting Dutch–Taiwan cultural ties.

The Real Taiwan and the Dutch covers the core Dutch area of Tainan, the Penghu Islands (strategically located midway between China and Taiwan, the Dutch had settled there briefly), the East Coast, Chiayi, and Pingtung, as well as a chapter on "Other Places" (including Danshui and Keelung, northern outposts where the Dutch built forts). Of Danshui's old fort, Goedhart says the name often used, Fort San Domingo, is wrong. This earlier Spanish fort was destroyed and the current building completely Dutch, so it should be called Fort Antonio after Governor General Antonio van Diemen. Sounds reasonable to me, though I'm of course partial to Antonio van Diemen; it was his drive to explore the Pacific that led to Abel Tasman discovering my native land of New Zealand in 1642. Note how Fort Zeelandia in Tainan and New Zealand share a common etymological origin, being named after Zeeland ("Sea Land"), the westernmost province of the Netherlands.

Co-author Cheryl Robbins is a Taiwan-based writer and translator. While working as a reporter for the English-language *Taiwan News*, she interviewed Goedhart several times and discovered a mutual interest in the country's aboriginal cultures. Robbins and Goedhart started doing research trips and writing the book before finding a publisher. Coverage in Chinese-language newspapers on Goedhart's project led Taiwan Interminds Publishing to approach Goedhart. They published a Chinese-language version of the book at the same time as the English version. (Yes, now all the restaurant coverage and food photos make sense!) No Dutch-language edition was produced, or needed; the English version was sold in the Netherlands, a credit to the exceptional English-language ability of the Dutch.

Robbins followed up this project with a trilogy of bilingual guidebooks for tourists looking to visit Taiwan's aboriginal areas: *A Foreigner's Travel Guide to Taiwan's Indigenous Areas.* The three volumes are: *Northern Taiwan, Central and Southern Taiwan,* and *Hualien and Taitung.*

Although casual in style, the historical information in *The Real Taiwan and the Dutch* is top-notch. I was amazed (and slightly embarrassed) to learn about an important Dutch site just a twenty-five-minute drive from where I live. Goedhart tells the forgotten story of Fort Vlissingen, in the village of Haomeili in Budai Township, Chiayi County. Built in 1636, on a sandbar in the estuary of the Bazhang River, it was destroyed in severe flooding in 1644. A replacement fort was built on the opposite bank upon safer ground. Nothing remains of Fort Vlissingen, though Goedhart was able, with the help of an enthusiastic local researcher, to discover the likely site, now marked by a stand of old banyan trees. Goedhart also relates a story he heard from the Haomeili locals about how a Mazu statue (perhaps dating to the 1580s and the among the oldest in Taiwan) was brought inside the fort for protection during a flood and thus saved, then given the moniker "Governmental Mazu."

As with Fort Vlissingen, going on the trail of Dutch-era ruins requires a talent for DIY augmented reality. Outside of the forts in Tainan and Danshui, there are few physical historical remains to see, so you have to superimpose the ghosts of yesteryear onto the often-uninspiring modern landscapes and cityscapes.

During Goedhart's travels he was surprised by how widely the Dutch had explored and settled and by how many people claimed to have Dutch ancestors, something of which they were proud. He was welcomed on his explorations with great warmth, being adopted as a member of the Tsou tribe in Chiayi, made a chieftain of the Rukai, and an honorary citizen of Tainan.

Black-hearted cynic that I am, I take the rose-tinted Dutch connections with a healthy dose of salt. The Dutch were more ruthless tax collector than benevolent older brother. When Koxinga and his troops landed, the aborigines in the area – the VOC's first native allies – immediately went over to the new arrivals. As Andrade writes in *Lost Colony*: "It was astonishing how fast they switched sides."

Thirty-eight years of VOC rule, more than a generation of missionary work, and how little it counted when it really mattered; there were no loyal legions of natives rising up to help their Christian brothers and preserve the blessings of Pax Hollandia. The tribesmen were instead collecting Dutch heads in exchange for reward money.

Chiu Hsin-hui, an assistant professor of history at National Tsing Hua University, writes in her superb but expensive (US$125 for the e-book, anyone?) ***The Colonial "Civilizing Process" in Dutch Formosa, 1624–1662***: "Being freed of the obligation to attend school, the Southern Plains Formosans were jubilant as they destroyed their textbooks replete with Christian edification and went out headhunting Dutch residents." The romanized script of the Siraya language used in these books would eventually become a sacred memory but was obviously not so treasured at the time.

3

Qing Rule in Taiwan, 1683–1895

WHEN the Qing defeated the heirs of Koxinga and came into possession of the short-lived Kingdom of Dongning, the new masters were faced with a choice of what to do with the island. The resulting debates and decisions are well covered in MIT professor Emma J. Teng's *Taiwan's Imagined Geography: Chinese Colonial Travel Writing and Pictures, 1683–1895*, a relatively readable book for an academic work that began life as a doctoral dissertation. The period covered is when Taiwan (or at least the western lowland areas) was under the dominion of China's Qing dynasty.

On the question of what to do with the newly conquered territory, the Kangxi emperor is reported to have told his officials: "Taiwan is no bigger than a ball of mud. We gain nothing by possessing it, and it would be no loss if we did not acquire it." He favored abandoning Taiwan (after repatriating all the Chinese). Keeping the island would be an economic burden, a needless expenditure for what was considered a wild land of tattooed cannibals, dangerous terrain, and disease. Kangxi had – as did his predecessors – a continental mentality; his eyes were on expansion into Central Asia, not turned toward maritime horizons.

Admiral Shi Lang, the man responsible for capturing Taiwan, thought the island worth keeping, and it was his side – by stressing strategic considerations – that eventually won the debate. Having decided to keep Taiwan, the contention now shifted to whether it was fit for colonization or not.

As Teng says, the Qing had not set out to acquire Taiwan permanently and in effect ended up as "an accidental colonizer." The rulers in distant Peking would continue to feel ambivalent about Taiwan. Unlike the Zhengs, and the Dutch before them, the Qing did not seek to develop the island. They followed a policy of quarantine, restricting Chinese immigration to Taiwan, and did not seek to extend control over the entire island. Instead, they sought to restrict Chinese infiltration into aboriginal areas, with the aim of avoiding frontier disputes.

The Qing rulers did not initially allow women to cross the strait, hoping to keep the men tied to the mainland. The expectation was that most of the men would return home to their families after the fall harvest and then go back for the spring planting. Permission from port authorities was needed for travelers sailing to Taiwan, and the required papers were invariably an opportunity for official graft. Of course, as ever, it was cheaper and easier to do things outside the law. The emperor was far away and enforcement difficult.

In 1722 the Chinese authorities established a north–south boundary line the length of Taiwan. Stretching along the western foothills, this demarcation line – mostly existing as ink on maps, but marked by fifty-four steles in strategic locations – prohibited the Chinese settlers from moving into the mountain areas. Encroachment did occur, however, and the line was redrawn higher up four times during the century. Eventually ditches were dug and some guards posted to mark and better enforce the line.

As Taiwan developed and became more attractive a destination, the pro-colonization camp eventually won the debate. As Teng writes: "By the nineteenth century, Chinese attitudes toward Taiwan and the material conditions of the colony had changed so dramatically that 'the ball of mud' was now considered a 'land of Green Gold'" (i.e. tea).

The Qing were unable to stem the flow of Chinese immigrants, and – fearing Japanese interest in the island – decided to bring the entire island into the fold. In 1875, the Qing began the "Open the Mountains and Pacify the Savages" policy, permitting Chinese settlers – backed with Qing military might – into formerly off-limit aboriginal lands.

Taiwan's Imagined Geography excels at showing history in all its messy complexity and dynamism. We come away from it with a more nuanced understanding of the Qing period, of how events were sometimes happenstance, how widely perceptions varied, and how contentious policies were. It's also refreshing to see Qing China portrayed as the empire it was; Europeans didn't have a monopoly on imperialism. Given the Chinese Communist Party's continual bleating about the humiliations suffered from Western imperialism, it's always useful to point out that China was itself – and continues to be – an imperial power. Teng's book is not a polemic against Chinese imperialism, though; a strong takeaway from it is that Qing rule over Taiwan was no worse than what Europeans were doing elsewhere at the time. And rather than the Chinese having a monolithic view of non-Chinese peoples as savages, they had a range of views that changed over time.

* * *

Another excellent book covering Taiwan's formative years is **State-craft and Political Economy on the Taiwan Frontier, 1600–1800** (1993), by John Shepherd. It's not just required reading, but required repeat reading. Is "repeat reading" a backhanded compliment? Well, like Teng's book, *Statecraft and Political Economy on the Taiwan Frontier* is an academic publication that was originally a doctoral dissertation, so it is heavy going at times but packed with fascinating details – things like the nature of land rental regulations – that reward a second look.

Shepherd's was one of the first books I read on Taiwan and a revelation, correcting the oversimplified assumptions I had about early Taiwan; the idea that Chinese settlers had turned up and driven the aborigines – by conflict, force of numbers, and development – into the mountains, and that the Qing authorities had largely ignored the island. Shepherd emphasizes the importance of plains aborigines in the process and how government "neglect" actually involved continued surveillance and interference in a "rationally calculated policy of indirect control and quarantine."

* * *

For me the most memorable account of the early Qing era is Yu Yonghe's **Small Sea Travel Diaries** (English translation 2004). Yu, an adventurous literati or official – we lack biographical information about him – happened to be traveling in Fujian when the need arose for a brave volunteer. In the winter of 1696, the Imperial Chinese gunpowder stores had exploded. Sulfur was required to manufacture a new supply of gunpowder. Taiwan, recently coming into Qing hands, was said to be rich in it. Yu stepped forward to go there and oversee the mining of the sulfur.

It turned out to be a grueling ten-month mission. In the early spring of 1697 (the thirty-sixth year of the Kangxi emperor's reign) he first sailed to the city of Taiwanfu (Tainan). After two

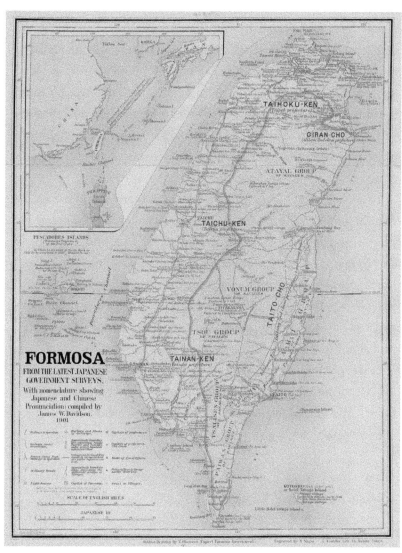

A 1901 map from James W. Davidson's opus The Island of Formosa,
Past and Present. *The bold line shows the "Approximate boundary line separating Savage District and Territory under actual Japanese administration."*

months, he set out in an ox cart, "accompanied by fifty-five troops, servants, aborigines and workers" along the western plains. Three weeks later he arrived in Beitou, where he set up camp and began bartering goods for sulfur brought in by the aborigines. Yu was appalled by the aboriginal women's state of dress or lack of it, and was happy to be trading cloth for the sulfur so that the aborigines could cover up. Although he thought some of the younger women very pretty, they had the unfortunate habit of putting "deer oil in their hair, which smells just horrendous and one can't even get near them."

Yu found traveling in Taiwan arduous; there was the impenetrable jungle, the merciless sun when not in said impenetrable jungle, and insects: mosquitoes and flies "like hungry eagles and tigers." And there were snakes, to which Yu had an Indiana Jones-strength aversion: exaggeration-prone and paranoid on this subject, he mentions snakes crying in the night, sometimes snoring like oxen, and small ones that chase people which are as fast as "flying arrows."

Some of the native inhabitants were equally formidable. Yu Yonghe, using the thinking and terminology then current, divided them into two categories: the plains savages ("cooked") and the wild savages ("raw").

> The wild savages live in holes in the ground and they drink blood and eat hair…. The cooked savages fear them and do not dare enter their territory. The wild savages are especially fierce and strong; they often come out to burn houses and kill people. Then they return to their lairs so there is no way to get near them. When they kill, they take the head, and when they return they cook it. They strip the skull and sprinkle it with red powder, setting it before their door.

Yu expressed admirable concern for the aborigines. He was critical of earlier mistreatment against them by the Dutch and Zheng regimes and also of current mistreatment by Chinese settlers, whom he saw as the cause of frontier disputes. Yu was hopeful about civilizing the aborigines, estimating it would take between thirty and one hundred years to do this. "Then what will be the difference between them and Chinese?" he asked.

The Yu Yonghe story is told in two books by historian Macabe Keliher: *Out of China or Yu Yonghe's Tale of Formosa: A History of Seventeenth-Century Taiwan* (2003) and *Small Sea Travel Diaries: Yu Yonghe's Records of Taiwan* (2004). The first has extracts of Yu's account with significant commentary; the second comprises Yu's diaries in full, translated from the original literary Chinese and annotated by Keliher. I recommend both books, and in the order of publication. *Out of China* gives excellent background information and explanations for the text, and is a great introduction to *Small Sea Travel Diaries*, a more immersive book. Yu's writing is mesmerizing and otherworldly, transporting the reader in time and space – reading it is like stepping into an ancient Chinese ink scroll.

* * *

Out of China and *Small Sea Travel Diaries* were published by Taipei-based SMC (Southern Materials Center), and both books are lovely productions full of fascinating old illustrations and maps. Another beautifully illustrated SMC production of note is Jerome F. Keating's **The Mapping of Taiwan: Desired Economies, Coveted Geographies** (2011). The book chronicles the development of Taiwan in increasingly detailed maps through the ages.

Keating is an old Taiwan hand who first came to Taiwan in 1988 from Texas on a two-year contract with an engineering firm working on the construction of the MRT, Taipei's mass rapid transit system. He fell in love with the country and has been here ever since.

The Mapping of Taiwan is his fifth book about Taiwan and I think his best. The maps, starting from a horribly inaccurate 1570 map by Flemish cartographer Abraham Ortelius, show Taiwan through the centuries as a "desired economy, coveted geography" (that is, a desired source of goods and a strategic location). Drawn by colonizers and would-be colonizers, the maps highlight the aspects that were most important to them, and reveals their state of knowledge at the time. Looking at Taiwan through maps also reminds us that Taiwan is a maritime nation, part of the Pacific story.

Keating ends with a call to arms; after centuries of having their island mapped by others, Taiwanese are at an important crossroads. "Taiwan's future and its economy are for the first time in its history in the hands of its citizens; it can continue to create and control a clearly Taiwanese imagined community. It can map its own future."

Some of the maps and illustrations in the book are from the private collection of Wei Te-wen, the founder of SMC Publishing and probably the best-known map collector in Taiwan. (By the way, the small SMC bookstore, in an alley near the main entrance to National Taiwan University, is a must-visit for bibliophiles.) Wei started collecting antique maps in 1990 after coming across a map of Hsinchu – where he was born in 1944 – in an antiquarian bookshop in Hong Kong. He now has more than one thousand antique maps.

Wei Te-wen founded the SMC in 1976, after having studied pharmacy at the Medical University of Taipei and then working in the pharmaceutical industry for a few years. SMC's titles include important works on Taiwan's history and culture. He has won awards for his books and contributions to the country. Although SMC's English-language titles constitute a mere fraction of the publisher's catalog – and an unprofitable one at that – these books have been a lifesaver for foreigners interested in Taiwan.

SMC reprints of old, out-of-print Taiwan books – in particular *Pioneering in Formosa* – were life-changing for me. Without them, I think I would have moved on from Taiwan after a few years. In those early years in Taiwan I was focused on reading and writing about Burma and Mongolia. SMC's reprints opened up a wonderful lost world of adventure: no longer was Taiwan just an overcrowded factory island. I won't go into details about these books or the authors, because I did so in *Formosan Odyssey: Taiwan, Past and Present*, but brief outlines are deserved.

Pioneering in Formosa: Recollections of Adventures Among Mandarins, Wreckers, & Head-hunting Savages, by William Pickering, is a swashbuckling account of a young Englishman's adventures in Taiwan during the 1860s. Published in 1898 it combines the red-blooded arrogance of youth and deep knowledge that came from the author writing the book after additional decades of experience among the Chinese.

After six years of sailing the high seas, the twenty-two-year-old William Pickering joined China's Imperial Maritime Customs Service in Fujian in 1862. He was in Taiwan from 1863 to 1870, first in Kaohsiung and then in Anping (the port near the old capital city of Tainan), where he was in charge of customs and later worked for British trading companies.

The Taiwan of Pickering's day was a wild frontier, with the mountainous interior the domain of headhunting tribes and the coastline notorious as a mariner's graveyard. Pickering traveled widely – invariably armed with "a Colt's revolver, a double-barrelled fowling-piece, and a seven-shooter Spencer rifle," – and made several important expeditions into the mountains and the southern coastal areas. Pickering was often in the thick of the action. His knowledge of the island and language skills resulted in several adventures on behalf of the United States government. Following the killing of crew members from the shipwrecked American vessel *Rover*, he was invited to accompany an American punitive naval expedition as the interpreter. He later helped U.S. Army general Le Gendre secure a treaty from the "savages" that would guarantee the safety of shipwrecked crews. Later, during disputes over the camphor trade, a bloody standoff resulted in him fleeing for his life, a five-hundred-dollar bounty on his head, and the British dispatching gunships to the island.

From Far Formosa: Its Island, Its People and Missions (1895), by George Leslie Mackay, tells the story of the Canadian Presbyterian's work in Danshui and northern Taiwan. He arrived in 1871, aged twenty-seven, the first missionary to preach in northern Taiwan since the brief colonial period of the Dutch and Spanish centuries before, and stayed until his death in 1901; today he lies buried in a shady cemetery on a hill overlooking the town, a household name in Taiwan. An old missionary account might not sound appealing, but make no mistake, this is compelling reading, for which much credit should go to the editor, Rev. J.A. MacDonald.

William Campbell, another Presbyterian missionary and a Tainan-based contemporary of Mackay's became a great authority on the Dutch history of Taiwan, wrote several books – I recommend *Formosa under the Dutch* (1903) and *Sketches from Formosa* (1915) – and translated others. He established a school for the blind and did extensive mission work. On one of his trips into the mountains he became the first European to reach Sun-Moon Lake and named it Lake Candidius after the first Dutch missionary to the island.

* * *

In compiling *Taiwan in 100 Books* I have chosen the best and most important works, and also a few that while informative I can't with a clear conscience recommend actually reading. The next two works belong to this last category, the culprits being two entries from Elisa

Giles' *China Coast Tales* series: ***Formosa: A Tale of the French Blockade of 1884–1885*** (1906) and ***Playing Providence*** (1897).

If you've ever read or watched a modern depiction of treaty port life and thought the portrayals were unfairly harsh (with current sensibilities applied, it seems merely having servants is a damning proof of moral failure) then *China Coast Tales* will come as a shock. This series of ten stories by Elisa Giles, wife of the British consul in Danshui (Tamsui), is an absolute birch flogging of her Western contemporaries, a scathing look at the petty jealousies and ambitions of treaty port expat life.

The books were published by the Shanghai-based Kelly and Walsh in six volumes between 1892 and 1906, and came out under a pen name, Lise Boehm. All ten stories in the six volumes focus on expat communities, particularly missionaries, the customs and consul staff, and expatriate wives. The few Chinese characters are typically servants. The plots are similar too: characters behave badly and then people die. Two stories end with a suicide, another two in deadly riots, one in death by drowning, and so on.

Drama in the stories is often provided by the arrival of an outsider, and such is the case in the novel *Formosa: A Tale of the French Blockade of 1884–1885*. Although published as a book in 1906, it first appeared in 1890 as a serialized story in Shanghai's leading English-language newspaper, *The North China Daily News*.

The subtitle, *A Tale of the French Blockade of 1884–1885*, is misleading because the blockade, which was of Danshui and other major ports in Taiwan as part of the Sino–French War (also called the Tonkin War), is covered only sparingly. The actual focus of *Formosa* is the battle between two Western wives: Patricia Drury, the nasty, domineering wife of the commissioner of the Imperial Chinese Maritime Customs, and Isabel Reynolds, the newly arrived flirtatious young wife of the British consul.

By convention, the consul's wife should have held the leading position in the small expatriate women's circle. However, as a young newcomer of dubious background (a comic actress) who is unwilling to conform to etiquette, Isabel instead finds herself ostracized by Mrs. Drury and her clique. For Isabel there's solace in the company of a sympathetic Mr. Drury. This developing affair ends when the subtitle-suggested conflict finally makes an appearance as a *deus ex machina*; the lovers are killed by a shell during an artillery bombardment by the French. (Note: I wouldn't have given away the ending like that if I thought the novel worth picking up and readers able to get to the end.)

"Playing Providence" (1897) is the second of the two stories in volume two of the *China Coast Tales*. The title refers to the controlling, nosy Mrs. Delane, who, like Mrs. Drury in *Formosa*, is the wife of the commissioner of customs in Danshui. The plot revolves around Mrs. Delane's obsession to unveil the mystery surrounding Mr. Smith, a customs clerk whose background is unknown. Of all the other expats she had, "found out, sought out, wormed out, ordered out, every little private detail, every aspect of family or of bachelor life; each dead, or alive and secretly-cherished, love-story. In short, she knew every single circumstance, trivial or important, about every single mortal."

But try as she might, Mr. Smith's past remains elusive, and not knowing proves unbearable: "Mrs. Delane actually began to grow thin under the mental torment which this mystery gave her."

She resorts to intercepting Mr. Smith's mail, and learns that he is in hiding from a wife. Against his wishes, Mrs. Delane arranges for the wife to come. It's not a happy reunion, but at least the story ends without fatality.

The women in these stories – malicious gossipers and meddlers – are representative rather than extremes of *China Coast Tales*. Giles clearly didn't think much of her fellow expatriate wives. Mind you, she didn't spare many people from her cynicism and scorn. And Giles herself makes it clear at the start of *China Coast Tales* that she is not exaggerating for effect but rather attempting to accurately illustrate treaty port life: "no attempt has been made to caricature individuals, but rather to portray types of ordinary occurrence."

Her greatest disdain is for missionaries, which was not an altogether uncommon view. Although expatriates would not run down their fellow Europeans in front of the natives, many were critical among themselves (and later in books) of missionaries for being tactless, upsetting customs and communities, and causing unrest (which consuls like Herbert Giles had to deal with). And the missionary work, noble from a distance as in newsletters back to a congregation, seemed closer up to consist, in effect, of bribing followers – their converts being "rice Christians." The expat elite considered missionaries lower down the social ladder and resented missionary denunciations of popular expat pastimes: drinking, socializing/whoring, and gambling (cards and, in the bigger treaty ports, horse-racing).

When writing *Formosa* and "Playing Providence," Giles was drawing heavily on her own experiences. She came to Danshui shortly after the French blockade as the second wife of the British consul, Herbert A. Giles (1845–1935). He was a leading China expert of the late nineteenth and early twentieth centuries; his system of romanizing Chinese—the Wade-Giles system—was the standard for decades. Herbert Giles was promoted to consul at Danshui in 1885 and transferred to Ningpo in 1891. The following year he retired because of ill health, and the couple moved to Scotland.

Although Elisa Giles' novels are extremely dated, the trashing of one's fellow expats still rings bells. The fact that I've given the endings away should indicate my feelings as to whether you need to read the stories for yourself. If you're looking for a novel set in Taiwan during the Sino-French War, there's Thurlow Fraser's *The Call of the East: A Romance of Far Formosa* (c. 1914), but once again I can't recommend it to the general reader. On the upside, this means there's an opportunity for someone to write a novel on the period.

* * *

A good non-fiction alternative to *Formosa* is *The Witnessed Account of British Resident John Dodd at Tamsui* (2010), by Niki Alsford. The book gives the original journal of John Dodd, notes, background on the times, and bibliographical information. Invaluable reference material at the end of the book includes a list of foreign residents in Taiwan from 1858 to 1895, important ships, and a map of the foreign cemetery at Danshui and a list of those buried there.

John Dodd (1838–1907) was one of the earliest merchants to settle in the treaty port of Danshui, arriving in 1864 in the employ of Scottish trading firm Dent & Co., and was an important figure in developing the export of Taiwanese tea to the West.

4

Japanese Taiwan, 1895–1945

IN 1894 Japan and China went to war over control of Korea. China lost this First Sino-Japanese War, and in the Treaty of Shimonoseki, concluded in April 1895, Peking ceded Taiwan – along with the Pescadores (Penghu) Islands – to Japan "in perpetuity." A coalition of outraged Taiwanese declared the short-lived Republic of Formosa. Resistance to the Japanese, which was disorganized and sporadic but fierce, lasted until about 1902 in the lowlands. It would take decades to bring the aborigines in the mountains – for the very first time – fully under control.

Modernization efforts which had begun under late Qing dynasty rule were built upon by Japan. Taiwan was Japan's first taste of being an imperial colonizer, and Japanese leaders were determined to show that they were the equal of the European powers.

The outstanding non-fiction work of the early Japanese colonial period is the 700-page *The Island of Formosa, Past and Present* (1903), by James W. Davidson, a war correspondent who witnessed the first eight years of Japanese rule. This period makes up nearly two-thirds of his book. Pre-1895 Taiwan gets the remaining third, with little good to say about Chinese rule. Davidson's book was the first comprehensive study of Taiwan to appear in English, and, as a result, was influential in shaping opinions.

Davidson was only twenty-two when he arrived in Taiwan in March 1895, a short time before the cession. He covered the Japanese military occupation and the Taiwanese resistance, then remained in Taipei (renamed Taihoku), becoming the first U.S. consul to Taiwan in 1898 and serving five years until his departure. He decided early on he wanted to write a book on Formosa, and was able to draw on a wide range of sources and contacts, as well as his personal experiences of the war and travels around the island.

Davidson's account of the Japanese takeover is gripping but one-sided. He sees the Republic of Taiwan and the armed resistance to the Japanese as something of a joke. The brave, competent Japanese are compared to the fickle rabble. In fact, there was significant resistance, an untold story deserving of a book.

Davidson also had strong views and biases in favor of material progress, championing the Japanese plans for economic development. His interest in having the island's resources utilized starts with the long subtitle to his book: *History, People, Resources, and Commercial Prospects. Tea, Camphor, Sugar, Gold, Coal, Sulphur, Economical Plants, and Other Productions.*

Progress is afoot and Davidson is complimentary to those bringing it: the Western merchants (and trade in general); the Japanese; and the late-Qing official, Liu Ming-chuan, the first governor of Taiwan ("intelligent, liberal-minded, and progressive," and one of just two Chinese he has praise for, the other being Koxinga).

The Island of Formosa, Past and Present was published by Macmillan & Company and Kelly & Walsh, the latter a Shanghai-based publisher founded in 1876. No new English-language work on Taiwan as epic as this has been published in the century since. Forget a large 700-page book with illustrations and maps; major publishers are reluctant to take on even medium-sized books, or those of any size. This is because the market for English-language books on Taiwan is small. Academic presses aim for high profit per book over volume, though the days of easy sales to university libraries are ending. All this means that the majority of Taiwan books are self-published. Although long dismissed as vanity publishing, self-publishing has gained some respectability in the last ten years or so. With the rise of online retailers like Amazon, e-books, and print on demand (which removes the necessity for print runs) it has never been easier or cheaper.

* * *

Self-publishing is nothing new. And for Taiwan aficionados an interesting example of such a work is **Letters of Gilbert Little Stark, July 23, 1907–March 12, 1908** (1908), a collection of long letters home from a young American traveler who passed through Taiwan as part of his Asian travels.

Gilbert Little Stark

In the summer of 1907, Gilbert Little Stark of Saginaw, Michigan, and three fellow graduates from Yale University set off for Japan, the first leg of a year-long adventure around the world. Like Gilbert, his companions were from wealthy, established American families: Hervey Perrin, Arthur Stout, and Amasa Stone Mather from Cleveland. Gilbert and Amasa's travels are chronicled in two separate self-published books. Both accounts are well written and informed, reflecting the extensive reading they did in preparation before embarking and also during their globetrotting, and the tone is modest, the young men aware of the modernity of the new century. This was an age of travel made easier by networks of steamships, trains, and telegrams, and the Yale men didn't see themselves as explorers. They did, however, with a concern still felt by their modern counterparts, strive to be travelers rather than tourists and to get off the beaten track.

Amasa's father apologized for the vanity of privately printing his son's account, *Extracts from the Letters, Diary, and Note Books of Amasa Stone Mather – June 1907 to December 1908* (1910). The father wrote that the book was his idea, a result of the family finding his son's letters interesting and thinking they would be better preserved in book form.

> Trips around the world are now such every-day occurrences, that a narrative of one, can hardly be expected to contain anything new, or be interesting to any outside one's own family, and yet, inasmuch as these young men did have one or two experiences somewhat out of the common – particularly in Mongolia, Formosa, the Shan States, and my son, later, in British East Africa – I have ventured to assume that perhaps a few of his and my particular friends might be interested also in a perusal of his narrative.

In fact, Amasa and Gilbert's ascent of Mount Morrison (Mount Jade or Yushan), Taiwan's highest peak, was a rare accomplishment, and their accounts of it remain valuable. And despite downplaying the risks, travel was still dangerous, sadly shown in the sudden illness and death of Gilbert Stark in India. (It was Gilbert's father who was behind the printing of his son's book.)

The four graduates had a flexible travel schedule, which they altered as they went. And the young men did not travel together the whole time, separating and reuniting along the way as their diverging interests led them. Amasa, for example, was a keen hunter, whereas Gilbert was not. They could part ways temporarily and still keep in touch with letters and telegrams – the Internet of the time.

The Taiwan adventure involved two of the four young Yale men, Amasa and Gilbert. While in Peking, they had at their disposal an excellent library thanks to Mr. Jamison, an American architect and engineer. It was among these books that Formosa seized them as a place worth visiting. Amasa writes:

Gil and I were browsing lazily in deep armed chairs before Mr. Jamison's library fire in Peking. I had Colquhoun's meaty tome The Mastery of the Pacific across my knees, and my hair was slowly rising on my head as I read his lurid account of the untamed headhunters of Formosa. I read one sentence aloud:

The savages, however, far from being subdued, have so far as one can learn, been rather more troublesome of late years.

It was like waving a red rag at a bull, and Gil closed his book with a bang. "Go on," he said, leaning forward with that keen glitter in his eyes, which I knew meant that he was already longing for fresh worlds to conquer.

"There will be plenty of time to assimilate the scanty facts and meager, though thrilling account, which this book gives, later," I observed. "The present point is, where is it?"

"An island off the South China Coast, somewhere."

"Full of wild-eyed head hunters, the book says."

"And primeval jungles and snakes!"

"Terra-incognita to tourist and globe trotter."

"When shall we start?"

"By the next boat."

"Leaving?"

"There is one tomorrow from Ching-wan-tao to Shanghai."

"We're off!"

Gilbert's letter to his parents, sent from Shanghai, was a little less gung-ho on the sudden change of plan to ditch the Philippines for Formosa: "After long deliberation on our schedule and talks with many men, we are not going to the Philippines, although it costs us a good deal mentally to cut it out. We leave to-night by steamer for Foochow, China, and on the 21st leave Foochow by steamer for Formosa!"

Gilbert mentions having letters of introduction to Mr. A— (Mr. Julean H. Arnold) the American Consul in Danshui, and that despite being entirely off the beaten tourist track, "the trip is as safe as living in Saginaw." Perhaps he shouldn't have included all of the following quote as he did from James Davidson's *The Island of Formosa*:

Of all the dominions which have ever acknowledged the authority of China, no corresponding portion of area can be compared with Formosa in interest and future importance, and that equally whether we consider the richness and variety of its soil, its stores of mineral wealth, its scenery, grand and picturesque; or the character of its inhabitant tribes of savages, as wild and untamed as can be found in all Asia and sufficiently unknown to please the wildest ethnologist.

Davidson's book is a doorstopper of a work, and I'm sure anyone who's held a copy can sympathize with Gilbert's decision not to buy a copy as it was "too bulky to carry around."

Gilbert's first Taiwan letter is from October 25, 1907, written at the European-style Shoto-yen Hotel in the hot springs resort of Hokuto (Beitou). The Americans arrived with their Chinese servant Lin, but "minus Am.'s [Amasa's] gun and my revolver, which the police have seized for the time being."

They met with the American ambassador and his wife, and learned that they could tag along on a trip to the central mountains. After calling on the minister of police (a Japanese Harvard graduate) for the necessary permission, they headed south by train. Gilbert was ecstatic at his good fortune – "the opportunity of a lifetime" – in being able to have a crack at the highest mountain in the Japanese empire. "Only about five Europeans, maybe not so many, have ever done it." He tells his parents that "a private individual could never do it now, and it has taken the consul a year to arrange it."

The next letter, written in the Taiwan Strait aboard the *S.S. Joshin Maru* and mailed from Hong Kong, is brimming with details of a trip that exceeded their "most enthusiastic expectations."

The expedition to Jade Mountain consisted of a main party of five: consul Arnold and his wife (and their two fox terriers, Peanuts and Dusibus), Hall ("Harvard '04, who is out here learning the tea business"), Amasa, and Gilbert. In tow was a Chinese cook, "the real true hero of the party," and their Chinese servant Lin.

The main railway line from Taihoku (Taipei) to Takow (Kaohsiung) was completed in 1908, and the party rode it halfway south, a ten-hour journey to Toroku (Douliu), where they spent the night. In the morning they backtracked a little north, departing from the railway line at Rinnai (Linnei), Yunlin County, for nearly two hours on push rail cars across the rice fields, and then continued on foot from Rinkiho (Zhushan) in Nantou County.

Accompanying the group were five Japanese and two local policemen, along with eighteen coolies to carry the luggage. They walked late into evening, and once over a ridge the next morning "left the outposts of civilization behind us, and for nine days we did not see a cultivated field, a water-buffalo, or a Chinese house." It was wild, beautiful territory, a botanical wonderland of lush foliage. The climb on the second day was hard work, alongside a river, and in the water so often that they discarded their shoes and "adopted Japanese *tabi*, socks with the big toe separated from the rest, and *waraji* or straw sandals." Rather predictably, changing to unaccustomed footgear left them with "a plentiful crop of blisters, skinned toes, and embryo stone-bruises."

At a Namakama police post they swapped Chinese bearers for aboriginal ones. Their servant Lin, "frightened and very much exhausted" would liked to have turned back, Gilbert says, if he had known the language. However,

the Formosa Chinese speak the Amoy dialect, and Lin talks only Mandarin and Cantonese. It was funny to hear him talking with the cook in pidgin-English, their only means of communication. The cook, bless his soul! was a rock of determination; it was a bad business, but he would see it through; and every night, when we straggled into camp and dropped on our blankets, tired out, there he was blowing his fire and opening tins of food. The only answers he ever gave to our commands were, "Awright, Master," "Cando, Cando," or, "That belong proper."

And up they continued. The male aborigines wore tight caps "of leather, with a flap hanging over the back of the neck and on to the shoulders" that tied like a bonnet. On their bodies they wore wide belts pulled tightly, loincloths at the front, a long knife in a sheath, (and in cooler weather would don trousers and deerskin jackets). An interesting costume but not necessarily what you want for your hiking companions, especially during an uphill trek: "It will be noticed that, from behind, the male attire appears to consist only of a wide belt about the waist."

On the fifth day a hard climb took a smaller party of eighteen to the summit, through a wild landscape of gorges, rivers, tall grasses and trees, cliffs and boulders, the last thousand feet over rock being the easiest. The weather was good – for half an hour before clouds rolled in – and the view magnificent; a glorious sea of mountain peaks, and both east and west beyond "quivered a hazy ocean."

They had climbed the second-highest peak, a couple of hundred feet lower than the main peak of 4,200 meters. Gilbert says they were the first foreigners and the second group to do so – a Japanese party had made it the previous year – and the fourth to try; two English attempts being thwarted by bad weather and in another the leader of the expedition, a Captain Goodfellow, falling into an aboriginal animal trap and needing hospital treatment. (The highest peak itself had already been scaled by a German expedition and two Japanese ones.) Another first was Mrs. Arnold being the first woman to summit the peak, though for me much of that honor is deserved by the bearers, as she did most of the trip being carried upon a "shelf" contraption. Neither Gilbert's or Amasa's account gives any indication of how heavy she was.

The climbers were saved the trudge of retracing their steps by taking a different route back to the plains, going by Alishan and Kagi (Chiayi) through gorgeous forest scenery and the lands of a different aboriginal tribe. The Arnolds continued south to Tainan as part of their six-week trip, while Hall and the boys headed back up north, Amasa reading a copy of *Anna Karenina* from Hall's stash of books during the train trip.

Gilbert's last letter is from March 12, written on the eve of a ten-day slow-boat journey down the western coast of India for Colombo, Ceylon. He was travelling alone but hoping to soon meet up with Amasa and Purdy, "Although I would not have missed India for worlds, I am delighted to be through with it; it has not been a pleasant month and I have been dreadfully homesick, although my health is excellent."

The last message from the road in the *Letters of Gilbert Little Stark* is Amasa's cable from the city of Mangalore in southwestern India: "Mangalore, India, March 26, 1908. Gilbert M. Stark, Saginaw, Michigan. Gilbert died to-day. Everything possible done. Immediate funeral necessary. We separated three weeks ago and only rejoined him to-day. Mather. Stout."

Gilbert Little Stark was twenty-two years old. There is no indication of what illness he died from – nothing mentioned in the newspapers, his Yale obituary, or the two travel accounts. Amasa himself was to survive his friend by only a dozen years, dying in 1920 from influenza.

* * *

The Japanese era has long been contested in Taiwan, with a general split along ethnic lines, with older mainlanders being anti-Japanese and native Taiwanese pro-Japanese. For the latter, Japanese development of the island between 1895 and 1945 is contrasted with centuries of neglect during the Qing dynasty and the corruption, chaos, and repression of the early decades of rule by the Chinese Nationalist Party, the Kuomintang (KMT). The mainstream public, academia, and media opinion of the Japanese colonial period is mostly positive. It doesn't hurt that modern-day Japan is such a beautiful, clean, safe, and civilized place to visit – by far Taiwan's favorite travel destination – and that the country is an important strategic ally.

A fascinating case of the subjective historiography of the Japanese era is the relatively little known Tapani Incident of 1915. Named after the village of Tapani (Yujing) east of Tainan, it was the largest single act of Han Chinese armed resistance during the Japanese colonial era; more than a thousand died in fierce fighting and hundreds from executions or during imprisonment.

The rebellion started with a former policeman, Yu Ching-fang, a self-appointed savior chosen by heaven to rally the forces of righteousness and drive out the Japanese. The messianic rhetoric of apocalypse and salvation tapped into old beliefs in the region, and specifically drew on those espoused by a secret society that Yu had belonged to and been jailed for his involvement with. Once freed, Yu associated himself with Xilai Temple in Tainan, where he raised money, recruited followers, and found co-conspirators. Yu's followers had to kneel before him, and – if they wanted immunity from the enemy's bullets – purchase magical amulets, and worse, follow a vegetarian diet for forty-seven days. The planned resurrection was derailed by the Japanese authorities making arrests, and the rebel attacks on police stations ended with a decisive one-sided battle in Tapani. The rebellion, which saw aborigines allied with Han Chinese, lasted a little over a month. Yu was arrested and executed.

Yu Ching-fang, photographed after his arrest

57

Paul Katz, an American social scientist interested in the history and religion of Taiwan and China, has delved into the story of the incident in **When Valleys Turned Blood Red: The Ta-pa-ni Incident in Colonial Taiwan** (2005). The title comes from a contemporary Taiwanese intellectual's description of the carnage: "Corpses clog the streams, valleys turn blood red."

Katz's account follows Paul A. Cohen's approach to the Boxer Rebellion in China, *History in Three Keys: The Boxers as Event, Experience, and Myth* (1998). Katz is interested in the religious aspects of the Tapani Incident and sees similarities between the two uprisings in this regard. As well as examining the factors contributing to the uprising, the rebellion itself, and the aftermath, he looks at its historiography, showing how the event was interpreted to suit political purposes at various times. For the Japanese authorities, the uprising was banditry; the KMT preferred to see the rebels as patriots inspired by the Xinhai Revolution of 1911, which brought about the Republic of China; more recently the trend has been to downplay the uprising or see it as the resistance of Taiwanese elites to foreign rule.

Observers of Taiwan's history tend to see things through a prism of nationalism – either resistance to or acceptance of Japanese rule, resistance to or acceptance of KMT rule, and either support for independence or unification with China. This focus is hardly surprising, as a change of national rulers is no trivial matter; you get a change of permitted customs and languages, and a drastic change of personal and family fortunes.

Nationalism is not the main focus for Katz. He sees the motivations for the uprising – like the Boxer Rebellion – as a combination of millenarianism and economic dislocation, the latter point involving the sugar monopoly, land taxes, and confiscation. The spark for the rebellion was religious but didn't happen out of thin air, instead coming from deep religious customs and a tradition of revolts.

* * *

Perhaps the most fascinating book on the Japanese era is *Among the Headhunters of Formosa* (1922), by the feisty American anthropologist Janet Montgomery McGovern, who made numerous visits to aboriginal areas during her two-year stay from September 1916 to September 1918.

It was Taiwan's scenery, first seen from the ship on her way to Japan from Manila, that had interested McGovern in visiting the island:

> Indeed, it was the beauty of Formosa that first attracted me. I shall never forget the first glimpse that I caught of the island as I passed it, going by steamer from Manila to Nagasaki. There it lay, in the light of the tropical sunrise, glowing and shimmering like a great emerald, with an apparent vividness of green that I had never seen before, even in the tropics.... The glimpse which I caught that day of the shining island with its vivid colouring, and seemingly wondrously carved surface, remained with me as a pleasant memory during the several years that I spent in Japan.

During her residence in Japan teaching English and studying Buddhism, she gave little thought to Taiwan, as it was off limits to anyone not on business; and the handful of travelers who did manage to visit were kept under strict Japanese supervision. While she was studying in Kyoto, a lucky break came in the form of an offer from a Japanese official to teach English in a government school in Taipei. She eagerly accepted the invitation. School holidays and a four-day work schedule left McGovern with plenty of time for exploring, though this was done in the face of constant official displeasure. When passing through the "squalid and dirty ... sordid ... hideous" port of Keelung on one of her excursions into the countryside, she was stopped by a Japanese policeman:

> Clanking his sword as he spoke, he demanded my name and address; also he peremptorily demanded to know what I meant by coming to take photographs in the great colonial port-town of his Imperial Majesty, and asked if I did not know that this made me guilty of the unspeakably abominable crime of lack of respect for his August Majesty. I explained that I was not taking pictures in Keelung, had not done so, and had no intention of so doing; that there was nothing there worth photographing.

Thanks to two sympathetic officials, McGovern was able to get the necessary permission to make trips into the mountains. She mostly travelled by push-car railway, and would then set out on foot. The warm receptions she invariably received and the close relations she managed to forge so quickly with the aborigines were, she believed, due to the fact that they regarded her "as the reincarnation of one of the seventeenth-century Dutch, whose rule over them, three hundred years ago, has become a sacred tradition." Oral history said that the Dutch had treated the aborigines well, and even taught them to read and write their own language in the "sign-marks of the gods" (i.e., the romanized script developed by missionaries).

Despite the "headhunters" title, McGovern downplayed the practice of headhunting, which was then on its way out among the three tribes still practicing it, by comparing it favorably to the mechanized mass murder of the First World War. "What is war between 'civilized' races, except head-hunting on a grand scale," she asked. The Japanese were succeeding in stamping headhunting out; though some of the bloodier customs associated with it continued with substitutes for human flesh. The Paiwan, for example, had a game – played once every five years – in which a bundle of bark was tossed in the air and warriors tried to lance it, the winner being the first warrior to catch it on his bamboo spear. Formerly an enemy's head had been used.

The neighboring Piyuma tribe had an annual ceremony in which a live monkey was tied before the bachelor dormitory, and young men killed it by shooting arrows into the unlucky creature. Tribal elders explained that in the good old days a prisoner (some unfortunate from a rival tribe) was used, but now they had to make do with a monkey. And the animal was a lousy substitute because it couldn't act as a messenger to the afterlife, whereas with the human sacrifice each of the arrows carried a message to an ancestor in the spirit world.

The Atayal marriage ceremony had a rather macabre conclusion, the bride and groom drinking together from a skull, preferably one the man had collected himself. McGovern found that the majority of Atayal grooms had indeed taken heads. Men in other tribes made do with skulls taken by their father or grandfather. The Ami and Piyuma made do with monkey skulls, "for which effeminacy they are held in great contempt by the Taiyal [Atayal]."

McGovern's account and the author herself are of such interest that you could easily write a whole book, either a broader biography of McGovern or a narrower concentration on her time in Taiwan. I hope one day a female English teacher in Taiwan – ideally an anthropology major – reads *Among the Headhunters of Formosa* and sees a kindred spirit and feels inspired to put pen to paper. There's even a bit of stardust for the project in the connection to Janet McGovern's famous son, William Montgomery McGovern

1897–1964, a notable explorer and professor who is often cited as a likely inspiration for the film character of Indiana Jones.

Turn to the front matter of *Among the Headhunters of Formosa* and you'll see she dedicated it to her son: TO W.M.M. MY SON AND THE COMPANION OF MY WANDERINGS. Elsewhere in the book he gets only one brief mention: "Sometimes accompanied by another English teacher and a servant, sometimes by my son or secretary, sometimes quite alone, I went up into the mountains."

Dedications tend to be a little dull, predictably made to a spouse in appreciation for emotional and practical support during the writing of the work, and also from guilt in ignoring the family, or maybe placation for the next book. Sometimes, however, as in McGovern's case, there's an interesting story behind the dedication.

Janet Stuart Blair Montgomery McGovern, born in 1874, graduated from Shorter College in Georgia and worked as a journalist in New York City. She married Felix Daniel McGovern (1873–1934), a journalist and later an army officer, but divorced after William was born.

Mother and son remained together and were very close. While Janet was teaching English in Japan, the teenaged William was also there, studying Buddhism, an interest that came from his mother. Before moving to Asia, she had been immersed in Eastern religion and occult teachings. After graduating with the equivalent of a doctor of divinity from Nishi Hongan-ji monastery in Kyoto in 1917, it seems William joined his mother for some of her Taiwan adventures. After Formosa, we next find the pair studying at Oxford University (and William also teaching Mandarin at the University of London). In 1922, the year *Among the Headhunters of Formosa* was published, William received his doctorate and embarked on a lengthy expedition to forbidden Tibet. Denied formal entry, he disguised himself as a Tibetan and managed to sneak into the sacred city of Lhasa, an adventure recounted in *To Lhasa in Disguise: A Secret Expedition through Mysterious Tibet* (1924).

* * *

A much more positive testimonial of the Japanese era is Owen Rutter's travelogue **Through Formosa: An Account of Japan's Island Colony** (1923), based on a brief trip the Englishman and his wife made in April 1921. They arrived in Kaohsiung, travelled up the west coast to Taipei, and departed from Keelung. At that time, the country was virtually closed to tourists; but Rutter, a colonial administrator and later a rubber planter in Borneo, was able to get an official invitation through a friend.

Rutter described his account as "the work of a passer-by," which is a statement of fact rather than modesty; real modesty would have been not writing a book after a two-week visit. A travelogue based on so whirlwind a trip might be annoying for a modern writer expected to ratchet up creditable length-of-stay points, but forgivable with Rutter because his book is well written, generally informative, sometimes funny, and a rare look at the country in the 1920s.

Rutter was given rose-colored glasses in the form of a guide-interpreter, C. Koshimura of the Foreign Section, and a carefully controlled schedule designed to show the colony at its best. It included tours around schools, a prison, a sugar factory, a model aboriginal settlement, and some of the usual tourist sites. He and his wife also received a free train pass and red-carpet treatment: officials meeting them at train stations, invitations to dinner, and an endless exchange of cards and little cups of tea. At the end of his trip he says, "I counted up the visiting-cards I had acquired, I found that there were a hundred and twenty-nine."

The Englishman had a keen eye for the details of administration, but his account often gets bogged down in observations about accommodation and meals. Mind you, when trying to turn such a short stay into a book, it would be hard not to prominently feature such things. And there's a fair bit of information filler. We get many pages on the story of the clash between Koxinga and the Dutch, but only a few paragraphs on Rutter's visit to Fort Zeelandia. The site wasn't very impressive: "The waste of mud flats, where three hundred years ago the Dutch squadrons rode at anchor, presented a dreary spectacle. Even Fort Zeelandia, over whose battlements the blood-flag had floated defiantly for eight months, was as depressing as the rest; it lies neglected, with crumbling walls, from one of which grows a great banyan tree, its strange roots twisting among the bricks."

As they were looking about the ruins of the fort, two police officers suddenly appeared and took them to see the salt-making process. A brief description ensues, and then we get the history and current practice of the salt monopoly, and other monopolies.

Rutter came away from his trip greatly impressed by Japan's stewardship of the island: "During the twenty-eight years Japan has been in possession of the island she has succeeded in developing it in a manner which must be almost, if not quite, unparalleled in the history of civilization."

There was one major exception though: the forced assimilation of the aborigines. Rutter's stage-managed travels to the aborigines, brief as they were, couldn't prevent him from feeling that Japan's handling of the tribes was a failure. The problem stemmed, he thought, from a lack of sympathy because at heart the Japanese despised the aborigines as savages. And unfortunately the "native problem" didn't draw the best and brightest personnel. In British colonies, the romance and adventure of serving in aboriginal areas attracted more able young men than needed. As a former district officer in Borneo, Owen had personal experience with a successful model for dealing with aborigines. District officers would visit the villages in their area of responsibility on foot, live among the people, learn the language and customs, settle legal disputes, and protect them from exploitation. In other words, Rutter's solution was to employ more chaps like himself.

The 1920s were in many ways the halcyon years for Japan's showcase colony, an Arcadian paradise on the cusp of modernity, not yet under the shadow of 1930s Japanese militarization. Photographs from the period show regally costumed aborigines, idyllic rural scenes, new railways and schools, and orderly cities with imposing boulevards and neo-classical architecture. *Through Formosa* is illustrated with photographs taken by Mrs. Rutter. Largely unremarkable pictures in themselves, they are actually quite special for another reason. The Japanese authorities were paranoid about foreigners taking photographs, and either discouraged or prohibited it, softening the blow by providing high-quality officially approved images. For example, every single photograph in an exquisitely illustrated forty-five-page *National Geographic* article from 1920 ("Formosa the Beautiful") came from Japanese government sources.

* * *

An excellent comparison piece to Rutter's *Through Formosa* is Harry A. Franck's **Glimpses of Japan and Formosa** (1924). Franck (1881–1962) was a prolific American travel writer of more than thirty popular travel books, starting with *A Vagabonding Journey Around the World* (1910). For his Taiwan travels there was insufficient material for a single volume and he added his account to the end of a travelogue on Japan. His Taiwan section is middling; we get straight descriptions of towns, some opinions, and background information, which sometimes feels like filler reworked from other sources; but there's little in the way of first-person adventures. He travels along the west coast main railway line and makes a couple of minor side trips to the interior; however, he's not always clear about places and dates – so it's impossible to know exactly where he went and how much time he spent there. Taiwan was a frustrating destination for Franck, which shows in the tone and effort of his writing. The root problem perhaps was that the country was a poor match for his casual (and frugal) vagabonding style; the colony was expensive, subject to Japanese restrictions, and much of it off-limits.

Further coloring his views were the comparisons he made with China. Franck arrived in Taiwan having come from southern China rather than Japan, and as such was struck by the Japaneseness of the place and also the reduced benefit of being a Westerner. "After the often Elysian freedom of life in China – for the foreigner enjoying the rights of extraterritoriality – the realization came almost with a shock that I was back in a mikado-ruled land again."

The cost of travel was an unfavorable contrast: "prices are approximately twenty-five per cent higher than in Japan itself, and to the traveler from China they are atrocious."

Franck got off to a bad start in the port of Keelung, where he was delayed because of bureaucracy, which kept him "courteously but firmly imprisoned on the ship during the two hours necessary to telephone the 'foreign office' in the capital and get me 'special permission' to land."

The rigid, military-like atmosphere of Taihoku he says seemed strange after months in China: "for here all is orderliness in complete contrast to Chinese disorder on the other side of the channel, a Prussian exactness which Prussia never attained. Japanese life makes one direct from China feel very staid and orderly."

One of the highlights of Franck's account is a conversation he had with a Spanish priest (unnamed in the book but probably Bartolomé Martinez). The Spaniard had been on the island for forty years, and thus long enough to compare Japanese rule with that of the preceding

Qing. While praising certain aspects of Japanese colonization, he was generally critical; there had been material gain but a great moral sliding: "Formosan girls of the class which a generation ago would have been immaculate in social behavior parade the streets in gay, insufficient garb, most of them ready at anything like sufficient provocation to give or sell their favours to any male who longs for them." One suspects a case here of damning the modern; after all, female fashions of the 1920s – short hair, bare arms, and raised hemlines – were as dramatic a shift in clothing tastes as we've ever seen.

The author was not convinced by the priest's viewpoint and was instead happy to see more "spontaneous gaiety" and freedom among the young generation. "I had myself seen no small number of these Formosan 'flappers,' girls above the peasant and coolie class, gaudy and conspicuous in their numerous hair ornaments, their flower-embroidered silk jackets, and trousers reaching hardly below the knees — perhaps this was what the padre referred to as 'insufficient' — their silk stockings ending in little gay-colored cloth shoes." It was certainly better than foot-binding.

Another of the padre's bitter complaints against the Japanese was their paranoid suspicion of foreigners. Despite decades of good works, he was still treated like a threat: "Every time he left town to visit one of his out-stations, when he went on any journey whatever, he had to give the police authorities detailed information as to where, when, and why he was going; and still they never failed to send spies behind his back to ask whom he had talked with, what he had said, and so on to the end of patience."

This seemingly insane level of xenophobic control is revealing; it suggests (and is supported by evidence) the extent to which Japanese citizens in foreign countries were engaged in collecting intelligence for the empire.

* * *

The Japanese were not xenophobic when it came to adopting certain Western customs, baseball being a prime example. The sport played an important role in the forging of Taiwan's identity, a story told in Andrew D. Morris' *Colonial Project, National Game: A History of Baseball in Taiwan*, published in 2010 by the University of California Press.

Although baseball is considered Taiwan's national sport, finding physical evidence of its popularity on the ground isn't easy. Go to a park on the weekend and basketball is what you see kids playing. Baseball is, however, Taiwan's most popular spectator sport, and the only one with a professional league (though a league of only four teams it has to be said).

Despite being more watched (and bet upon) than played, baseball has a special place in Taiwanese history and the national psyche, which Morris examines in great depth from its origins to the present day. Baseball was brought to Taiwan via Japan, where it had been first introduced into schools in the 1870s by an American professor teaching English in Tokyo. During the Japanese period of colonial rule, the sport evolved from a Japanese preserve to a deeply embedded part of Taiwanese life.

For the colonial authorities, baseball was a useful means of "Japanizing" the locals, in particular the troublesome aborigines. The first great Taiwanese baseball arose in the 1920s, the Nōkō Baseball Team from the remote east coast town of Karenko (Hualien). Comprised of Ami aborigines, the team achieved national success, which led to a celebrated tour of Japan, where four of the team's star players remained, accepting offers to play for a Kyoto high school. In 1927 and 1928 the Ami players helped take the Kyoto team to the most prestigious tournament in Japan, the Kōshien High School Baseball Tournament. If winning a high school contest sounds underwhelming, author Morris provides some useful context, describing the Kōshien tournament "as a cross between the Super Bowl, NCAA 'March Madness,' and *American Idol* in its centrality to Japanese popular culture."

Japanese "civilizing" efforts against the aborigines at that time included a system of reservations and forced resettlement. Resentment at heavy-handed rule boiled over into the Wushe Rebellion in 1930, the last major uprising against the Japanese. Several hundred Seediq warriors descended on the village of Wushe, killing more than 130 Japanese, most of whom were there for an athletics meeting at the elementary school. The Japanese retaliation was shift and brutal, and included bombing with mustard gas, arguably the first use of chemical weapons in Asia. Resettlement and assimilation was stepped up. The Wushe Rebellion – and the brutal response to it – shocked Japan and Taiwan, destroying the illusion of Japan's seemingly successful and benevolent colonial experiment. Baseball would, however, soon help to heal the wounds. A highlight of *Colonial Project, National Game* is the Kano team episode, the story of how a ragtag band of players from a two-bit school on Japan's colonial fringes defied the odds to reach the 1931 Kōshien final (where they lost 4–0). The Kano story had – and still has – the perfect ingredients to capture both the Japanese and Taiwanese public imagination. The team's unusual tri-ethnic composition – Japanese, Aborigines, and Han Taiwanese – made it a symbol of harmonious assimilation; for the Japanese audience, the Kano team was exotic and validation of the civilizing colonial project. Additionally, the team came from the backwater of Chiayi City and a low-status vocational school without a baseball pedigree. They didn't even have their own baseball field; daily practice involved a bicycle ride across town to a municipal field. And then there was the tough Japanese coach, Kondo Hyotaro, straight out of central casting, who took a losing side and whipped them into champions. He's fondly remembered as exemplifying Japanese qualities of strictness, self-sacrifice, and integrity. It was the bushido spirit applied to baseball, boot-camp machismo best enjoyed at the safe distance of nostalgia.

The Kano story is ready-made for the big screen, and the only surprise about the 2014 film *Kano*, which became one of the all-time best performing domestic films, was that it hadn't been made earlier.

Readers, however, should not approach *Colonial Project, National Game* expecting a rousing, cinematic tale. It is an academic book, and if you're as allergic to academic jargon as I am you may find your facial muscles twitching at phrases such as "colonial discourses," "mode of assimilation," "hegemonic colonial implications," and "postcolonial hierarchies." In addition, Morris is more interested in tangential subjects than the actual baseball. Don't expect player profiles or blow-by-blow game commentary on the epic clashes. He looks at the game in terms of something he calls "glocalization," that is, how various local and global forces interacted. All that aside, the book is packed with factual and anecdotal nuggets, which is why – though I'm not a fan of the sport – I've included it despite covering another baseball book (*Playing in Isolation*), which we will encounter later on.

* * *

Although there was never ground fighting in Taiwan, the island was deeply involved in the Second World War. Taiwanese served in the Japanese military, and the island was an important base for aerial operations, especially against China, and then against the approaching American naval push northward. From 1944 it was on the receiving end; targets of military value in Taiwan were heavily bombed by American planes. Downed American fighter pilots and bomber crews were treated as "war criminals" rather than as prisoners of war and were imprisoned in Taihoku (Taipei) Prison.

Fourteen airmen were executed there on June 19, 1945. Eleven others were released soon after the Japanese surrender.

Taiwan was also home to fourteen POW camps, a few of which provided temporary quarters for prisoners being transported from Singapore or the Philippines to Japan or Manchuria, a couple for senior officers, and the others slave labor camps, such as the notorious Kinkaseki in the northeast, where prisoners were put to work in copper mines. In total about 4,400 prisoners did time on the island, with – according to Japanese records – around ten percent dying, though this was much higher at the worst camps such as Kinkaseki.

Taiwan's Second World War experience is screaming out for a book. At the moment, the only offerings are five POW memoirs: *Banzai, You Bastards!* (1991), by Jack Edwards; *One Day at a Time: A British Prisoner of War's Account of 1300 Days in a Japanese Slave Labour Camp* (1993), by Arthur Titherington; *Tomorrow You Die: The Astonishing Survival Story of a Second World War Prisoner of the Japanese* (2012), by Andy Coogan; *Out of the Depths of Hell: A Soldier's Story of Life and Death in Japanese Hands* (1999), by John McEwan; and *Three Heroes of Kinkaseki* (2015), by Philip and Patricia Andrews (the three prisoners covered being Harry Brant, George Horton, and Joseph Walker).

The best known of these is *Banzai, You Bastards!* I recounted the author's experience in *Formosan Odyssey*. Welshman Jack Edwards (1918–2006), a sergeant in the Royal Corps of Signals, was taken prisoner at the surrender of the "impregnable fortress" of Singapore in February 1942. He was shipped to Taiwan later that year, marched from the port of Keelung to a camp at Kinkaseki (now Jinguashi) and put to work in a copper mine. Work and living conditions were hellish, made worse by sadistic guards – both Taiwanese and Japanese – who took every opportunity to beat prisoners.

The bombing of Hiroshima and Nagasaki brought about a sudden end to the prisoners' ordeal. The Japanese in Taiwan surrendered quietly to the arriving Americans, and the POWs were evacuated by the U.S. Navy.

5

2-28: A Bad Beginning

THE false certainty of hindsight makes it seem inevitable that
the Japanese colony of Taiwan would, after the Second World
War, come under the control of the Chinese Nationalists; and it was
surely logical that Chiang Kai-shek and the KMT would, several
years later, flee to the island in the dying days of the Chinese Civil
War and make it the new seat of the Republic of China, a fortress
from which to contemplate retaking the mainland. How different
things were in reality, how much more complicated and interesting were the many twists and turns. In *Accidental State: Chiang
Kai-shek, the United States, and the Making of Taiwan* (2016),
Taiwanese historian Hsiao-ting Lin – drawing on both English- and
Chinese-language archival materials, including newly released
official files and personal papers – convincingly argues that the
formation of a Nationalist state in Taiwan was far more "accidental"
than the result of any deliberate planning by the various players.

China showed no interest in regaining Taiwan until the early 1940s. After war broke out with Japan in 1937, Chinese talk of reclaiming lost territories centered on areas in Manchuria. Taiwan – which China's Qing dynasty government had ceded in perpetuity to Japan in 1895 following defeat in the first Sino-Japanese War – was not an issue. This changed, however, with the December 1941 Japanese attack on Pearl Harbor, bringing the Americans into the conflict. In the lead-up to the Cairo Conference of November 1943, when Chiang Kai-shek met with Franklin D. Roosevelt and Winston Churchill to decide on the post-war reshaping of the world, the Nationalists were forced to decide exactly which territories to insist on reclaiming. They considered asking for Korea and the Ryukyus (the island group containing Okinawa that stretches between Taiwan and the main islands of Japan) but decided this was not practical; in the case of the latter, the fact they had no navy deterred them. In a fascinating side note – and *Accidental State* is full of such treasures – we learn that President Roosevelt, "was more than pleased to have the Ryukyu Islands return to postwar China, an idea he had advanced to the Nationalists in 1942."

Chiang left the Cairo Conference with broad promises that his government could take over the island of Formosa after the war. The communiqué stated that: "Japan shall be stripped of all the islands in the Pacific which she has seized or occupied since the beginning of the first World War in 1914, and that all the territories Japan has stolen from the Chinese, such as Manchuria, Formosa, and The Pescadores, shall be restored to the Republic of China."

Not everyone in the American government favored Taiwan being handed to the Republic of China. An important figure was George Kerr, an American who had lived in Japan and colonial Taiwan, and who served during the war years as a Taiwan expert.

Kerr drafted a memorandum for the War Department exploring post-war possibilities for Taiwan: independence; immediate transfer to China; and third, a temporary Allied trusteeship, during which time the Taiwanese could hold a plebiscite to decide their own future. The last option is what Kerr favored, as did Taiwan's early independence supporters.

Following the dropping of the atomic bombs on Hiroshima and Nagasaki (August 6 and 9) and the Soviet Union's declaration of war and immediate invasion of Japanese-controlled Manchuria, Japan surrendered on August 15. The transfer of power on Taiwan from the Japanese to the Chinese Nationalists was achieved with American assistance. Chiang Kai-shek appointed Chen Yi as governor, an ominous beginning as Chen's leadership over Fujian Province had been ruinous. Chen was escorted to Taiwan by George Kerr to accept the Japanese government's surrender. The official handover was on October 25, 1945, a date from then on celebrated as Taiwan Retrocession Day. It's worth noting that Japan did not formally relinquish sovereignty over Taiwan until the Peace Treaty of San Francisco in 1951 and that the treaty does not hand the country over to the Republic of China (ROC). Given the lack of subsequent international treaties to settle Taiwan's status, its sovereignty remains undetermined under international law.

Taiwan's retrocession was initially greeted with enthusiasm by most Taiwanese. The early years of KMT rule of Taiwan, however, were a disaster; it wasn't long – February 28, 1947, to be exact – before corruption, mismanagement, food shortages, and hyperinflation led to mass discontent that boiled over into an uprising called the 2-28 Incident (or 2-28 Massacre). The spark was harassment of a female street cigarette vendor by Tobacco and Alcohol Monopoly officers, and the subsequent shooting by police of a member of the crowd that gathered in protest.

In *Formosa Betrayed*, George Kerr's account of 2-28, he uses the term "the March massacres," which gives a more accurate impression of what happened. Giving a specific date (i.e., February 28) implies a single outburst of violence rather than a longer, calculated campaign of terror. After the initial violence on 2-28 and the following days there was a lull while the authorities bought time with conciliatory promises. ROC troops were steaming toward Taiwan. When they arrived on March 8, the killing resumed. Alongside the random shooting of civilians, there was more organized carnage; lists of opponents had been drawn up – the people on them were now taken away and executed. The ranks of Taiwan's best and brightest were decimated, the survivors silenced for more than a generation. Estimates of the total "incident" fatalities range from ten thousand to thirty thousand. The KMT government brushed the incident off as a Communist- and Japanese-inspired insurrection. Public discussion of it was forbidden.

Accidental State author Hsiao-ting Lin makes it clear that Taiwan's fate after the Second World War was never a straight choice between Chiang Kai-shek and Mao Zedong. If the KMT had not moved to Taiwan (or done so under different leadership), the island would most likely have come under an Allied or U.N. trusteeship. This was an idea promoted by the Taiwanese political elite and several American advisors, including George Kerr, who had been the American vice consul in Taipei.

As the Nationalists' hold on China slipped in the late 1940s, some American officials – who expected China to split between a communist north and anti-communist south (as would later happen to Korea and Vietnam) – looked to bypass the Nationalist leadership and directly work with and aid regional anti-communist allies.

As part of this regional story, Lin gives a previously untold account of an abortive Yunnan independence attempt, highlighting the complicated multi-player intrigues of the time. Chiang was hoping to make the southwestern province of Yunnan a bastion from which to resist the advancing People's Liberation Army. Unlike Taiwan, Yunnan's sovereignty was settled (Japan had still not formally relinquished its rights to Taiwan). The Nationalist governor of Yunnan Province, Lu Han, had other ideas than hosting Chiang; he secretly sent a request to the U.S. government. If the United States backed him, he would declare independence. Washington turned down the offer, and the governor promptly handed the province over to the Communists on December 9, 1949. The next day, with his last hope for a base on the mainland gone, Chiang flew from the wartime capital of Chongqing to Taipei, stopping briefly in Chengdu, the last time he would stand on Chinese soil.

On January 5, 1950, the American government washed its hands of him and the KMT, U.S. president Truman issuing a press statement to the effect that the United States would not intervene in China and would not provide military assistance to the Nationalists in Taiwan. The Americans changed tack six months later with the start of the Korean War.

Accidental State is a book that invites counterfactual history speculation. Would Taiwan as a protectorate (of either the United Nations or the United States) ended up more like Japan or the Philippines? If we're doing "what ifs" for the entire stretch of Taiwan's history, then the big one is the Dutch in Taiwan: What if Koxinga had not decided to come to Taiwan, and, on the Dutch side, what would have happened if the VOC leaders in Batavia had been more supportive of Governor Coyet? But going back to what ifs surrounding the early KMT hold on Taiwan, one spy case stands out.

On October 1, 1949, Mao stood atop Tiananmen Square's Gate of Heavenly Peace in Beijing and declared the founding of the People's Republic of China. His triumphant armies still had some unfinished business on the edges of the empire; a week later the PLA invaded Tibet, and on October 24 a large force landed on Kinmen, a small island near the Fujian city of Xiamen. But the PLA forces invading Kinmen were defeated in a fierce three-day battle. This gave temporary halt to Chinese plans to take Taiwan, an eventuality most contemporary observers thought was inevitable. The start of the Korean War in June 1950 would change that. However, as described in Ian Easton's *The Chinese Invasion Threat* (2017) the little known Cai Xiaoqian spy case was an important factor in deterring an invasion during those dangerous months when Taiwan stood alone.

The Communists had a large network of agents in Taiwan. Their primary mission was to recruit ROC military commanders who would defect – ideally with their troops – when the Chinese landed. Secret agents were also used to stir social unrest, for sabotage, and to build up networks of influence.

The spymaster running operations in Taiwan was Cai Xiaoqian, a Taiwanese who in the 1920s had moved to Shanghai to study. He joined the Communists and proved a skilled propaganda officer. After World War II he returned undercover to Taiwan and developed a spy network. Easton says that by December 1949, he may have had as many as thirteen hundred undercover operatives under his control, and preparations were taking shape nicely. Spymaster Cai "recommended that the invasion be launched in April 1950, when the weather would be most favorable for amphibious operations."

One of Cai's prized assets was a two-star ROC general, Wu Shi, who had access to and handed over strategic secret documents. But Chiang Kai-shek's intelligence agents were closing in. "Having experienced a fatal hemorrhaging of intelligence and the defection of key military units in mainland China, he was determined to eradicate undercover spies who had infested Taiwan. It was a race against time."

After uncovering a spy ring in Keelung in September 1949, the spy catchers worked their way up, threads taking them to Cai himself, who was promptly arrested. Cai was an expert interrogator, and managed to convince his captors he would defect and assist them. He made a daring escape but was eventually cornered and captured, importantly not choosing to commit suicide. Easton says, "Cai still had too much to live for. He was desperately in love with a young girl who had been captured by counterintelligence officers."

March 1, 1950, was a pivotal date in the history of cross-Strait relations. That evening, after a long interrogation session, Mao's spymaster in Taiwan cracked under pressure and defected. He became a ROC military officer and, in return, gained his girlfriend's freedom, a huge sum of gold, and a high-ranking position in the military. To earn his generous reward, Cai fingered General Wu Shi and Agent Zhu Fengzhi, and revealed the identities of his other collaborators, exposing every major communist officer on the island. Cai's information allowed MND officers to make a clean sweep, clearing out enemy spy rings and underground cells across Taiwan.

* * *

Two-two-eight – the original sin, and the most dramatic event, of Taiwan's modern history, shorthand for the decades of KMT repression known as the White Terror – has been the go-to choice for novels in recent years: *The Third Son* (2013), *The 228 Legacy* (2013), and *Green Island* (2016). All three were written by Taiwanese-American women; echoing this, the stories take place in the United States as well as in Taiwan.

The Third Son begins in 1943 during an American bombing raid. An eight-year-old Taiwanese boy, Saburo, saves a fellow student, the lovely Yoshiko. It's the start of a romance. As suggested in the title, Suburo is the third son of a traditional family, and as such neglected. Despite numerous handicaps, his intelligence and determination gains him a coveted scholarship to the United States, where he eventually ends up working in the new field of space rocket technology.

The political dramas of the time – World War II, the transition from Japanese to KMT rule, 2-28, the White Terror – are covered but are not central. The authoritarian nature of traditional Chinese family values come in for harsh appraisal.

Reviewer Bradley Winterton described it as "the best novel featuring Taiwan" he had ever read: "A few others have perhaps more thoroughly worked up particular incidents in depth, but none has been as professionally constructed and as lucidly written as *The Third Son*." While I agree the novel is excellent, especially for a debut work, I wouldn't go quite that far: for a book to wear the crown of best Taiwan novel, I would – on top of plot, characters, and writing quality – like its entire story to be set in Taiwan; additionally, I've never been able to buy early childhood romance as being meaningful.

With Jennifer J. Chow's *The 228 Legacy* (2013) the White Terror is dealt with indirectly – how it affected one family living in 1980s California. Only a few pages are set in Taiwan, covering a three-day sightseeing trip by a main character, whose husband was murdered during the 1947 uprising. The story is narrated in the present tense – a personal bugbear – and is rather dour reading. Anyone looking to learn about Taiwan would be better off with *Green Island*.

* * *

Shawna Yang Ryan's **Green Island** (2016) is the star Taiwan novel of its decade, a deserved popular and critical success. Writing it was a fourteen-year project, which included extensive research in Taiwan and the United States. The titular island, off the southwest coast of Taiwan, is where many political prisoners were sent during the martial law era.

Green Island tells the story of a family scarred by 2-28 and the White Terror. The novel opens with the birth of the unnamed female narrator, the youngest child of the Tsai family, born on the night of February 28, 1947, as revolt breaks out on the streets of Taipei. She is delivered by her father, Dr. Tsai, who two weeks later is arrested for publically expressing mild criticism of the Nationalist government, and sent to Green Island. His long absence – like that of so many others, who were either killed or imprisoned – is a dark secret, a topic not to be raised. The author makes an excellent choice in not having her father a fiery revolutionary and noble martyr; instead he returns home after ten years as a broken man, a spectral presence in the family. The father carries the black mark of having been imprisoned, and also the suspicion of his survival having come from being an informer.

When the protagonist narrator emigrates to the United States, politics follow her as a result of her husband's and her friendship with a Taiwanese pro-democracy dissident. For me the U.S.-based passages diffuse the story slightly but are an understandable choice; the author is herself Taiwanese-American, and they make the story more accessible for the target audience.

Green Island is epic without being overly heroic, and all the more moving for having good yet flawed characters. For them there is merit in surviving, in getting on with life, but a sadness pervades: the wearying, ever-present shadows of 2-28 and the silent complicity with authoritarian rule. As the protagonist says near the end: "Nothing sublime hid in the pain we found in one March decades ago, a month that went on and on beyond the boundaries of the calendar."

Both a family history and a political history of Taiwan, *Green Island* spans the decades from 1947 to the 2003 SARS crisis. For such a novel, how to handle the political arc presents a challenge. The end of authoritarianism and the triumph of democracy was anti-climatic: gradual and largely peaceful, with no storming of the barricades, no extracting of justice from a tribunal, and no obvious event to bookend the 2-28 incident. Even picking a date for when Taiwan could be called democratic is tricky. This quiet, successful transition might be one of the reasons the country hasn't received the international media attention it merits.

* * *

The first English-language White Terror novel was ***A Pail of Oysters*** (1953), by Vern Sneider (1916–1981). Unlike Sneider's previous novel, the humorous 1951 bestseller *The Teahouse of the August Moon*, this has a dark tone. Set against the political repression and poverty of the early 1950s, *A Pail of Oysters* tells the moving story of nineteen-year-old half-Hakka and half-Aborigine villager Li Liu and his quest to recover his family's kitchen god – a framed picture of a god – stolen by Nationalist soldiers. Li Liu's fate becomes entwined with that of American journalist Ralph Barton, who, in trying to shake off his government minders and report honestly about KMT rule of the island, is drawn into the world of the Formosan underground.

A Pail of Oysters is a landmark work from a time when novels were often seen as a moral force (and novelists could actually make a living). The book was taken seriously and became part of the debate on China and Taiwan. Banned in Taiwan, in the United States the novel received generally positive reviews but was denounced by the powerful China lobby, an unofficial and disparate collection of individuals (most famously Henry Luce of *Time* magazine) and special interest groups that sought to influence American opinion in favor of the KMT. In his detailed introduction to the

2016 Camphor Press edition of the novel, Jonathan Benda describes how *A Pail of Oysters* was brought to the attention of a 1954 U.S. Senate subcommittee session on the "Strategy and Tactics of World Communism." John Caldwell, a former director of the U.S. Information Service in China, testifying on the effects of communism on U.S. publishing, presented *A Pail of Oysters* as an example of anti-KMT bias, calling it "the most recent effort to smear Chiang" and a "thoroughly dishonest book."

Caldwell's assertion was wrong. Sneider was accurately informing Americans readers that Taiwan was not simply a matter of the Communists versus the KMT; he was writing about and for the forgotten, oppressed Taiwanese majority. While Sneider gives a damning portrayal of the Nationalists, his book is far from a polemic; American journalist Barton encounters sympathetic soldiers and, when secretly meeting an underground figure, he's told that Taiwanese hopes lie not with rebellion but moving forward with progressive leaders in the KMT. Here Sneider was thinking of Governor Wu (Benda says Sneider had originally even included Wu's name in the manuscript), whom he had interviewed during a 1952 research trip to Taiwan.

Vern Sneider

Although the three-month summer trip was Sneider's first visit to Taiwan, he was not unfamiliar with the island. During the Second World War, he served with the U.S. Army in the Pacific and was then sent to Princeton University to study for a possible invasion and administration of Taiwan; when the island was instead leapfrogged in favor of Okinawa, that's where he went, his war-recovery work becoming the subject of *The Teahouse of the August Moon*. Sneider was next sent to Korea, where he met a Taiwanese who served as his inspiration for *A Pail of Oysters*; a short story of the same name was published in 1950 in a literary magazine.

* * *

Just as *A Pail of Oysters* is arguably the most important English-language fiction work about Taiwan, **Formosa Betrayed** (1965), George H. Kerr's detailed and impassioned account of KMT misrule, has a good claim for the non-fiction equivalent. Even today it sells well – especially the version translated into Chinese – and retains its political power. In 2014 it was in the Taiwan news headlines when, during the Sunflower Movement protests, a young protester threw a copy at President Ma Ying-jeou.

The "betrayed" in the title refers not only to the Taiwanese people's crushing disappointment when they realized that KMT rule was worse than that of the Japanese, but also to American culpability. The United States was in large part responsible for handing Taiwan over to Nationalist control and for the KMT maintaining power. The U.S. government ultimately ignored the pleas for self-rule, and it's heartbreaking to read how so many Taiwanese wanted and thought they might get independence as a United Nations trusteeship under American guardianship.

George Henry Kerr, born in 1911 in Pennsylvania, was the son of a Presbyterian minister. He had no interest in religion, but visitors to the manse included missionaries on furlough from exotic lands, China among them and the seeds of fascination for East Asia seem to have been planted. Kerr studied Mandarin and Japanese, and was in Japan studying for two years before moving to Taiwan in the summer of 1937 to teach English, replacing a friend who had had fallen ill. Intending to work for only half a year, he ended up staying three, before leaving in 1940 for doctorate studies at Columbia University. Kerr's knowledge of the region took on unexpected value when the Japanese attacked Pearl Harbor, bringing the United States into the Second World War. Kerr became a "Formosa Specialist," first for the Army and then the Navy, preparing for a possible invasion or at least eventual occupation of the island.

In October 1945 he returned to Taiwan as an assistant naval attaché, escorting KMT appointee for governor Chen Yi to Taipei to formally accept the Japanese government's surrender. The following year Kerr was appointed a vice consul at the American consulate in Taipei.

The Horrifying Inspection, by Huang Rong-can

After the KMT were in possession of Taiwan, the looting began. Kerr describes how there were three stages:

From September, 1945, until the year's end the military scavengers were at work at the lowest level. Anything movable – anything lying loose and unguarded for a moment – was fair prey for ragged and undisciplined soldiers. It was a first wave of petty theft, taking place in every city street and suburban village unfortunate enough to have Nationalist Army barracks or encampments nearby.

The second stage of looting was entered when the senior military men – the officer ranks – organized depots with forwarding agents at the ports through which they began to ship out military and civilian supplies. Next the Governor's own men developed a firm control of all industrial raw materials, agricultural stockpiles and confiscated real properties turned over to them by the vanquished Japanese. By the end of 1946 these huge reserves were fairly well exhausted, and at last in early 1947 the Governor's Commissioners imposed a system of extreme monopolies affecting every phase of the island's economic life. This was Chen Yi's "Necessary State Socialism" in its developed form and the ultimate cause of the 1947 rebellion.

This Necessary State Socialism was complete statist control whereby the authorities seized the means of production and infrastructure and turned the economy into a series of monopolies. This was accompanied by inflation, food shortages, and mass unemployment. Kerr gives dozens of detailed example of enterprises being taken over and run into the ground, and when no longer working, dismantled and carted away to be sold as scrap metal: "Factory after factory simply disappeared. The principle seemed to be that 'If you can't sell the product, sell the plant.'"

Kerr even has a minor but telling example of KMT misrule related to books:

> Some newcomers were unfortunate enough to be assigned to administrative jobs which were not directly associated with production and commerce. They had to devise their own ways of milking the economy. I discovered one of these by curious chance, a minor one, but important in consequence.
>
> My home lay on the principal boulevard leading from town to the Shih Lin suburb. One day a heavily loaded bullock cart broke down at my gate. In passing I noticed that it was loaded with books which had been stripped of hard covers. They were being taken, I was told, to a small pulping mill at Shih Lin. When I discovered that one of my acquaintances was employed there it was arranged for him to set aside and sell to me any interesting book having to do with Formosa. He told me that each week the pulping mill received many tons of books and statistical records – anything made of paper – and that the bulk came from school libraries and minor office files which had been taken over by the mainland Chinese. Many, indeed, bore the stamp of well-known institutions, from primary schools to high Government offices. The newcomers could see no use for the books (written in Japanese) and so were selling them out the back door, to be pulped, pocketing the money for themselves.

Kerr personally witnessed far worse things during the March massacres. One day, watching from the relative safety of the Mackay Mission Hospital, he "saw Formosans bayoneted in the street without provocation. A man was robbed before our eyes – and then cut down and run through. Another ran into the street in pursuit of soldiers dragging a girl away from his house and we saw him, too, cut down." The city was soon littered with bodies, including those of two students who had been beheaded near his front gate. And after the random violence came a period of deliberate organized violence; executions of the Taiwanese elite – a generation of leaders, doctors, lawyers, academics, students, and others silenced.

Kerr, who had warned in writing that a violent crisis was brewing and been denigrated for it, left the diplomatic service after the Nationalist crackdown. He returned to the United States in 1947, taking on a succession of university teaching positions. His anti-Chiang Kai-shek stance caused problems for him, though he was still able to get work in academia and, in cooperation with U.S. government, do fieldwork on Okinawa. His *Okinawa: The History of an Island People*, published in 1958 by Charles Tuttle, became the standard work on the island. Kerr spent most of the last decades of his life in Hawaii. Taiwan lay just halfway across the Pacific, but he never returned. Kerr died in 1992.

There is an obvious question about *Formosa Betrayed*'s publication: why the long gap between Kerr's departure in 1947 and publication in 1965? In fact, Kerr had set out to write a book right away, starting in May 1947 for an academic and policy organization. Benda says that after a long silence on the manuscript, Kerr learned that the institute had sent it to the State Department, which was unhappy with it. Kerr retrieved his manuscript – with some difficulty – just as McCarthy was kicking off his anti-communist witch-hunts. Publication was a non-starter in such a climate for anyone with career aspirations, especially for a known critic of the KMT and a homosexual.

Kerr was certainly not being paranoid in worrying about how he and his book would be treated. In 1960 Ross Y. Koen's *The China*

Lobby in American Politics was suppressed. Two weeks before pub-lication, the KMT threatened legal action over Koen's assertions of their involvement in smuggling narcotics into the United States. Koen says he agreed to water a few things down but balked when asked for further concessions. The publisher, Macmillan, withdrew the book before it was on the market, and tried to recall those already sent out to libraries and reviewers, destroying over four thousand copies. The author got the rights to his text back in 1968, after agreeing not to mention Macmillan or details of the suppression. The book was eventually released by Harper and Row in 1974; in the introduction Richard C. Kagan says that many library copies were stolen by right wing groups and that the KMT put pressure on the publisher via the CIA and the State Department.

In the mid-1960s, conditions were better for Kerr to publish a book on Taiwan but still problematic. Benda says that "Kerr faced pressures not to publish – not only from the Cold War political atmosphere but also from his own traumatic memories of 228."

An author finally holding a physical copy of his new book is often compared to the joy and satisfaction of becoming a parent. In reality, it's usually a bittersweet moment – as there's usually some nasty surprise. So it was with Kerr; he was horrified by the "cheap and tawdry look" of the cover, which showed an orange dagger piercing the word "Formosa."

Formosa Betrayed received mixed reviews. The *Christian Science Monitor* accurately called it "partisan" but "well worth reading" and also "particularly timely" because of the contentious status of the PRC and ROC at the United Nations. Kerr had not aimed for a balanced account of the recent history; instead, he wanted to tell the untold story and saw no need to repeat the pro-KMT perspec-tive when the China lobby was doing this so well. Some reviewers questioned its relevancy; Taiwan had moved on and improved, and it was too late to undo events. Benda says there were even accusations that Kerr was a spy or a CIA agent and that he was behind 2-28 in some way, encouraging Taiwanese dissatisfaction with Chen Yi's government and instigating "traitorous" petitions to the United States and international organizations for intervention.

Despite the only moderate success of *Formosa Betrayed* with American readers, the book was a sensation among pro-independence Taiwanese living overseas. A Mandarin translation was published in 1973; it took six and a half years for the main translator, Ron Chen, and several fellow graduate students helping to complete the translation. Benda writes "It was a dangerous task – if the student spies that the KMT had operating on campuses around the country found out about the work, the translators could have lost their passports and their family members back in Taiwan could have been persecuted." Although banned in martial law Taiwan, copies of pages and later an official abridged copy circulated in the activist underground. Martial law ended in 1987, but it took several years for many restrictions to be lifted. *Formosa Betrayed* was legally published in Taiwan in 1991, and a new, improved Mandarin translation was published in 2014.

* * *

If *Formosa Betrayed* is notable for the long time it took to get published, there's another English-language witness account of 2-28 that took much longer: **Formosa Calling** (1998), by Allan James Shackleton, who was in post-war Taiwan as an officer with the United Nations Relief and Rehabilitation Administration. *Formosa Calling* describes how the KMT pillaged the island: "the Formosans soon found that property was not safe when soldiers were about and that they had no redress at law for any robbery committed by the military." The theft wasn't just hungry soldiers pilfering their next meal. Shackleton wrote that it was looting on a large scale and "done, not only to make good deficiencies in food and equipment, but also with the idea of re-selling and making money. Therefore, nothing was really exempt from the attentions of the soldiers. But more serious was the fact that there were lying about the streets in the mornings, the dead bodies of important people who had been dragged from their houses at night and shot."

Shackleton tried for years to get *Formosa Calling* published, but it was deemed too politically sensitive. After the author died in 1984, the family kept the manuscript in a trunk with other papers. And that's where it sat until 1997, when Stanley Liao, then president of the New Zealand Taiwanese Association, was preparing a memorial event in New Zealand to mark the fiftieth anniversary of 2-28. He was told that George Kerr had mentioned a New Zealander surnamed Shackleton as an information source in his 1965 *Formosa Betrayed*. Looking for a Kiwi connection for the fiftieth commemoration, Liao turned to the country's telephone directories and started calling listings for "Shackleton." Over a hundred calls later, Liao reached the family and was richly rewarded for his perseverance to learn of the existence of the manuscript. It was published by the California-based Taiwan Publishing Co in 1998, fifty years after it was written.

6

Fortress "Free China"

THE Nationalist retreat to Taiwan and the Korean War (June 1950 to July 1953) meant an unprecedented burst of print coverage for Taiwan. James A. Michener, a household name after his bestselling *Tales of the South Pacific* (1947), included a chapter on Taiwan in his ***The Voice of Asia*** (1951). This non-fiction work consists largely of interviews with representative people in each country. Michener stresses that he talked to ordinary people rather than politicians and other elites. For the Taiwan chapter there are four main subsections and interviewees: "Indian Summer in Formosa" (Y.P. Tom, air force pilot), "The Governor's Mansion" (Edith Wu, the wife of K.C. Wu, the highly regarded governor of Formosa), "The Hard Way" (Liu Ping, an impoverished refugee student at the most prestigious college, National Taiwan University), and "The Tank Commanders" ("four young fellows, tough, straight and aching for a fight" who show Michener a pledge to retake the mainland, signed in blood).

Michener doesn't say how the interviews, which took place in Taipei in 1950, were set up; but we can assume they were arranged by the Government Information Office. Every single interviewee is a mainlander, not even a token Taiwanese in the mix; and all are recent refugees desperate to get back to China, even if that entails another world war.

In the Taiwan section, Michener begins with seven questions, then has the interviews, and concludes with answers to those earlier questions. Here are the questions and answers combined and paraphrased (with the exception of the fourth).

1. *Could Chiang's troops invade mainland China without large-scale American assistance?*

   This is an absolute impossibility because the Nationalists lack the manpower (with, at best, a quarter of a million troops) and have insufficient ships and airplanes to transport and support troops.

2. *If the Nationalists were put ashore with American help, would the people of south China rise up and support them?*

   Maybe.

3. *Once in China, would Chiang's troops go over to the Communists, as many did in the last years of the Chinese Civil War?*

   The collapse of Chiang's army in 1948–1949 is unlikely to be repeated, with his soldiers better trained, armed, led, and more motivated than before.

4. *Is the Nationalist government now on Formosa a responsible one, which has addressed its weaknesses that contributed to it losing the mainland?*

   "It is probably the most efficient government in Asia today, not even excepting Japan's. It has solved the food problem. It has rationed goods so that everyone gets a fair break.

It polices the island so that even white men can move about at night without risk of murder. It has launched an education program, prints liberal newspapers and insures just trials. Furthermore, in order to erase evil memories of the initial Chinese occupation, the Government has specifically worked to protect the indigenous Taiwanese population."

5. *If Russia and China start World War III, should we transport KMT troops to the mainland and support them?*
   Yes.

6. *If the preceding case occurs, should we help reinstate the KMT as China's government?*
   Yes. Although Chiang Kai-shek is past his use-by date, his government is currently the best choice.

7. *Is it really possible to defeat China, a nation of 463 million people?*
   Yes. The idea of it being unconquerable is wrong. The Mongols did it, as did the Manchus, and the Japanese might well have done it had they not been at war with the United States.

Michener says he is against going to war with China, but if the United States were pushed into it, then victory would be far from impossible: "I should judge it somewhat less difficult to subdue China than it was to defeat Japan in 1941."

The author's assessments of the feasibility of rolling back the Communist victory in China and of the nature of Chiang's regime on Taiwan cannot be dismissed as cheerleading from a China lobby hawk. Michener was a liberal Democrat (in fact, a decade later he would run unsuccessfully as a Democratic candidate for a seat in the U.S. House of Representatives). Because he was a moderate, his writing made for more effective propaganda (and propaganda it was, with KMT talking points given and certain glaring realities ignored).

For me, the most striking line of the book is in the section titled "The Governor's Mansion," where Edith Wu apologizes for some unfinished work on her new house with the prophetic, "we do not think of this as our permanent home." Of course, this was meant as an expression of belief and determination that they'd soon be returning to the mainland. Indeed, Edith and K.C. Wu would leave in 1953; but instead of returning to China they fled to the United States, fearing assassination by Chiang Kai-shek.

Despite all of Chiang Kai-shek's talk of retaking the mainland and his American supporters pushing for him to be unleashed, the reality was rather different. In *Accidental State: Chiang Kai-shek, the United States, and the Making of Taiwan*, which we encountered earlier, author Hsiao-ting Lin rewrites these assumptions with a revisionist look at Chiang Kai-shek's determination to take the fight back to the Communists during the Korean War years (1950–1953). Hawkish rhetoric was useful for propaganda purposes and for securing U.S. aid, but Chiang was half-hearted at best.

A crosscheck of both Chinese and English declassified documents now reveals that as the Korean War entered a stalemate, it was actually the military and intelligence chiefs in the Pentagon who took the lead in transforming the Nationalists' grandiose but empty "military rollback" slogan into detailed courses of action for the purpose of U.S. geo-military interests in the Far East. While Washington urged Taipei to launch a military counteroffensive against the Communist-controlled territories of Hainan Island and the Southeast mainland, it was Chiang Kai-shek who now tried to avoid such an operation so as to keep his military supremacy intact within the Nationalist hierarchy, in addition to assuring Taiwan's defense interests. In other words, in the early 1950s, when the American-favored General Sun Liren remained a perceived threat, Chiang placed political deliberations ahead of any other issue, giving priority to the consolidation of his Taiwan power base without truly thinking about a genuine counterattack on the mainland to overthrow Mao Zedong.

General Sun Liren (1900–1990), a graduate of the Virginia Military Institute, whose fighting successes had earned him the nickname "the Rommel of the East," was arrested in 1955 on fabricated charges of planning a coup. He remained under house arrest until released by President Lee Teng-hui in 1988. President Ma Ying-jeou made a public apology to Sun's family in 2011.

Another example of Chiang Kai-shek's political maneuvering described by Lin is his use of a secret Japanese military unit (called Baituan) to help train and indoctrinate soldiers. The purpose was "to counterbalance the strong MAAG [American] influence and, more significantly as it turned out, to checkmate such Nationalist military leaders as Sun Liren, who had American support."

The secret Japanese unit was also involved in military planning. They devised a counteroffensive plan for the mainland. Requiring a five-year preparation period, the end date was the spring of 1958, with the beachhead and base of operations to be the Pearl River Delta. This kind of planning was largely for political reasons. After the Korean War, the Americans weren't interested, and Chiang knew – contrary to the public messaging – that he would end his days on Taiwan.

* * *

To see what a full-blooded pro-KMT work from the era looks like, let's turn the cover of John C. Caldwell's *Still the Rice Grows Green: Asia in the Aftermath of Geneva and Panmunjom* (1955), from the Henry Regnery Company, a conservative publisher.

The first sentence of the prologue gives us some inkling how the book is going to play out: "If the day be bright and clear, the pilot flying the lonely skies from Formosa westward to the China Coast sees the mainland of Enslaved China even before the lofty peaks of Free China recede into the haze."

In the first chapter we're with the American author on board a Nationalist P-6 gunboat, feeling "much a part of the motley crew of guerrillas, regulars and commandos," as they take part in raids on Communist shipping along the coast. It had been an exciting and dangerous afternoon: "We had chased and captured a Communist junk out of Amoy."

As a newspaper correspondent and former State Department officer, Caldwell was on a month's tour of disputed islands, from tiny Tungting Island – defended by "fifty men from twelve different provinces" – to the fortress of Kinmen, seventy square miles "supporting a population of 41,000 civilians and 75,000 troops and guerrillas." But more than mere numbers, more than a mere island, in Kinmen lay the possible future "of all Chinese, free and enslaved, indeed ... all Asia.... It is an idea and an ideal; in its future are wrapped the hopes and fears of millions."

Rousing stuff. Time to hit the brothel. With so few women on the island, and as the author says, the Chinese having a realistic view of human nature, the authorities had established a giant house of prostitution. Caldwell, the son of missionaries, visited it on a Sunday afternoon. "There are seventy-five girls there, but few were busy. The price is cheap, thirty cents for an enlisted man, who draws his partner by lot; seventy-five cents for the officer, who can make a face to face choice."

Caldwell was a die-hard "retake the mainland" guy, claiming that it was a realistic goal given sufficient will. His hopes were for a two-punch attack from Korea and Taiwan, with the southern bridgehead most likely in Fujian. It would take genuine backing though, not the "hollow talk" and half-hearted support of the United States government. A less hostile American press would help too. Among the publications that come in for Caldwell's criticism is Vern Sneider's newly released *A Pail of Oysters*, which Caldwell read shortly before his Taiwan travels. The book, he says, "took some pretty terrific swipes at Free China's government and particularly at the military.... And so I began everywhere to ask about the conduct of Chinese soldiers. I watched them, officers and enlisted men. Later on Kinmen and other guerrilla islands I had opportunity to talk to the soldiers themselves, literally hundreds of them."

Caldwell says he was impressed by the soldiers; their behavior had been bad previously but changed around 1951; they now paid for their food, were kept busy, and caused little trouble. Yes, there were arrests and executions for national security, but "absolutely no evidence of any reign of terror on Formosa."

"The Nationalist Government does not run a police state," he asserted, no doubt having in mind an article in *Look* magazine from June 1954 by K.C. Wu titled "Your Money Is Building a Police State in Taiwan."

It would be easy to dismiss Caldwell as a partisan McCarthyite hack, a naïve American being led around and fed Free China propaganda, eyes and ears closed to anything that ruined the China lobby fantasy of a Christian Chiang Kai-shek ready to retake the mainland, but that is far from the truth. Caldwell was a child of China, born to missionary parents across the water from the offshore Matsu Islands. Indeed, there's a moving passage in *Still the Rice Grows Green*, when from a seaplane leaving Matsu, he could gaze along the China coast, the stomping grounds of his early life. And what an early life it was! His Methodist missionary father was a keen naturalist – together they wrote *South China Birds*

(1931) – and hunter. Asked by the local villagers for help, his father had shot numerous man-eating tigers that plagued the region. His fame had spread far and wide, and especially so when one of the great adventurers of the age, Roy Chapman Andrews, wrote about hunting with him. It was a *Boys' Own* childhood for John Caldwell, which he wrote about in the delightful *China Coast Family* (1953).

John Caldwell served in China as an agent of the U.S. Office of War Information during World War II. One of his brothers was a U.S. Air Force pilot, lost in action fighting the Japanese. The other brother, Oliver J. Caldwell, worked for the Office of Strategic Services (a forerunner of the CIA) and was an important figure in the wartime capital of Chungking; he advised Roosevelt to look for an alternative to Chiang Kai-shek and later wrote a book critical of Chiang's government.

Born and raised in China, the Caldwell boys were a special breed of foreigner, with a level of involvement, knowledge, and investment difficult to find an equivalency with today. They had been born into the great American missionary project in China, and their lives and hopes for the future were wrapped up in the fate of the country. Caldwell was no stooge. For him there was no choice but to support the KMT as the lesser of two evils. Perhaps he was so desperate to believe – to hope – that he was blinded in his judgment. Not only had he lost his family home to the Communists, he had lost his new home in Korea to them as well. After the Second World War, Caldwell was with the U.S. Information Service in Korea, nation building and helping hold elections. His translator there was Elsie Fletcher, the daughter of a missionary family with long ties to the country; they married in 1949. They evacuated Korea together in 1950 and settled in Tennessee, from where he wrote travel books and conducted tours to Asia. He died in 1984.

Caldwell doesn't give the KMT a pass on its failings, though these are viewed as having been largely in the past. He says that China was lost because of corrupt generals and officials. "In my home province of Fukien I saw the Nationalist government at its worst, saw Governor Chen Yi and his henchmen milk the province dry. Was Chen Yi dismissed? No, as was so often the case, he was promoted! Generalissimo Chiang Kai Shek made him Formosa's first governor at the end of World War II. And the exploitation of the island has left scars that will require a generation to erase."

His criticism of Chiang Kai-shek is part praise, that he "trusted old friends too much, has been so blinded by personal loyalty that he could not see their incompetence and corruption." The truth is Chiang Kai-shek knowingly chose corrupt, incompetent yes men because of his lust for power, treated the country like his own property, and always put his own grip on power before national interests.

Turning to contemporary Taiwan, Caldwell mentions his two favorite generals: Major General Chow Mei-yu, a director of nursing in her forties with master's degrees from both MIT and Columbia; and Chiang Ching-kuo (CCK), Chiang Kai-shek's oldest son. Caldwell cites the negative press on Chiang Ching-kuo: how he "heads the secret police ... and is building a machine to take over, to become a dictator." (This, of course, was accurate; he removed any rivals and took over from his father as dictator.) Caldwell also mentions *Look* magazine running a story in which it stated fears that the younger Chiang would sell out to the Communists if given the opportunity. Although this would not come to pass, there were secret talks on possible reunification held in the following years, so these fears were justified. The imagined betrayal of Taiwan by Chiang was actually the subject of a 1965 thriller called *The Jing Affair*, which we will look at a little later.

When Caldwell met Chiang Ching-kuo at his home office, they used an interpreter; the incompatibility of Chiang's Chekiang patois and Caldwell's Foochow dialect a reminder of how linguistically diverse China used to be. Caldwell describes CCK as a small, soft-spoken man who smiled frequently. They discussed resettlement of Korean POWs, propaganda work (leaflet and food drops), and the education of Chinese GIs. He presents CCK as tough but reasonable:

> "There are things about my work I do not like," the young general said frankly. "I am responsible for seeing that security measures are maintained here. We have had to arrest people, we have had to execute some people too. It is not a pleasant job, but it is a necessary job."

* * *

Despite close ties between the United States and Taiwan during the early Cold War decades, relations were not always smooth. In 1957 the American embassy in Taipei was overrun and ransacked by rioters, and the American staff beaten and forced to flee for their lives. Taiwan had turned on its ally, generous benefactor, and protector. This historical episode, known as the Liu Ziran Incident, though largely forgotten, shook U.S.–ROC relations, and is the subject of Stephen Craft's excellent *American Justice in Taiwan: The 1957 Riots and Cold War Foreign Policy* (2016). It's an eye-opening, detailed yet highly readable account of the tensions between the American military and their hosts in the late 1950s, when there were about eleven thousand Americans on the island. The book explores issues of extraterritoriality and justice, both in Taiwan and elsewhere in Asia. What could be a tinder-dry read on international law becomes an often-gripping story because of the wonderful framing of the topic around the killing of an ROC citizen by American serviceman Sergeant Robert G. Reynolds and his subsequent trial by an American military court. (It was Reynolds' acquittal that sparked the riots.) The mysteries surrounding the killing and riots add complexity and interest.

On the night of March 20, 1957, forty-one-year-old Sergeant Reynolds confronted a local man who was watching his wife take a shower through the window of their house. The man allegedly attacked Reynolds. The American shot him with a .22 revolver and then asked his wife to call the Foreign Affairs Police. Returning to the injured man, Reynolds fired a second shot when the man stood up and began approaching him again. The attacker, thirty-three-year-old mainland Chinese Liu Tzu-jan (Liu Ziran), fled into a side street and soon after died from his wounds.

Reynolds, a career soldier who had enlisted in 1945, had served in Taiwan for just over two years as a member of the U.S. Military Assistance Advisory Group (MAAG), and was preparing to return to the United States with his wife and daughter.

The ROC authorities and the American military began investigations to determine what had happened. Was it murder or justifiable self-defense? The case fell under U.S. jurisdiction. American military personnel and their families enjoyed diplomatic immunity, thanks to the 1951 Mutual Defense Assistance Agreement, which in effect treated U.S. military personnel as members of the embassy. An amendment extended that immunity to MAAG dependents. MAAG also permitted advisors to keep weapons in their homes if they were registered.

Author Stephen G. Craft, a professor of security studies and international affairs at Embry-Riddle Aeronautical University in Florida, does a good job of placing American diplomatic immunity in context and showing how it compared to similar agreements elsewhere and historically. I hadn't, for example, been aware that this practice existed in the United Kingdom during the Second World War.

Given the Chinese sensitivity to extraterritoriality – so painfully reminiscent of the "unequal treaties" and treaty port justice – why had the ROC agreed? Simply put, the government was desperate for American military and financial aid. The ROC did, however, continue to push for a status of forces agreement (SOFA), which would give it more control in crimes where locals were the victims. (It was not until 1965 that the United States and the Republic of China finally signed a SOFA limiting American immunity to that allowed in agreements the United States had signed with its European allies.)

The Reynolds killing of Liu was to stress test American justice in Taiwan. Things got off to a bad start with the ROC authorities being uncooperative with the investigation. Craft describes – and this will be all too familiar to anyone who has dealt with passive-aggressive Chinese bureaucracy – how they stonewalled the Americans in sharing their results from both an autopsy and a ballistics test.

On several occasions the provost marshal attempted to meet with the director of the Foreign Affairs Police, only to be told that the appointment had been cancelled because the director was "ill." When documents were released to the Americans, they were always in Chinese and without English translations. The excuses for not providing translations became comical. On one occasion, a Foreign Affairs Police official said that he had the translations in his desk but the drawer was locked and he did not have a key.

One of the many frustrations was the ROC officials' refusal to say who Liu was or what he did for a living. When Lieutenant Colonel Salonick from the military police headquarters asked the chief of the CID (Alien Criminal Investigation Division) "point-blank for the dead man's name and whether he served in the military or had a police record, he received only silence for an answer." Craft believes that "Claims that Liu Ziran was in fact a security or intelligence agent seemed plausible."

The Reynolds case was widely reported in Taiwan's newspapers. Coverage was very hostile, and the press readily spread unfounded rumors, such as that Reynolds had been drunk and that both men had been engaged in black market activities.

The American investigation concluded that Reynolds had shot in self-defense and that he would not be prosecuted. However, after repeated requests from the ROC Foreign Ministry, the Americans decided to reexamine the case. The new investigating officer, Lieutenant Colonel Ross R. Condit, believed that Reynolds had fired the first shot in fear but could have retreated after wounding Liu. Condit recommended that Reynolds be tried for voluntary manslaughter.

The court-martial of Sergeant Reynolds was held on May 20, 1957, at the MAAG-Taiwan headquarters in Taipei and was open to the public, with members of the local press and ROC Ministry of Justice attending. Twelve jurors were whittled done to eight: five colonels and three sergeants. (Craft explains: "Since the Fifth Amendment of the U.S. Constitution does not apply to those in the military, a court-martial, unlike a criminal trial, does not require a full jury of twelve peers.") The proceedings ended with a secret ballot and the jury returning a "not guilty" verdict.

The Taiwanese public reaction was one of shock and anger. Compared to the offense of peeping at a woman, the response (i.e., shooting the perpetrator dead) seemed ridiculously disproportionate. Cultural differences regarding justice also contributed to the outrage. According to Chinese thinking, killing a person – even in self-defense – is a crime that carries an element of blame. For most Americans, the lack of witnesses and the concept of "reasonable doubt" made it very hard for the jury to find Reynolds guilty. On top of this, the American ideas of the right to bear arms and the right to stand your ground were not ones enjoyed or understood by the locals. Another sore point was the lack of compensation for the widow and her children. In Chinese culture it was – and still is – a matter of expressing sympathy, but it was resisted by the Americans, thinking that it would look like an admission of guilt.

Author Stephen Craft believes that the court martial was not properly handled, suggesting the Americans could have done more to give the impression of a fair trial, by having twelve jurors, not eight, and less partial ones by flying jury members in from southern Taiwan instead of having "men who lived and worked in fairly close proximity to Reynolds, and probably were under considerable peer pressure to vote not guilty."

The day following the acquittal, hundreds of protestors surrounded the embassy, where that morning eight Americans and twenty-three Chinese employees were working inside. The crowd quickly grew to thousands and the mood became angrier. A prolonged barrage of stone-throwing shattered all the front windows. Some protestors tried to storm the gate but were held back, but soon the weight of numbers saw the mob force their way through.

Rioters rushed into the compound, overturning and smashing cars and ransacking the first floor while American and Chinese personnel gathered in an air-raid shelter on the second floor.

Over the next two hours, nine waves of rioters forced their way into the embassy for durations of ten to fifteen minutes.... The crowd outside cheered as rioters hurled objects out the windows. A rioter cut down the U.S. flag, which was torn to shreds by the mob below. When an ROC flag took its place on the pole, "hysterical cheers" could be heard. Rioters hung a second ROC flag from the embassy balcony. One cried out, "Long live the Republic of China."

Some rioters discovered the eight foreigners and pelted them with objects at hand:

> The eight ran for blocks with the rioters on their heels, including one rioter who had already inflicted injury with a hammer. From time to time one of the Americans got in a good punch against a rioter, but they suffered more than they dished out from a mob that clubbed, kicked, spat upon, and stoned them.

A state of emergency was called in Taipei. Two army divisions were deployed, and the chaos subsided. As well as damage to the embassy building and various other American buildings, the incident raised numerous questions: Were the riots planned, and if so, by whom? Why had the authorities been so slow to respond? "Were the riots an expression of anti-Americanism or did they reflect an internal political struggle within the ROC government?"

The lack of hard evidence means we are left with various fascinating possibilities rather than concrete answers. One line of explanation has it that the riots were instigated by PRC forces, either saboteurs or in collaboration with the ROC. Secret talks took place in 1956 and 1957 between the KMT and the Chinese Communist Party about unification; obviously, proponents of such a move had an interest in undermining ROC–U.S. relations. Furthermore, the CCP was upset by the increased American military presence in Taiwan, in particular the deployment of Matador missiles, which were capable of carrying nuclear warheads.

Much more likely was ROC involvement, though how high up and how organized it's hard to know. The deceased man, Liu

Ziran, worked for the Institute for Revolutionary Practice, which was involved in this kind of agitation propaganda work. Was it a case of government mobilization getting out of hand? Were Liu's colleagues at the Institute for Revolutionary Practice behind the riots? Anticipating a not-guilty verdict had they prepared for demonstrations at the embassy, and then, with a growing crowd and only a light police presence, had things spiraled out of control?

Many Americans suspected Chiang Ching-kuo was behind it, as did some ROC officials, who thought he was looking to create a rift and discredit more liberal, pro-American leaders in the cabinet. Another possible explanation was that the protests and riots related to the Reynolds case were an attempt to make an issue of American extraterritoriality, and a push for a status of forces agreement. While Craft is cautious not to present a definite conclusion, all in all he thinks the evidence suggests that the protests were not completely spontaneous and had some level of instigation from the authorities for political reasons, but that they got out of hand.

Regardless of government involvement in the riots, there was undeniably real public anger, both at the Reynolds case specifically and also from wider pent-up resentment against the American presence on the island because of their relative wealth and privilege, and their contempt for the fighting qualities of the Nationalist leaders and troops, as well as cases of black market profiteering, womanizing, drunkenness, disorderly conduct, and dangerous driving.

Although the sacking of the embassy could have led to a diplomatic rupture between the countries, the tensions receded without serious long-term damage. The KMT was lucky that no American had been killed. Timing played a part in putting the incident quickly behind them; the Second Taiwan Strait Crisis of 1958, initiated by an intense Chinese artillery bombardment of the island of Kinmen, prompted greater U.S.–ROC military cooperation. The Americans, for example, secretly supplied the ROC Air Force with AIM-9 Sidewinder missiles for their F-86 Sabres. (In a series of aerial engagements against MiG-15s and MiG-17s, this was the first use of Sidewinders in air-to-air combat.)

Author Stephen Craft first came to Taiwan in 1986, living in Luodong, Yilan County, for a year teaching English and working at a children's orphanage as part of a college internship. He returned to Taiwan, living in Taichung from 1993 until 1997, during which time he married a Taiwanese woman, worked on his dissertation, and taught history and English. *American Justice in Taiwan* was a long-term project, one that involved trips to archives in various countries in the 2000s. Craft's research was aided by the historic election victory in 2000 by the Democratic Progressive Party, which opened archives related to the case.

* * *

A Pocket Guide to Taiwan (1958), published by the United States Department of Defense a year after the riots, reflects the desire for a less abrasive American presence on the island. The guide gives upbeat background information on the land and people, the island's history and culture, and places to visit, and it encourages readers – Americans stationed on the island – to be sensitive to their hosts. The unnamed author praises the Taiwanese people as shrewd, industrious, thrifty, and well worth getting to know; they make considerate, generous friends and have a good sense of humor. There's sensible advice on being courteous (especially to the elderly), showing respect for local customs and religions, and the importance of face. A strong admonition is made against racial prejudice: "The Chinese judge a person by his actions – not by the color of his skin. You would do well to follow their example." Racial slurs are to be avoided: "If you're in the habit of referring to foreigners with some handy slang names, forget them right now! *You're* the foreigner on Taiwan." Complaints about strange aspects of Taiwan are to be avoided too; yes, the place might stink, but the author optimistically assures his readers that they'll eventually get used to "the smells of the open sewers and from the fertilizer on the rice paddies surrounding the cities."

In a section titled "Legal Status," the guide says that although military and civilian personnel of the Military Assistance Advisory Group enjoy, in effect, the privileges of diplomatic immunity, this should not be abused; local customs and laws are to be respected. "This means the traffic laws, too. When you drive a motor vehicle, always bear in mind that human life is just as important to the Chinese as it is to you."

A Pocket Guide to Taiwan outlines numerous possible activities, in particular for the greater Taipei area; there are excellent hiking opportunities, floating picnics on Green Lake (Bitan, Xindian), temple sightseeing, and shopping for curios on Haggle Row (the west side of Zhonghua Road, which, in *A Pail of Oysters*, is where Li Liu finds his stolen kitchen god). Or you can go swimming at the "clean, beautiful, and unspoilt" ocean beaches near Danshui. And nearby there's even golf to be enjoyed on an eighteen-hole course. Here, once again, the author is keen to stanch any possible cross-cultural misunderstandings. Of the local players he says, "rules of sportsmanship differ slightly from our own. Take it in your stride." The neighbors' farm animals are to be considered too. "Not infrequently livestock from surrounding farms wander onto the fairways. Should your ball strike one of these animals so violently that it dies, an unwritten ground rule requires you to pay for the animal but does not give you the carcass."

I'm all for placating possible native uprisings but this seems gullibly overgenerous. When you pay compensation for an accidentally killed beast, you should at least get the choice cuts of meat for barbecuing; to do otherwise is to risk an epidemic of mysterious golf ball deaths.

* * *

Another title from 1958 is Lillian Dickson's **These My People: Serving Christ among the Mountain People of Taiwan.** Lillian came to Taiwan in 1927 in her mid-twenties with her missionary husband, James Dickson, who taught in Danshui and later Taipei. They were both Americans but attached to the Canadian Presbyterian Church. Lillian found the life hard; suffering two miscarriages during her first three years on the island made for an inauspicious beginning.

Western missionaries came under increasing scrutiny in the 1930s, and the Dicksons left the island in 1940. After spending the war years doing missionary work in British Guiana, they returned to Taiwan. This time Lillian was determined to be more than a missionary's wife; she threw herself with relentless energy into a host of projects: distributing medicine, training and setting up clinics in the mountains, building churches and kindergartens, helping run a leper colony in a suburb of Taipei, and providing treatment for blackfoot disease patients on the southwest coast.

She did this under a charity she founded called Mustard Seed. Funding was based partly on Lillian's writing prowess, honed by years of writing letters to the congregation back home. Her friendly, anecdotal style touched American readers, of whom there were many. Her newsletters had an enormous reach – twenty-five thousand sent out monthly to supporters – and were immensely effective; her fund-raising, which included speaking tours in the United States, helped to consistently bring in a quarter million U.S. dollars a year, a colossal amount for the time, and one that went an enormous way in low-cost Taiwan.

These My People has the flavor of newsletter pieces; written for a Christian audience, it contains too much carrying the light to the heathen and uplifting vignettes of grateful reception for modern agnostic tastes. This slight book of 121 pages concentrates on her missions to the aborigines, often on foot into remote mountain areas; Dickson's work with lepers is covered in her *Loving the Lepers* (1953, 1983). She was the subject of a biography, Kenneth L. Wilson's *Angel at Her Shoulder: Lillian Dickson and Her Taiwan Mission*, published by Harper & Row in 1964. Dickson passed away in 1983 and was laid to rest in a grave next to her late husband in the garden of the Taiwan Theological College and Seminary in Shilin, Taipei.

Christian endeavors to improve the health, education, and well being of the people were an inspiration for Buddhist organizations. The most important Buddhist charity in Taiwan is Tzu Chi, founded in the small city of Hualien in 1966 by Buddhist nun Cheng Yen. Today Tzu Chi has millions of members worldwide, providing humanitarian aid – medicine, education, disaster relief, and culture – making it the largest non-governmental organization in the Chinese-speaking world. The rise and operations of the organization are detailed in *Tzu Chi: Serving with Compassion* (2010), by Mark O'Neill, a Hong Kong-based writer who has also written about Taipei's National Palace Museum: *The Miraculous History of China's Two Palace Museums* (2015).

* * *

In the years after China's "Liberation" (as an aside, this "liberation" should always be used with quotation marks), a steady stream of leftist visitors paid court to Mao Zedong's People's Republic of China and came away enthusiastically repeating CCP propaganda. Likewise, there were many "useful idiots" on the right who returned from stage-managed tours of Taiwan evangelical in their praise of Chiang Kai-shek and his "Free China." One of my favorites of these propaganda accounts is a forgotten book called **Flight to Formosa** (1958), by Frank Clune (1893–1971), a staggeringly prolific Australian travel writer and popular historian.

Clune, who churned out bestsellers from the 1930s through the 1960s, came from a poor family of Irish stock. Leaving school at fifteen, he lived an adventurous vagabond life, which would provide the material for his memoir *Try Anything Once* (1933), its success starting him on a writing career of sixty-six books in thirty-seven years.

Flight to Formosa, the last of his foreign travel books, describes a five-week trip around the country in winter. The subtitle gives a strong hint of the flavor: *"A Holiday and Fact-finding Tour of Nationalist China's Fortress of Freedom and the Ports of Hong Kong and Macao."* I love the odd mix of informality and earnestness of "A Holiday and Fact-finding Tour;" and "Fortress of Freedom" accurately predicts that alliteration will be more prevalent than nuance. Clune says he was in Taiwan "to find out the facts, by independent investigation on the spot." The veteran of Gallipoli (wounded and invalided home) was angry that despite Australian troops fighting the Chinese Communists in Korea only five years earlier, newspapers were running "puff pieces" on the PRC and maligning the ROC.

Clune travelled to Taiwan with his wife, "an extra pair of eyes, observing things from the feminine angle" and also providing some comedy in the role of the hapless tourist reacting to exotic color such as a terrifying pedicab ride and unmanageable chopsticks. The couple were met at Taipei airport by Sampson C. Shen, the director of the Government Information Office, and driven to the Friends of China Club (on Huaining Street), the usual accommodation for foreign correspondents, and where the character Barton stayed in *A Pail of Oysters*.

After a round of visits to various officials, the Clunes headed south by car along the west coast plain: down to Hsinchu, Miaoli,

Changhua, Taichung, inland to Sun-Moon Lake (foggy in winter), and then Chiayi, Tainan, and Kending. They visited factories, farms, and fisheries, and they talked to foreign missionaries – contrasting their persecution in China with the religious freedom on Formosa. Into the 1980s there were quite a few missionaries living here who had colorful tales from China; they'd lived through civil war, World War II, and early Communist rule.

The author was impressed with what he saw: "Formosa has been transformed into a well-managed and highly productive democratic country, prosperous and unified." One of the things that struck him most was the intensive nature of farming, and it's interesting to think that despite the population having doubled since then, the rural population has shrunk and the fields are much emptier. The farming population was so congested on the west coast plain that he likened it to "one big outer suburban area or continuous market-garden." The farmers' "industry, patience and ingenuity in tilling the soil are beyond compare."

He was also impressed by the lack of drunkenness. His visit to a government rice-wine factory in Puli prompts a comparison of Chinese sobriety with his fellow countrymen, whom he declared the "heaviest booze-guzzlers in the world." During his five weeks on Formosa he "didn't see even one person drunk."

When Clune visited the Hengchun Peninsula, Taiwan's southernmost point, he mentions a whaling station operating (a recently started joint venture with the Japanese). Near Hengchun he had a lunch of eels and shrimp at a warm-water spring and a Japanese-style inn. In an example of his grimace-inducing wordplay he describes the waitress serving them: "Golden Lily is a comely wench with a golden smile, caused by three gold teeth which glitter like the rising sun when she grins. She wore a jade-green jacket and Chinese-style slit dress, showing bare leg thigh-high on the port side."

After the road trip back to Taipei, the Clunes had an audience with Chiang Kai-shek on the first day of Chinese New Year, the honor of being his first guests of the year. Clune was impressed by Chiang's good health, with the leader sprightly and younger than his seventy-one years: "His eyes are bright, keen and kindly. But his bearing is soldierly, erect and firm."

Arrangements were made for the Clunes to see the work in progress on the epic Central Cross-Island Highway being built across the Central Mountain Range by army veterans. From Taipei they flew in an Air Force DC3 to Hualien, "a clean, thriving town" buoyed by investment on the highway, and then traveled by jeep through coastal plains of sugarcane and peanuts to Taroko Gorge, and "lunched with the road-workers in their barracks on the summit of Ho Huan Pass." Construction on the highway started in 1956, and the road opened to traffic in 1960. It was a stunning achievement through almost impossible terrain, and a journey along it is one of the world's great road trips.

Clune ends his Formosa section with another highlight, a trip to Kinmen, then one of the true hotspots of the world. There he met the "doctor-priest" Reverend Father Druetto, a Franciscan of French nationality.

Of all his travels "in Formosa, land of democracy" Clune says he could "roam at random, unsupervised, as freely as in any other country outside the Red Curtain." He never mentions 2-28 or the White Terror, even indirectly.

Clune's writing is a strange mix of cheesy informality and political punditry. It also focuses on the practical – notes on fertilizer production are more likely than glowing descriptions of scenery. *Flight to Formosa* casts the inquiring tourist as hero, championing the common sense of the Australian everyman over the snobbery and elitism of the "parlour pinks" and "eggheads." He even takes several swipes in the foreword at "critics who sit on their backsides and sling off at my travel books for being too slangy or autobiographically egotistical." But "they get their copies free," unlike the many Australians who buy and read his books he says. Clune aimed for mass-market appeal, and it worked. It's worth noting that he was far from being a hick; he lived in a wealthy Sydney suburb and through his wife, a sculptor and artist who ran a gallery, mixed with the art set.

Although terribly dated, *Flight to Formosa* has lasting value because of its very disposability. The author put relatively little work into it; he had little inclination or time to check the information provided to him and the pat stories he was told by his government minders. Written to appeal to contemporary readers without an eye on posterity, it gives us a snapshot of the time.

* * *

Readers were taken to the frontline islands of Kinmen and Matsu in **The Odd Day** (1962), by DeWitt S. Copp and Marshall Peck Jr. Copp was an air force veteran and writer of non-fiction and fiction on Cold War and aviation themes. Marshall Peck Jr. was a journalist.

The title of the book comes from the bizarre aftermath of the Second Taiwan Strait Crisis of 1958; following an intense forty-four-day bombardment of the island of Kinmen, the PLA switched to artillery shells containing propaganda leaflets and shelling only on odd-numbered days. The book tells of such a day. (The situation would continue for two decades, until U.S. president Jimmy Carter established diplomatic relations with the PRC in 1978.)

With the help of interpreters, the two Americans interviewed a hundred and fifty individuals, mostly mainlanders and military, choosing the most interesting and/or informative cases for the book. Real names are used – with only a few exceptions for security reasons. (Tracking down the people featured and their offspring would make for an interesting follow-up book.)

Despite all that reporting, *The Odd Day* involves some fictional sleight of hand, though how much isn't made clear. In the foreword we are told that "All of the statements and all of the opinions expressed by everyone in this book are authentic.... However, their actions have been woven into a twenty-four-hour sequence."

The story begins on the Fujian coast in the early hours, with a fisherman attempting to escape to Kinmen with his wife and baby daughter. Later in the day we are in Matsu, where we meet "the Mudcats," American advisors in the Matsu Defense Command Assistance Team (MDCAT). An American colonel tells the authors how vital the islands are: "Lose the offshore islands, you lose Taiwan. They'd be right on Okinawa's flank then, looking down on the Philippines.... All it takes is just one breach in the line ... it's the difference between having our Pacific defense out here or in California."

On the "bastion" of Taiwan there are some moving conversations with a pedicab driver, whom you feel sorry for with his "I'm going back someday" optimism. A KMT soldier recently discharged after eleven years of service, he'd saved hard to buy his pedicab and the rights for a station in front of Taiwan Normal University, and was earning NT$1,500 a month working fifteen-hours shifts.

We meet Ah Chi Yu, a beneficiary of the land-reform program, the poor tenant farmer once in debt to his landlord now master of his own land. Here the writing is so romanticized it's condescending, with old-fashioned, folksy, wording à la a poor man's *The Good Earth*. "His son-in-law was a good man, a steady worker. But his son-in-law was not the son of his loins, the son of his name."

The last profile in *The Odd Day* is "The Overflight Pilot," an exciting story about a C-46 transport plane deep in China dropping food parcels and being pursued by enemy fighters; it's a riveting adventure, but you suspect you might be reading fiction.

The book closes with a return to the opening story, and it's a happy ending: the fisherman, his wife and child safely reach an outer island of Kinmen. *The Odd Day* makes for reasonably good propaganda, but propaganda it is, every so often a line jumping out: "Green Island, where Communists were sent for rehabilitation." Or when the authors push the fiction that the restrictions of the 1954 Sino-American Mutual Defense Treaty are holding the ROC back from taking the fight to China.

Authors Copp and Peck do not give a real cross-section of people or opinions. There's a token anti-KMT voice, in a chapter called the "The Opposition Leader," featuring an opponent of the government – under the alias Tuan – and he is presented as a delusional and dangerous pro-independence hothead. Tuan is on a train preparing to meet a sympathetic local journalist and hand over an illicit book wrapped in a fake cover. The book is described as: "From a source in Japan he had recently received a copy of a book that was a best seller in the United States." Tuan, who had taught himself English was obsessed with the book, which criticized American foreign policy and the KMT regime. "He had read and reread the chapter that dealt with Taiwan until he could quote entire passages from it. Nothing patterned his own outlook more thoroughly. The book was with him now in the small wicker traveling case he had set beside his leg."

The smuggled book mentioned in *The Odd Day* is almost certainly William Lederer's **A Nation of Sheep** (1961). Lederer was a big name at the time; with co-author Eugene Burdick, he had written *The Ugly American*, a 1958 novel lambasting U.S. diplomats and U.S. foreign policy in Southeast Asia. Originally nonfiction, on an editor's suggestion, the authors turned *The Ugly American* into a novel, with the protagonists battling a communist insurgency in the fictional nation of Sarkhan. The book was a sensation – selling about five million copies and shaking up the U.S. government so much that it is often cited as an inspiration for the Peace Corps. The title even found a place in the English language as a phrase for boorish Americans abroad, though its usage is rather ironic considering the original context: the "ugly American" in the novel was actually the hero, and the ones criticized in the story were the diplomat elites, not loudmouth tourists.

A Nation of Sheep is a polemic against bungled American involvement in Asia. Lederer damns the U.S. military, diplomats, press, and ultimately the American public – the "sheep" of the title – for their ignorance, gullibility, and apathy.

Taiwan is covered in the third chapter, "What We Aren't Told about Formosa." Its opening pages are astounding – an old-fashioned Orientalist portrayal of China's eternal civilizational qualities, including its leaders as being ruthless manipulators skilled at wrapping themselves in piety. "This play-acting, this political masquerade, is typically Chinese." The Chinese understand the fakery, Lederer says, but foreigners do not. Oversimplified and borderline racist, yet there's more than a kernel of truth to it.

The author presents Chiang Kai-shek as an example par excellence:

He may have sometimes worn Western clothes, but in his mind and marrow vibrates the accumulation of 4,000 years of Chinese warlord sagacity, ruthlessness, and public piousness.... Even now, in adversity – cooped up on the tiny island of Formosa, his strength gone, his political machinery rusted away, his once vast armies dissipated – even now he struts and crows, telling the world that he ultimately will regain those things so dear to him; power over vast China and the concomitant riches. But being completely Chinese, his grasping-for-power is done in the name of public morality. In this instance it is called democracy and freedom, two things about which this politician knows nothing; nor has he ever practiced their principles. Yet so skillful are he and his family at political charades that for decades he has used freedom-loving America as the golden compost from which he derived nourishment and protection.

Lederer outlines Chiang's corruption, incompetence, and deceit. He mocks the idea of his army recovering China. The false promise and accompanying bloated military is a means to milk the United States, retain importance, and to maintain rule over the island.

According to the author, Chiang's propaganda machine had been leading America "by the nose" for twenty years. Lederer says the KMT in Taiwan were good at laying out the welcome mat for visiting politicians and media people. Flattery and presents were liberally given to Americans: "almost every high official stationed in Taiwan receives a suitable engraved silver service or a medal – or both."

A Nation of Sheep suffers from bias and hyperbole, tainting some valid points with ill-informed criticism. Lederer says the offshore islands of Matsu and Kinmen should have been abandoned to the PRC. (In this, however, he was not alone: Eisenhower among other leaders wanted Chiang to give them up.) Lederer believes the Americans were fools to become entangled in the islands. His assertion that the KMT holding them was of major propaganda value to the CCP as they served as proof of aggressive American intentions is foolish; handing them over to the PRC would not have tempered Beijing's belligerence. Thank heavens for Chiang being a stubborn old bastard. Kinmen and Matsu were more than just brilliant photo-op publicity stages and morale boosters; these heavily armed holdouts were – and continue to be – formidable obstacles to any Chinese invasion of mainland Taiwan.

In *The Chinese Invasion Threat* (2017), author Ian Easton cites internal Chinese military writings, which indicate an invasion of Taiwan would begin with attacks on the island fortresses: "PLA writings portray it as essential to rapidly storm Kinmen and Matsu, paving the road to Z-Day. These islands are a key to success because they sit within range of the ports and airstrips where China would likely assemble its invasion armadas. Unless completely neutralized, Taiwan's defenders could use their frontline island perimeter to mount missile strikes, commando raids, and helicopter assaults on the mainland."

* * *

Along with Taiwan's mountain areas, the offshore islands are, in my opinion, the country's best travel destinations, each a unique combination of beautiful scenery, traditional culture, and fascinating history. Despite similarities between Matsu and Kinmen – close proximity to the Chinese coast, a similar military history and sites to prove it – they are sufficiently different to make visiting both worthwhile. Kinmen has lovely clusters of historic architecture – better than any of the meager offerings on mainland Taiwan. The less developed and less touristy Matsu archipelago has more impressive scenery and nature.

These islands are featured in ***The Islands of Taiwan*** (2014), by Englishman Richard Saunders, who has done more to get his fellow expats exploring the island than any other person or organization. He is the founder of the group Taipei Hikers, and has regularly led day and weekend hikes around Taipei, as well as longer treks to Taiwan's 3,000-meter-plus mountains. Saunders has written hundreds of travel articles and numerous guidebooks, including *Taipei Escapes* (two volumes), *Yangmingshan: The Guide*, and his magnum opus, a beautifully illustrated two-volume guide to the country, *Taiwan 101: Essential Sights, Hikes and Experiences on Isla Formosa.*

Saunders started writing walking guides out of frustration. After arriving in Taipei in 1993, he soon became "annoyed at friends constantly complaining that there was nothing to do in the Taipei area. I had an old scooter and was already discovering the trails around the capital, and started writing my first book, *Taipei Day Trips*, on a typewriter in my apartment at Muzha to prove them wrong."

He loves all the offshore islands but when pushed for favorites names Lanyu and Matsu; Lanyu, off the southeast coast of Taiwan, for its magnificent rugged volcanic scenery and unique aboriginal cultural; and the Matsu Islands for their southern Fujian-style architecture, stunning views, island-hopping possibilities, and awesome subterranean military structures, the most impressive of which is a series of flooded tunnels used to shelter ships.

* * *

In John Slimming's **Green Plums and a Bamboo Horse: A Picture of Formosa**, published in 1964 by John Murray, we head to Kinmen and Matsu in the excellent company of an accomplished writer. The Englishman's four nights on Kinmen and week on Matsu are the pick of written accounts of the islands.

Slimming arrived in Taipei in June 1962 and stayed into early 1963. He gives a casual explanation for his extended stay. He and his wife Peksee were passing through Taiwan from Japan to Hong Kong, and then onward to home in Malaya. Peksee (English name Lucy), an ethnic Chinese from Malaysia three generations removed from Canton, was looking for the Old China and she suggested they stay on longer. Visiting her ancestral home in China was off-limits, so Formosa was the best substitute, though Taipei was still very Japanese, and as Slimming remarked, "The Chinese ideal in Formosa is being quickly replaced by the American." Peksee studied Mandarin in the morning with a softly spoken septuagenarian, a former Buddhist monk who came to the house thrice a week dressed in a full-length gown. An exile from Peking, he had not heard from his family there in over fourteen years.

Green Plums and a Bamboo Horse opens in winter – the coldest ever Taipei January then or since recorded – cruelly felt in their old-fashioned single-story Japanese-era house complete with tatami mats and sliding doors opening to a walled garden. The house was cold and noisy, the chorus of morning sounds a kaleidoscopic alarm clock: "Food sellers calling out as they pass the gate; tea barrows, fire-stoved, with large whistling kettles, shrilling a hiss of steam; the bread sellers and the *bau-tze* stalls; the rag man, with a bicycle cart, shouting at the new day; the sound of cycle bells and a taxi horn and the strained engine whine of next door's car which never starts easily. And beneath it all, the continuous noise of wooden clogs on stone."

Wooden clogs? I'd not have guessed that as a quintessential sound of Taipei so long after the Japanese period. The "clogs" are the Japanese *geta*, a kind of sandal with an elevated wooden sole and the foot held in by two strips of fabric straps like flip flops.

A neighbor had an old-fashioned gramophone, and among the scratchy old record favorites was a Cantonese love song, "Green Plums and a Bamboo Horse," based on a poem from Tang dynasty great Li Bai. It's fitting that Slimming chose a poetic reference for the title, as his writing is lovely – notable for descriptive poetry-like listings of the sights, sounds, smells, and colors of Taiwan. He is perhaps a little too fond of similes, but there's no denying they hit the mark. Of pressed pigs' heads in a Taipei grocery's shop: "The boned heads of pigs, pressed flat like masks, the snouts smashed in on themselves and wrinkled. What silly expressions these punched faces have – like cartoon drawings of defeated boxers." My favorite metaphor is in a description of a rural roadside scene on a summer's day, looking out of a train window as the locomotive awaits a signal crossing: "Sprays of bamboo arched out across the road, making a criss-cross abstraction of shadows, like melting calligraphy poured onto the ground." Melting calligraphy poured onto the ground – what wonderful imagery! Beautiful and true because that's what bamboo shadows look like.

Slimming's deepest contact with Taipei locals is with mainlanders, and these passages are a powerful evocation of the sadness of exile. One friend "lives only for the day he can go back to his own province" and carries keys of a house in Chengdu, "uselessly jingling on his pocket. Keys on a chain, worn smooth with continual handling, waiting to be used again." Slimming says of the refugees: "Every day there is talk of going back, of planning for the return, of returning, and the talk, even now, has the ring of hope, like a new sovereign spinning on a marble counter."

It's an obsession stoked by the government: "There are slogans, ten feet high, plastered on walls and hoardings all over town, politicians continually rededicate themselves to the cause of reclaiming the Mainland and every day newspapers are full of articles and editorials about the coming invasion."

Slimming mentions "a new Government tax on beer now, a 'Reclaim the Mainland' tax. So every bottle is worth a round of ammunition maybe, on some Fukien beach."

Slimming is generally sympathetic to the KMT, and dismissive of "malcontents" advocating Taiwanese self-rule, though he does mention 2-28, referring to it as "the incident" and calling it a bloodbath that resulted in seven thousand deaths and the loss of a whole generation of Taiwanese leadership. However, he puts the blame on the man on the ground, Governor Chen Yi, rather than Chiang

Kai-shek, and implies such a bad beginning makes the subsequent progress since 1947 all the more impressive. Slimming says the incident is being ignored and wiped from the records, and predicts: "Eventually it will be quite forgotten and no mention will be made of it at all." Although it might seem farcical for modern readers to call 2-28 "forgotten," – the events of 1947 dominate historical coverage of Taiwan – the silence Slimming predicted was indeed what happened for the next three decades.

There were two daily English-language newspapers, the *China Post* and the *China News*. Slimming describes the *China Post* as surprisingly anti-American considering the great amount of help received from the United States. "We read *The News* to find out what is happening in the world; we read *The Post* for amusement. *The Post*'s English is quaintly written with many mistakes and much slang. It obviously has a chip on its shoulder about something. Its voice is unformed somehow, like a child's whining."

One evening a local friend brought Slimming a cutting from a Chinese-language daily paper – it was the first installment of a serialized novel. "This is yours," he said, handing Slimming a Chinese translation of *The Pass*, a novel set in the Shan States of Burma, and drawing on the author's experiences there working for the British Council. This unapproved translation was news to Slimming, and there was nothing he could do about it because Taiwan had no copyright laws. At least Peksee found the daily installments of *The Pass* useful, going through them with her Mandarin tutor, and then translating them back into English as her homework.

The Pass (1962) was John Slimming's third book. Born in 1926, Slimming was just old enough to catch the tail-end of the Second World War, serving as a glider pilot. After the war, he found more adventure in the British colony of Malaya, as described in *Temiar Jungle: A Malayan Journey* (1958), a travelogue among the Temiar tribe, for whom he was responsible as an Assistant Protector of Aborigines; and *In Fear of Silence* (1959), an autobiographical novel about the Malayan Emergency, during which Slimming was badly injured in a Communist ambush, and forced to retire. In 1968 Slimming left Malaysia for Hong Kong, where he worked for the Government Information Service (GIS) and published a controversial account of the anti-Chinese riots of 1969 in *Malaysia: Death of a Democracy*. Slimming died in Hong Kong in 1979 from a heart attack. He is fondly remembered by friend and GIS colleague Peter Moss in his 2004 memoir *Distant Archipelagos: Memories of Malaya* as a great character and storyteller, a trained actor who could effortlessly quote Shakespeare but was otherwise tight-lipped and rumored to be working for British intelligence.

I wonder if there was an intelligence angle to Slimming's visit. Getting a visa for a long stay wasn't that easy. As the author says, Taiwan had great tourism potential; but the whole industry was based on transit passengers enjoying seventy-two-hour visa-free stays; longer visits required a visa application taking six to eight weeks and a guarantor. Slimming doesn't say how he obtained his visa – perhaps through his wife as an overseas Chinese. Then there was the Slimmings meeting Chiang Kai-shek – though just a handshake – and more than an hour talking to Madame Chiang, who the author describes as charming, knowledgeable, and possessing "an assumed air of royalty." However, the many bureaucratic hassles Slimming encountered with getting mountain permits and clearing books through customs (Shakespeare and Jane Austin being investigated in case they were communist) suggest he wasn't an official guest of the KMT.

7

Ghosts, Pirates, and Anthropologists

JOHN SLIMMING's wife had wanted to stay in Taiwan because visiting her ancestral homeland was impossible. During the years of Mao Zedong's rule (1949–1976) China was largely off-limits to Western journalists, missionaries, Sinologists, students, tourists – pretty much everyone except for the occasional leftist sympathizer. For many anthropologists, however, Taiwan provided an excellent substitute destination. Margery Wolf followed her husband, Arthur Wolf, an anthropology graduate student, to Taiwan, where they spent two years, 1959–1960, doing fieldwork in the farming village of Peihotien, southwest of Taipei.

Margery Wolf, who would go on to become a leading anthropologist, wrote a lovely account of the village: *The House of Lim: A Study of a Chinese Farm Family* (1968). It's a beautifully written book with use of dialogue, scenes, and narrative structure more novelistic than dissertational, a fascinating look at the private and public lives of a family, and the informal power of women in a village. The family members she writes about shine as individuals.

If you look for Peihotien on a map, you won't find it. Following standard anthropological practice, Wolf used pseudonyms for both the place and people in her book. The village was on the upper Danshui River in Tucheng District, now part of the greater Taipei urban metropolis. It was under an hour's journey from Taipei, half an hour by train and then the same on foot through the countryside ("one ride in an aged pedi-cab down a rutted country path is sufficient to discourage a second"). In 1959 this village of shady trees and traditional brick farm houses had a population of about five hundred. Despite being near Taipei, Peihotien seemed a world away; two old female residents claimed to have never been to the city.

The Wolfs rented a building from the Lims for themselves and research staff. (She doesn't mention the size of the staff, but it included a cook.) The Lims, the subject of Margery Wolf's book, were the largest, richest family (though not very rich, owning a modest twelve pigs) in the village, the embodiment of the Chinese family, three generations under one roof, fourteen people living as a single unit, sharing one kitchen. What made the family special was that it was a joint family, combining two family branches. Family members all contributed to the common pot and received from the common pot, with the senior male of the Lim patrilineage having the final word on allocation. It's easy to imagine that the system of a large family sharing hard-won profits would lead to resentments over contributing more than one's fair share, and indeed it did – making for great human drama in the book. The Lims had one advantage in terms of the two branches of the family keeping out of each other's hair: there was a division of work, with one side tending to the five acres of farmland and the other running a small cement-bag factory. The wives shared cooking duties on a five-day rotation. Even so tensions simmered below the surface, periodically erupting – as the author says this was a "family of strong-willed, hot-tempered personalities" – and the family would divide into two households just a few months after the Wolfs left.

For me the most fascinating aspect of *The House of Lim* is the description of *sim-pua* marriages, a practice also found in China but more common in Taiwan. A *sim-pua* marriage involved adopting a girl, raising the child bride in the family, and then, when she was old enough, marrying her to one of the sons. You've not misread that; the custom was in effect marrying your adopted sister – not exactly a recipe for conjugal fireworks. As Wolf writes with understatement: "The early and prolonged association of husband and wife often affects their later marital relationship." As you would expect, the fertility rate for such pairings was much lower than for regular marriages, and the divorce rate much higher. Why then was it so prevalent?

For poor families, getting rid of a daughter early (when old enough to work, or even after weaning) meant one less mouth to feed. Girls were adopted for domestic labor, as actual daughters, or as future wives. In the latter case, adopting a foster daughter early on meant a financial saving for the boy's family because of the reduced bride price paid to the girl's family. Also, there was no need for expensive wedding-related activities; bowing to the ancestors and a family feast was enough. Another advantage was that a girl could more easily be molded to the family culture (growing up in the family obviously meant an easier time adjusting to the marriage), and there would be fewer conflicts between mother-in-law and daughter-in-law than would occur when bringing an outsider into the family.

Still, it was recognized that *sim-pua* marriages were hardly ideal. The ill treatment generally afforded adopted daughters was proverbial; everyday phrases referred to being beaten or crying like an adopted daughter, and flustered mothers used adoption as an effective threat against recalcitrant children. Wolf says that contrary to her expectation that adopted girls would hate their foster parents, she was struck in numerous interviews that resentment was far greater toward natal parents for sending them away into their hard life.

Margery Wolf does a good job of capturing the centrality of the Chinese vice of gambling and makes the obvious comparison with the Western weakness for the bottle. She says a gambler in the family is often "as disastrous as a chronic alcoholic in an American family." Not just men either: "the disease is endemic among certain Taiwanese women. Many of them learn of its hypnotic fascination when they work as wine house girls or prostitutes; others discover it at New Year's festivals when it is almost a standard part of the celebrations."

The story of the problem gambler in the Lim family is told in a chapter, "Tan A-hong: An Adopted Daughter." Tan A-hong spent ten years in the Lim family; but when their own daughter, who had been given away as a foster child, was returned to the Lims, they found another home for her. The resulting marriage was short-lived and A-hong drifted into the life of a prostitute. A-Hong's daughter followed her into the trade. Wolf says that prostitution was not so looked down on. It was seen as driven by need, as a sacrifice for parents or children, and as long as they did not practice it back home in the village and were seen to support their family, then they were not ostracized.

Margery Wolf largely eschewed politics in *The House of Lim*. She did mention Taiwanese–mainlander enmity in relation to a marriage of one of the family, though it's rather cryptic stuff: "Because of several tragic events followed by innumerable misunderstandings, there exists on Taiwan an attitude of scorn and distrust between the Chinese native to the island and those who came after the establishment of the Communist regime on mainland China."

Wolf doesn't give readers much sense of the struggle the Taiwanese were having in adapting to new colonial masters and a new official language. On the contrary, she brings up and dismisses the young generation's nostalgia for the Japanese time, saying it was shallow and stemmed from images gleamed from Japanese pop culture.

"As the men of his grandfather's generation chaffed under the restrictions of a Japanese colonial government and longed for the return of a Chinese administration that they could not remember, so the young men of today look upon a past they were too young to know, as a time of freedom and plenty."

The Wolfs returned to the Peihotien area in 1968 for further fieldwork, this time basing themselves in the nearby town of Sanxia. Much had changed: Taipei was no longer a city of oxcarts and pedicabs, and development had spread out into the hinterland. Peihotien had lost much of its charm – chicken farms where once gleamed paddy fields, and ugly new concrete-block architecture among the graceful old farm courthouses. Most of the village's big old trees had been destroyed by construction or by the extreme winds and flooding of Typhoon Gloria, which killed about two hundred people when it hit northern Taiwan in 1963.

From this stay and a subsequent trip in 1970, Margery Wolf wrote *Women and the Family in Rural Taiwan* (1972). In this much more conventional anthropological work, she addressed an essential feature of Taiwanese (and ethnic Chinese) family dynamics: the especially strong relationship of the mother and son, for which she coined the term "uterine family." Consider, Wolf postulated, a young woman coming into a new family in a village. It was a harsh new beginning, any prior status or connections now of little use. The way forward was to bear sons and foster the loyalty of the boys; the long-term ideal was to have the son side with the mother over his wife.

Although the "Taiwan" in the title *Women and the Family in Rural Taiwan* was an improvement on the "Chinese Farm Family" used for *The House of Lim*, the assertion in the text itself that Taiwan was a perfect stand-in for China was overstated: "Taiwan is ethnically Chinese, just as Chinese as Peking is. To be sure, the Taiwanese have customs that differ from those in Peking, but so do the people of Shanghai, and so do the Chinese who live in small villages forty miles from Peking."

Margery Wolf was a professor of anthropology at the University of Iowa from 1985 until her retirement in 2001. During this time she wrote *A Thrice-Told Tale: Feminism, Postmodernism, and Ethnographic Responsibility* (1992), which used an experimental approach, retelling in three ways the same incident, that of the possible "shamanic possession" of a woman in a Taiwanese village in 1960, but ultimately judged by fellow villagers to be a case of mental illness. The book grew out of a paper, "The Woman Who Didn't Become a Shaman" (originally published in *American Ethnologist* in 1990).

* * *

Margery Wolf and her *A Thrice-Told Tale*, along with fellow American anthropologists, come in for harsh criticism in **Looking Through Taiwan: American Anthropologists' Collusion with Ethnic Domination** (2005), by Keelung Hong and Stephen O. Murray.

Looking Through Taiwan examines how American anthropologists, not able to do research in China, chose Taiwan as a substitute and through self-interest were happy to go along with the authorities' fantasy of Taiwan being China.

Co-author Keelung Hong, born in Taiwan in 1943, grew up resentful under what was in effect colonial rule. Like many

Taiwanese of that era, he "recalls being punished for speaking Holo [Taiwanese] as a schoolchild and thirsting for broadcasts in the majority language." Still, he excelled academically and did post-graduate studies in the United States, earning a doctorate in chemistry at Berkeley, and worked as a research scientist. The other co-author, Stephen O. Murray (1950–2019), was a scholar based in San Francisco with an impressive list of publications on sociology and anthropology.

Before completing *Looking Through Taiwan*, the pair had already worked together, including co-authoring *Taiwanese Culture, Taiwanese Society: A Critical Review of Social Science Research Done on Taiwan* (1994), which examines much of the same ground. Although controversial, the 1994 book was more ignored than rebutted. Veteran professor of East Asian studies Murray A. Rubinstein has called it "a declaration of war on mainstream scholarship about Taiwan." Speaking of a 1996 edition – toned down and with material added – Rubinstein says it "contains much that is useful, even if the rhetoric does sound somewhat strident at times."

Looking Through Taiwan presents several core arguments that are hard to refute. Hong and Murray say that American anthropologists overemphasized the similarities between Taiwan and China. The KMT was happy to have social scientists writing about "a timeless, essentialized Chinese culture and society in Taiwan." These researchers were happy to have something that could be labeled "China," treating Taiwan as if was "an embalmed Ming-Dynasty theme park for aliens to visit and make their careers writing about as 'Chinese.'" Hong and Murray also highlight anthropologists' choice of safe topics such as kinship and folk religion (ignoring covert protest aspects and presenting it as part of China's ancient tradition). While no individual anthropologist can be fairly faulted here, collectively it was a failure of the field.

Looking Through Taiwan is a book of startling intensity. It's extremely rare to see so much anger in an academic publication. Time and again as you make your way through the chapters you wonder if you've walked in on a personal squabble. More than a squabble, a feud even, in the case of the authors' animosity toward anthropologist Margery Wolf.

The multiple criticisms made against *A Thrice-Told Tale* seem damning. There are language problems with the original notes and interpretations – and ignorance of basic facts and terms related to the subject; most obviously the use of "shaman" in the Taiwan context. Taiwan doesn't have shamans – they are best described as "spirit mediums."

Keelung Hong says he wrote to Margery Wolf following the publication of her paper in *American Ethnologist*, but she did not respond. It was this unwillingness from her and other anthropologists to address criticisms and engage in discussion, which, he says, led to him writing *Looking Through Taiwan*.

While the book makes valid complaints, and is a must-read for anyone interested in the social sciences in Taiwan, I wish it were less polemic. Too often it is dialed up to eleven, such as the repeated charge that Americans "fled" democratizing Taiwan, and when Keelung Hong writes: "it seems that American anthropologists are afraid of democracy and believe that they must depend on authoritarian states to force people to be studied by ignorant aliens speaking (if usually awkwardly) the language imposed by that state."

Thankfully, the situation described in *Looking Through Taiwan*, whereby anthropological research on Taiwan was done through a prism of the country being a substitute for China, is much less of a problem today. However, the book remains relevant for two main reasons. First, researchers (and others) working in China today face choices that earlier generations of anthropologists had to make with regard to authoritarian-era Taiwan. And, second, the false equation of Taiwan with China continues to appear in a wide range of writing and this has done harm in fostering unrealistic expectations that an increasingly prosperous China will follow Taiwan's path to democracy. Yes, the two places share elements of history and culture, but the differences should not be overlooked: Taiwan's frontier history, the centuries of international maritime trade, its aborigines, the fifty years of Japanese rule, and American influences make it unique. The push for democracy in Taiwan had a central ethnic element – pushback against the domination over the majority Taiwanese by a refugee minority of mainlanders – that does not apply to China.

* * *

With its pretense to be the one true China, it's easy to dismiss Cold War Taiwan as a comic opera country; but it was indeed a lifeboat of culture – and at least one open to foreigners. Among those who came to Taiwan for that legacy, and who would go on to write about China – both past and present – instead of the reality of Taiwan, are three notable figures: Pierre Ryckmans, Bill Porter, and Daniel Reid.

Sinologist Pierre Ryckmans (1935–2014), a French-speaking Belgian with a Flemish surname, studied Mandarin and painting at National Taiwan Normal University (NTNU), arriving in 1958, the year of the Second Cross-Strait Crisis. Ryckmans' painting classes brought him into contact with Pu Hsin-yu, an eccentric master striving to preserve classical painting techniques as well as the philosophy and poetry related to the art. Pu was the cousin of Puyi, "the last emperor" of the Qing dynasty, and might himself have become emperor but for the Dowager Empress Cixi. Although Pu was a professor at NTNU, he worked off-campus from a Japanese-style house, where he taught carefully chosen students, with character being as important a prerequisite as talent. Pu refused to teach outside of his house, even when asked by Madame Chiang Kai-shek, a keen amateur painter, as lessons would have required him travelling to the Chiang residence. For the first year, his painting students could do nothing but calligraphy; and in the second year they moved on to rocks and trees. Pu Hsin-yu's methods came from generations of craft and from principles contained in an encyclopedic *Manual of the Mustard Seed Garden* from the late 1600s. Ryckmans would go on to write his doctoral dissertation on early Qing dynasty painter Shitao and have a celebrated academic career in Australia. In a series of books published in the 1970s and written under the pen name Simon Leys, he was at the vanguard of academics criticizing the Cultural Revolution and the idolization of Mao by fellow intellectuals.

Bill Porter is an American author and translator noted for his translations of Taoist and Buddhist texts and poems (which he writes under the pen name Red Pine) and travelogues exploring China's hermit heritage. After dropping out of Columbia University's graduate school and moving to Taiwan in 1972, his entry into the living world of Chinese letters was a one-year stay in Fo Guang Shan, a Buddhist monastery near Kaohsiung, southern Taiwan's largest city. He moved to a quieter monastery near Taipei for two and a half years, then lived in Bamboo Lake (Zhuzihu), a village up on Yangming Shan, translating ancient texts and teaching a few English classes down in the city to pay the bills. After getting married, he found a proper job at Taiwan's English-language radio station, ICRT, then headquartered up on the mountain. Porter moved back to the United States in 1993.

Daniel Reid's Taiwan stint was similar. He arrived in 1973 after completing a master's degree, and he spent the next sixteen years studying and writing about ancient Chinese culture, with a focus on Taoism and traditional medicine. His best-known work is

The Tao of Health, Sex, and Longevity: A Modern Practical Guide to the Ancient Way (1989), which we will look at later.

* * *

Colorful religious beliefs and practices are an aspect of Taiwan life that strike new arrivals to the island and lose little power to shock and confound no matter how long you stay. My favorite anthropological book on the subject is David K. Jordan's **Gods, Ghosts, and Ancestors: Folk Religion in a Taiwanese Village** (1972), which describes the religious beliefs and practices of an agricultural village called Bao'an (a pseudonym) near the town of Xigang in southwestern Taiwan. *Gods, Ghosts, and Ancestors* is one of the first books I bought in Taiwan. It was a revelation. I had done some background reading on Chinese religion before coming to Taiwan: Buddhism, Taoism (the classical kind rather than the folksy kind), and Confucianism, and also the customs associated with holidays like Chinese New Year and Tomb Sweeping Day – but it little prepared me for what I found on the ground, especially in the boonies.

In his book, Jordan explores religious belief at the family and village level. Of the three religious elements in the book title – gods, ancestors, and ghosts – Jordan wisely devotes the most space to ghosts. The gods, with temples dedicated to them, and ancestor worship, with altars for them in people's homes, are more visible, better known, and have been more extensively written about. However, the folk religion aspects associated with ghosts are more intimate and little known.

Although Jordan gives a general introduction to rural religious beliefs, the emphasis is on how beliefs and practices interact with the social structures of family and village. Rather than being a mere local catalog of customs, this is earthy Taiwanese religion woven into and interplaying with everyday life. *Gods, Ghosts, and Ancestors* captures the casual, messy nature of it.

The author, an American in his mid-twenties, arrived in the autumn of 1966 and stayed until the summer of 1968, conducting research for an anthropology doctoral dissertation, completed the following year at the University of Chicago. Jordan writes with admirable honesty of his language shortcomings and acknowledges the help he received. His pre-arrival language preparation was about five months of intensive Mandarin summer classes, insufficient of course to handle written materials. In addition, his village was a Hokkien-speaking one, although young people were comfortable with Mandarin, having learned it at school. The village was welcoming, the residents happy at his interest in Taiwanese culture and their village. Local leaders and officials were also helpful.

Jordan spent the first three months in the village quietly engaged in studying Taiwanese textbooks (largely self-study as these were in Romanized form, with which the locals were unfamiliar). After this, he hired a research assistant from a nearby town and began his fieldwork: census taking and interviewing. In summer he hired another man, and both of these assistants would continue working almost up until Jordan's departure a year later. He also hired a female assistant to interview women in the village about matters of a feminine nature. Not bad – in your mid-twenties and you've got three workers. Labor and living costs were extremely low at this time, especially in the countryside.

The village of Bao'an had roughly sixteen hundred people divided into 227 households. About two-thirds of the villagers had the surname Kuo (Guo). There was one temple in the village – a site for both religious and non-religious gatherings, with the paved area in front used for drying crops and as a playground for children. The temple was not specifically related to one god but was associated with various deities, most importantly Matsu (Mazu) and Marshal Xie. The statues of these gods, however, were kept for security reasons (the temple didn't have lockable doors) in residents' homes, and there was usually just an old Guanyin statue in the temple during Jordan's stay. The village's patron god was King Guo, whose main temple in Taiwan was Xiluo Temple in Tainan City, founded it was said in 1714 by transferring a burning pot of incense from its home temple at the Phoenix Mountain Monastery in Fujian. Every three years the statue of the god would go on a tour of villages and come to Bao'an.

About halfway through Jordan's stay in Bao'an, a boy drowned in a village fishpond. Drownings are to this day often attributed to ghosts, and it was especially so in this case as the boy could swim a little and the pond was shallow. Among the explanations were that a ghost from a previous death in the pond – a water ghost pulling the boy in – was responsible, or that ghosts from outside the village were to blame. Regardless, the spirit of the drowned child would now become a "water ghost" waiting in bondage to the water gods until a victim could be pulled in to take its place; this was so serious a threat that the villagers would not speak aloud the words "water ghost," instead referred to it as a "bad thing."

Five days later an exorcism was held. First a divination ritual was performed at the temple, where instructions were sought from the gods. The instruments of divination were two "divination chairs" – basically a small palanquin (i.e., a sedan chair) but with protruding arms, carried on two poles and a bearer front and back. Into the chair the presence of a god would materialize – seen in the bouncing, jerking movements of the chair. Upon a special table, protruding arms wrote the message. The first god, His Highness Chi, offered common-sense advice: the villagers should strive for harmony and keep the children away from the fishpond. The second chair, possessed by King Guo, gave instructions: the two gods (here represented by the divination chairs) would go to the pond and drive away the "bad thing."

Various precautions and preparations ensued, and then the chairs were taken to the pond, which they made frenzied dashes around and then moved in and out of the water, beating the surface while "the onlookers shouted high-pitched shouts, hurled burning firecrackers over the pond, and threw handfuls of sesame seeds into the water." All these things were designed to scare away the ghosts. "Sesame seeds?" I can hear you wondering. In a footnote, (and Jordan's footnotes are exceptionally good, being full of interesting asides and answers to sensible questions) he says he was told that the purpose of the seeds, "was that the bad thing would try to count the seeds, but as there were so many he would surely lose count. In a fit of frustration and pique he would run away and never return. It struck me as unlikely, but that is the only explanation I was able to elicit. Sesame was in season. As I understand it, any small seeds would do."

Among the most jaw-dropping sections of *Gods, Ghosts, and Ancestors* is the topic of marriages to female ghosts. Yes, it's always a pairing of flesh-and-blood male with a spectral female, because of ancestor worship being following the patrilineal family structure. If a woman is to be worshipped in the afterlife, she needs to have a husband and children; in this way, a ghost marriage is a lot like a girl being adopted into a family.

Although Jordan didn't witness a spirit wedding himself, that was mostly due to poor timing and finding out about it too late; they were relatively common at the time. He describes three ghost marriages from Bao'an. When I mentioned this custom to Taiwanese friends, I found out that one of my acquaintances had married a spirit, and I wrote about this in *Formosan Odyssey*.

Toward the end of Jordan's stay in Taiwan, he came upon and was shocked by a bizarre religious practice, and one that didn't make it into his book. Invited to a "phoenix worship" séance at a nondescript Mazu temple one evening, he found women in white robes, chanting, playing drums and flutes, and, at the center of the action were men going into trances, taking turns to write characters with a Y-shaped stick (a phoenix) on a leather pad atop a table. The writing was interpreted by a "temple officer" who called out each character, which was then written down in a book by a secretary. This continued at some length. Jordan learned that the spirit-writing took place every night. The writing was collated and subjected to spirit editing, and then published. Their last book, the third in a series – covering about three years' worth of revelations – had several thousand copies printed. Spirit-writing, normally employed as an oracle for believers seeking advice to personal problems, was here being done on a startling scale to produce "morality books" (*shanshu*), which contained religious instruction and exhortations to moral behavior.

Jordan visited more of these "phoenix halls" and found that they were quite common. However, with time running down and no such activity in Bao'an, he was unable to delve deeply into the phenomenon. Moreover, this cult activity was different from village-based religion tied to the cycle of the seasons, families, and communities, and so was not relevant to his doctoral research.

After finishing his dissertation, Jordan began work as an academic (this was back in the days when there was a reliable pathway from a Ph.D. to the lecture podium rather than to the coffee machine). He was able to take a sabbatical in 1976 and return to Taiwan to research spirit-writing cults. His research resulted in *The Flying Phoenix: Aspects of Chinese Sectarianism in Taiwan* (1986), co-authored with historian David Overmyer.

Jordan has enjoyed a long, successful academic career, though he will probably be remembered as the chronicler of folk religion in the village of Bao'an. His book is a bottled essence of rural Taiwanese life in the 1960s, containing some essential elements still recognizable today and others only of that time. I wonder if it's slightly grating to Jordan to be best remembered for his first work. Better that than obscurity.

A Chinese edition of *Gods, Ghosts, and Ancestors* was published in Taiwan in 2012, and the following year saw the publication of a detailed restudy of the same village by Professor Ting Jen-chieh (Ding Renjie) of Academia Sinica, Taiwan's leading research institute; *Restudying Bao'an Village* is available only in Chinese at the moment, but I'd love to see an English version.

Jordan has, since 1999, very generously made *Gods, Ghosts, and Ancestors* available for free online (http://pages.ucsd.edu/~dkjordan/ scriptorium/gga/ggamain.html). This favoring of readership over royalties is a fitting story arc, considering the publication history of the book. The first edition of *Gods, Ghosts, and Ancestors* was published in 1972 by the University of California Press. Priced too high to sell well, it faded slowly to the out-of-print graveyard. Meanwhile in Taiwan, there were several cheap pirated editions finding their way into the hands of appreciative readers, some of whom wrote to the author thanking him for producing such an informative yet accessible book. It was the enthusiasm of these readers and the continuing popularity of the pirated editions that led to the legal Taiwan printing of a second but this time affordable edition in 1985 by Taiwanese bookstore chain Caves Books.

This backstory to the second edition highlights an important facet of publishing in Taiwan from the late 1950s into the early 1990s. The country was once notorious for book piracy, and we're not just talking about niche anthropological works on Taiwanese folk religion. Taipei printing houses once throbbed to the sound of presses rolling out huge numbers of English-language books – best-selling novels, university textbooks, encyclopedias – for both local and, more significantly, the world market.

It was piracy on a massive scale, and out in the open. Although the KMT represented China at the United Nations and was accepted as such in many of the world's capitals, it had not signed any international copyright agreements. Consequently, a publisher in Taiwan could print its own version of the latest novel; no need for permission from the copyright holders, no need to pay royalties.

It reminds one of a century earlier, when Charles Dickens famously crusaded against the lax U.S. copyright laws, whereby domestic authors' works enjoyed some copyright protection but the works of foreign authors were unprotected and went unpaid in royalties. Likewise, in Taiwan, foreign works were free game whereas local registration of ROC copyright provided (at least in theory) protection. The obvious solution was for foreign publishers to register for local copyright in Taiwan. Easier said than done, however. Enter passive-aggressive Chinese bureaucracy. To say that the ROC government made things hard is an understatement. Encyclopedia Britannica, along with Webster's dictionary, and Gray's Anatomy, was among the first to realize the seriousness of the problem in the late 1950s. They tried registering their encyclopedias and eventually succeeded; but it was a long, frustrating process. A major obstacle was the censorship: the officials claimed that Encyclopedia Britannica had incorrect information on various subjects, such as Mao Zedong and Outer Mongolia (an independent country but still claimed by the KMT as part of the Republic of China).

Foreign publishers made the obvious deduction that the Taiwanese authorities were deliberately helping local printers and they urged the U.S. State Department to put pressure on the KMT to join the Universal Copyright Convention. The United States was, after all, bankrolling the very survival of the regime.

In the November 15, 1963, edition of *Life* magazine, a special report titled "Taiwan's Best-selling Pirates," gives a fascinating snapshot of the situation. The sub-heading, "A Clever Chinese Publishing Racket Gets Its Lumps," was in reference to a recent "crackdown" or at least a tightening of regulations whereby no pirated books were to be exported. The author of the report, Charles Elliott, mentions Chongqing South Road, which he'd visited when he was a correspondent in the Far East. Here were seven or so publishers, including the Tan Chiang Book Company. He gave some examples of their offerings: a hardcover medical textbook for $3, compared to $16.50 for the legitimate U.S. edition; and the full 24-volume set of the Encyclopedia Britannica for $40–$75 (depending on the binding), compared to $400 to $550 for the real thing. The books felt a little cheap – reflecting the lower grade of paper used – though the quality was reasonable. As well as winning on price, the pirated books were winning the race on speed to the bookshelves: "Faulkner's *The Reivers* was on display in pirated editions in Taipei within three weeks of its American publication, while shipments of the real article (at five times the price) didn't reach stores anywhere in the Far East until five weeks later."

The pirating process was straightforward. The publisher would have a copy of a new release sent by airmail from the United States or elsewhere. Upon arrival, it would be cut up and the pages photographed, and then those were turned into plates for use in a standard offset printing press. Usually every page was copied "faithfully," so the books came with the original copyright page, complete with "Printed in the U.S.A." The exception was for anything politically sensitive, which would be removed or blanked.

ROC officials countered complaints about book piracy with the line of defense that it was confined to poor university students, who couldn't afford to buy the legit books. On the question of the tortuous copyright registration, an official explained to Elliott "with a perfectly straight face," that a reason for the lengthy copyright process was that a book "must be examined carefully in search of violations of *somebody else's* copyright!"

When Elliot wrote his *Life* piece, it seemed American pressure was starting to pay off. Taiwanese concessions included promises to make registration easier, tighten copyright rules a little, and to treat the export of pirated books as smuggling.

Things did not improve. Taiwan's notoriety for illegal reprinting became such that the subject soon warranted its own title, **Book Pirating in Taiwan**, by David Kaser (1969). The author details, with remarkable sympathy for the Taiwanese position, the rise of book piracy in Taiwan in the 1950s and 1960s, the pushback from American publishers, and the attempted compromises.

David E. Kaser (1924–2017) was an American librarian and scholar who wrote extensively on the history of printing and libraries. Much of Kaser's goodwill for Taiwan's situation stemmed from his deep knowledge of the early days of the American publishing industry, when it was the world's most prolific book pirater. He knew better than anyone that America's championing of international copyright protection was a case of a poacher recently turned gamekeeper. The first international copyright protection in the United States came in 1891, but this was only for books manufactured in the country. Those brought in from overseas could be ripped off. Complete protection would have a long wait, coming in 1956 with the United States joining the Universal Copyright Convention, which had been drawn up by UNESCO four years earlier.

With funding from a Guggenheim Fellowship, Kaser spent much of 1967 examining Taiwan's book piracy. He traveled to the country, where he talked to numerous "gracious and hospitable" government officials and book printers.

Kaser describes how, as the piracy of Western books in Taiwan grew rapidly in the mid-1950s, American publishers were perplexed at what course of action to take. Similar piracy in Japan had been successfully stymied by allowing cheap local versions to be printed. This couldn't be replicated in Taiwan as the country was just too poor – textbooks selling at half the original price were still going to be way out of the reach of students and the great majority of the population. American publishers, "under the guise of corporate magnanimity, simply looked the other way and tolerated the piracy which they knew was taking place." This tolerance ended in 1960, when pirated books started coming into the United States, a phenomenon first noticed, by happenstance, at Iowa State University.

With tremendous charity for all parties involved, Kaser relates Taiwanese efforts to crackdown on book piracy. His trusting acceptance of ROC government explanations and promises is painfully amusing in its naïveté, and often turns a rather dry subject matter – details of proposals, negotiations, and agreements – into comedy gold. For example, he attributes the slow progress in combating piracy in part to the ancient ways of the East: "the Oriental concept of urgency differed considerably from that of the West; time perspective was different. Things generally have seldom been done there at the same rapid rate of accomplishment that is sought in the West...."

In particular, the wheels of the KMT bureaucracy turned slowly and involved "painstaking scrutiny" for every proposed change: "it required time, time, time, to bring together and appraise the multiplicity of diverse thoughts, considerations, and interests which would interplay with the changes to be made." As if an authoritarian state couldn't do things quickly when the leadership wanted action.

Kaser gives fascinatingly detailed examples of books that were pirated, such as *Death of a President*, historian William Manchester's account of the assassination of John F. Kennedy. It was published in the United States on April 7, 1967, where it retailed for ten dollars. Within eleven days a pirated version had been published by a book company in Taichung and was selling for about NT$70 (US$1.75). Before long, Taipei printers had two additional pirated editions on the market, and the price had now dropped to around NT$50. "Ironically but typically, the two new pirate printings were reproduced not from copies of the New York edition, but from copies of the Taichung reprinting. Thus pirates were pirating piracies."

Book Pirating in Taiwan is full of stories of false dawns of optimism. Following a crackdown, several book pirates were sentenced to prison terms of ten to twelve months.

Word of the convictions appeared the following day in *The New York Times,* and it inspired some in the American industry to think that perhaps the days of book piracy in Formosa were really coming to an end, although many old China watchers were frankly doubtful. Their doubts were confirmed when the full story became known several days later and it was determined that the convictions had been for pirating copy-righted *Chinese* books and that no Western reprints had been involved.

Kaser describes proposals for American booksellers to work with Taiwan printers and letting them produce low-cost editions. It was thought that by the mid-1960s Taiwan's consumers would have become sufficiently wealthy for this approach to work. The next chapter is titled "Dashed Hopes and Increased Chaos: The Situation

Worsens." Despite all the setbacks, the author finishes the book on a high-minded note; public opinion in Taiwan has, he believes, come around to seeing piracy as a problem and the ROC government is willing to act – all that is needed is for the Taiwanese and American publishers to work together "for the public good and for their mutual gain."

However, as William P. Alford wrote in the beautifully titled *To Steal a Book Is an Elegant Offense: Intellectual Property Law in Chinese Civilization* (1995): "the situation failed to improve appreciably. Nor did much-publicized additional governmental initiatives in the areas of enforcement and mass education, taken during the remainder of the 1960's or through the 1970's largely in response to intensifying U.S. pressure, prove any more effective."

The epicenter of the Taipei book trade was Chongqing South Road in central Taipei (a few minutes' walk southwest of the main train station). It was once known as "Book Street," which you wouldn't guess from the handful of bookstores still there. Its heyday was in the 1970s, when it was one of the great biblio-destinations in the world and lined with about a hundred bookstores. With China in the darkness of the Cultural Revolution, it had extra significance, and was arguably the premier book venue for the Chinese-speaking world. The rise of chain bookstores in the 1980s diluted the concentration of stores on the road; and, of course, the Internet has killed off most of the rest.

Book piracy was not exclusively the bane of foreign publishers. Even for local books, copyright registration was worth little on the ground. As Alford writes: "few among the more than 1,400 publishers and reprinters in business in Taiwan in the mid-1970s thought it worth the expense and effort to obtain copyright registration."

Nor was the piracy problem limited to books. Taiwanese entrepreneurs were increasingly churning out everything from pirated records and tapes, to pens, watches, and cameras. The ROC government turned a blind eye to (and perhaps even encouraged) the piracy because it was a good fit for their policy of import substitution and aggressive exporting.

In 1982 *Newsweek* described Taiwan as the counterfeiting capital of the world. Similarly, a 1986 article in the *New York Times* stated: "Until a few years ago, Taiwan was the undisputed counterfeiting and illegal-copying capital of the world."

Increased American pressure on the ROC – as well as local economic and cultural changes – led to Taiwan finally enacting proper copyright laws starting in 1992. No unauthorized copies of books were to be printed, whether for local use or export. Illegal printing still goes on – typically for expensive textbooks – but on a much-reduced scale and only for the domestic market.

* * *

A few years after Jordan was recording religious life in rural Tainan, another young American immersed himself in a small community, this time through a stay on a remarkable offshore island, resulting in *Song of Orchid Island* (2006).

Orchid Island (also known as Lanyu) lies thirty-nine miles due east of the Hengchun Peninsula. Rising dramatically up out of the Pacific, it's a volcanic creation of gnarled shores and steep emerald mountains, and home to three thousand Yami (Tao) people, the most distinctive of Taiwan's aboriginal groups.

The Yami are more closely related to the people on the Batanes Islands in the Philippines than to other aborigines in Taiwan, and are Taiwan's only maritime group. Life follows the rhythms of the ocean, with the year divided into three fishing seasons related to the flying fish. Boat building is a sacred and practical aspect of traditional life; the climatic event of the year is the boat ceremony, when the iconic Yami fishing canoes are launched.

Tao (Yami) boat-launching ceremony, from Song of Orchid Island

Onto this special island came Jesuit seminarian Barry Martinson in 1971, sent there to teach art and music at a primary school as part of his training. *Song of Orchid Island*, which describes his year with the Yami, is an ode to this beautiful island, its close-knit community, and the twilight of age-old ways. The island's isolation had long preserved their ancient culture, but things were starting to change.

Song of Orchid Island is neither a conventional missionary account (there's no mention of saving the natives from damnation), nor an anthropology text, though fascinating anthropological details are woven into the vignettes; we learn about the intricate customs regulating the catching, preparation, and eating of fish; superstitions concerning malignant spirits; and the naming practice whereby the names of parents and grandparents change after the birth of the first child.

Part of the attraction of the book is, like Jordan in the village of Bao'an, we have a man in his mid-twenties undertaking the kind of immersive adventure most of us have daydreamed about. Exotic travel is fun; but who wouldn't trade that for the deeper experience of staying in a remote, non-Western community and following village life through the seasons? On top of its vicarious pleasures, the book is important as a time capsule of a unique place at a specific time. It's also well written and in a lyrical style that matches the subject matter. Here's a passage describing the launching of a canoe:

> Ten of the men grasped the newly built canoe and heaved it toward the water, scraping its hull coarsely on the pebbles beneath. Together, they began to chant and with a thrust hurled themselves into the boat as it hit the water, striking the oars with rhythmic harmony. Out a certain distance the

men stood up in the canoe and called again to the flying fish. The endless sea stretched before them, answering their call with the silence of sun-filled stars sparkling on its early morning waters.

Martinson arrived on – and departed from – the island as the well-meaning Westerner, the very antithesis of a fire-and-brimstone preacher or a modernizing campaigner of muscular Christianity bringing the blessings of civilization and salvation. Martinson is tolerant of the islanders, admiring the simplicity and happiness of their ways, and seeking to offer them help they request rather than be an outsider imposing what he thinks is best for them.

A Taiwanese teacher at the school didn't share Martinson's views on the locals. While on a school outing, the teacher reacted to Martinson's expression of admiration for the Yami culture:

"Culture?" Big Lee stared at me in amazement. "These people have no culture. Look at what they eat. Sweet potatoes and taro. No vegetables. They won't use chopsticks. No matter how much we tell them, they still refuse to change. Sometimes the children are so dirty I can hardly stand it. They never wash before eating – only after. Do you call that culture?"

"I was thinking more of their way of life. It's so simple and rich in traditions – especially when you compare it to ours. Why change all that?"

"So you are content to let them remain in their misery. Maybe you would like to preserve this island as a reserve for anthropologists, like the Japanese did – or as a zoo for tourists! ... Oh? And then there are those like you who come along and say everything is perfect here. Orchid Island is a paradise and the people are saints. They can do no wrong. They don't need anything."

Big Lee's retort stung, partly because it was so unexpected and partly because there was truth in what he said. Was my attempt to love simply the vain quest of a romanticist? I tried to answer Big Lee, but could not find the words to express my feelings. There was an uncomfortable moment of silence. Then Principal Chen, who hadn't said much the whole trip, spoke earnestly for us both.

"Everyone has his own way. One likes to teach. Another likes to paint and sing. I like to build things. Each has his own way, and all the ways are the right ways. If all of us tried to change the Yami they would resent it. If all of us tried to accept them as they are, they would never improve. The right way is the way that is right for you."

Despite Martinson's sunny disposition and the poetic warmth of his prose, the account of his time on Orchid Island is balanced with honest observations of poverty, hunger, and illness – this was clearly no tribal paradise. A fierce typhoon the previous summer had blasted the hills with salt water, killing the sweet potato crop. For the past few months the people could eat only taro. Even for those with money, there was nowhere to buy provisions, so people came to the church asking Martinson for food. And while on Orchid Island, Martinson had need of a dentist. He had a broken filling – from crunching a betel nut – on one side of his mouth and then a cavity on the other. The island practitioner was away in mainland Taiwan; the pain drove Martinson to Taitung for a real dentist.

I'm glad Martinson describes the hardships of life on Orchid Island. As a curmudgeonly cynic (though I prefer to think of myself as a bruised romantic), I'm allergic to glowing descriptions of tribal life.

I always wonder why writers singing profuse praise for a people or place so seldom choose to stay on. As a long-term expat, I'm not impressed by a residency of a year or two. However, this does not apply to Martinson. Although he would not reside on the island again, this was hardly a case of parachuting in for a year of exotic deprivation and then returning to comfortable city life in the West, because he has – for more than forty years since his time on Orchid Island – been serving the aboriginal people in Taiwan.

In 1976 Martinson was assigned to the mountain village of Qing-quan (Chingchuan), in eastern Hsinchu County, to serve as parish priest to the predominantly Atayal aboriginal community. Since then, as well as administering to spiritual needs, he has been involved in educational and cultural work. Using his artistic talents, Martinson made stained glass windows for the church building and, to raise funds, painted murals in the village. He also set up a youth center and converted an abandoned church in a neighboring area into a tuition-free kindergarten.

Barry Martinson describes his first six years in the village in *Chingchuan Story* (2007). As with *Song of Orchid Island*, it's a series of unassuming, good-natured vignettes with restrained Catholicism and a tendency to lyrical naturalism. Published in English in 2007, *Chingchuan Story* originally appeared twenty-five years earlier in Chinese. This takes us back to the publication history of *Song of Orchid Island*. Despite a fair amount of competition — such as from the hoaxes of Psalmanazar and Robert W. Smith, the belated release of *Formosa Calling*, and explosive publications that were long banned, such as *A Pail of Oysters* and *Formosa Betrayed* — *Song of Orchid Island* has perhaps the most interesting backstory of all the works featured in *Taiwan in 100 Books*.

The book-origin story for *Song of Orchid Island* all began with a fortuitous encounter on the island itself. Martinson was in a back room of his church, drinking coffee with some friends, when two young Taiwanese women peered in. There was mutual surprise. The visitors were tourists staying at a new hotel nearby. During the next few days, the women visited several times. Echo, one of the women, was physically striking, "with long black hair and an infectious smile," and something of a force of nature. Martinson and Echo hit it off; before returning to Taipei, she gave Martinson her phone number and address, with an invitation to dinner at her home. Shortly afterward, Martinson moved to Taipei to complete his studies at the seminary, and he set up a meeting. Sadly, several mishaps, including a lost address, meant they didn't meet up. Their paths would not cross again for almost a decade.

During his first year in Taipei, Martinson wrote *Song of Orchid Island* and sent the manuscript – his one and only copy – to a publisher in San Francisco. Months dragged into years without a response. (It turned out the publisher had gone bankrupt.) A friend in the States helped Martinson recover the manuscript. Martinson writes: "Finally, a sheaf of yellowing paper with cigarette burns and missing pages was returned. I threw the unfortunate manuscript in a drawer and vowed never to write a book again."

Several years later, when Martinson was living in the mountain village of Qingquan, he received an unexpected package. It was a Chinese-language book titled *Sahala de Gushi* 撒哈拉 的故事 (1976; English edition, *Stories of the Sahara*, 2020). The author was Echo Chen, who had written it under the pen name of Sanmao. Published in 1976 and an instant sensation in the Chinese-speaking world, the book was part travelogue and part memoir, describing her marriage to Spaniard Jose Maria Quero y Ruiz and their life in Western Sahara (a Spanish colony at the time). They had married there in 1973. *Stories of the Sahara*, as well as numerous articles, had made Echo a writing celebrity.

She was free-spirited and pretty, a bohemian artist traveling and writing, and with an exotic marriage to a foreigner. It was an intoxicating mix for a readership longing for freedom and broader horizons.

Born in 1943 in the wartime capital of Chongqing, Echo moved to Taiwan with her family when she was six years old. Rebellious, intelligent, and a ferocious bookworm, she had trouble fitting in at school. Discipline problems meant she was home-schooled from the age of twelve by private tutors and her own father, who was a lawyer.

Echo moved to Europe to study when she was twenty. She would go on to travel to more than fifty countries and write two dozen complete works. With her charisma and captivating life story she was a fantasy figure for a whole generation of Taiwan girls and young women, and, a decade later, part of the great wave of Taiwanese music and literature that swept through China in the 1980s.

In his isolated aboriginal mountain parish, however, Martinson was unaware of her popularity. Now Echo was back in Taipei, though under sad circumstances, her husband having died in a scuba-diving accident.

As Martinson read through *Stories of the Sahara*, the simple, poetic style reminded him of his unpublished account of Orchid Island. Thinking it might interest Echo and bring back memories of her trip there, he sent the manuscript of *Song of Orchid Island* to her. "A few weeks after I had mailed Echo my manuscript, there she was again, poking her head through the door of my church." Echo told Martinson she had sent the manuscript to a publisher in Taipei and they wanted to issue it in Chinese. Echo translated the book, and it was published by Crown Press in 1982. In the lead-up to the book's release, excerpts were been published in newspapers and a magazine. The manuscript that had almost been lost, that had gathered dust for nine years, and that was now in another language became a bestseller, with the first printing of thirty thousand copies selling out. Martinson modestly writes: "The editors were quick to point out that this was not because my book was so great, but because San Mao was so famous." Echo and Martinson donated their book royalties to St. Mary's Hospital in Taitung, which gave free medical services to people from Orchid Island.

At Echo's prompting, Martinson took up writing again, starting with a memoir describing his first years in the mountains (*Ching-chuan Story*). She translated it into Chinese. More collaborations followed, and Echo was a frequent visitor to the mountain village. Eventually, "she moved on with her travels and her interests, restless and always searching, and we did not see her again. Then one day in wintertime I received word that she had died, and by her own hand."

San Mao committed suicide by hanging on January 4, 1991, at a hospital in Taipei. She was forty-seven years old. Why had this gregarious, successful woman, admired and loved by so many people, taken her life? Was it the fame, a fear of illness, or the lingering sadness of her husband's death? The reason for her suicide remains a mystery. On this question Martinson writes: "I wondered if the answer was somehow connected to the end of her favorite book, when the Little Prince allowed a snake to bite him so he could return to his star in the heavens. Echo always associated herself with that strange person from another planet. Maybe she thought that was a way – the only way she knew – to get home."

8

Cloak and Dagger Days

Iᴛ's amazing how few Cold War-era novels were set in Taiwan. The country offered the novelist an embarrassment of riches; invasion scenarios, ethnic tensions, exiles, clandestine military operations, Golden Triangle connections, gangsters, and spies, along with secrets and vendettas from the Second World War and the Chinese Civil War – all in a more foreign setting than British-influenced Hong Kong and Singapore. And yet this potential World War III flashpoint gave us only a few stories of that time, such as Vern Sneider's *A Pail of Oysters* (1953), D.J. Spencer's *The Jing Affair* (1965), and Christopher Wood's *Taipei: A Novel* (1981, Fontana). The last entry is from the English screenwriter for two James Bond movies (*The Spy Who Loved Me* and *Moonraker*) and also the author behind a smutty series of novels starting with *Confessions of a Window Cleaner* in 1971. As you'd expect, *Taipei* is low-rent entertainment, the plot involving a heist of priceless treasures from the National Palace Museum. It's ludicrous but fun escapism, or cringeworthy pulp, depending on your taste.

The Jing Affair (1965) is another matter completely. This riveting, pro-independence thriller contains the improbable heroics and love interest element common to bestselling page-turners but adds layers of authenticity and heart to a politically explosive work. No wonder the author – whose identity was unknown until a few years ago – wrote the novel under a pen name, D.J. Spencer.

The story revolves around a sellout of Taiwan by General Jing, the head of the KMT's secret police, "father of the Youth Corps, monitor of the island's political orthodoxy, inquisitor and jailer, not to mention judge," and "for all practical purposes, the most powerful man on Taiwan."

American surveillance reports come in of ROC troop buildups on islands near the Chinese coast, and of various signs indicating an imminent invasion of the mainland.

> New data began to flood in upon American intelligence from all sides. The first item came from a most unlikely source, Taiwan's fish markets. Over a period of two weeks, fish suddenly disappeared from the island's markets and from the island's dinner tables. The fishing boats, intelligence learned in late November, were going out, but they were not coming back. Reconnaissance planes of the Seventh Fleet patrolling the Taiwan Strait found the boats in a matter of hours: every available small craft out of Taiwan was anchored some twelve miles off the coast of Red China on the western side of China's offshore islands, just outside the port of Foochow.

There is also mysterious activity at General Jing's private resort lodge high in the mountains of central Taiwan. U.S. intelligence suspects Jing is preparing to betray Taiwan to China under the guise of an invasion. The Americans – openly, at least – are powerless to act. They have treaty obligations to defend Taiwan from foreign aggression but not from Nationalist intrigue. Things will have to be handled discreetly, for now. From Washington the call goes out to implement Contingency Plan S; long-dormant pro-independence Taiwanese leaders and fighters assemble in the foothills east of Taichung, while out in the Taiwan Strait aboard a U.S. Navy carrier Taiwanese-American air force pilot Johnny Hsiao prepares for a daring undercover mission. By the time we get to the end of the novel things will have escalated quickly, but I'll save the plot details for readers to enjoy on their own. Let's look instead at some of the characters.

General Jing is a not-so-disguised reference to Chiang Kai-shek's son, Chiang Ching-kuo (CCK); In Hanyu Pinyin romanization the spelling is Jiang Jingguo. Author Spencer was not alone in speculating about CCK's reliability. As the elder Chiang (born 1887) approached the end of his life, there were fears that Chiang Ching-kuo, the expected successor, might cut a deal with Beijing. As Stephen Craft writes in *American Justice in Taiwan*, there had been secret meetings held: "subordinates of both Chiang Ching-kuo and Chiang Kai-shek met with PRC foreign minister Zhou Enlai in July 1956 and April 1957, respectively, to discuss national unification and the idea of an autonomous Taiwan controlled by Chiang Kai-shek, but nothing came of the talks."

CCK was suspect because he had been involved in left-wing politics from an early age. Against his father's wishes, he went in 1924 to the Soviet Union to study. At that time the KMT was still in an alliance with the Chinese Communist Party and receiving aid from the Soviets. In 1927, shortly after CCK graduated from university in Moscow, his father launched a purge of the Communists, and CCK became something of a hostage. It was only in 1937 that the younger Chiang was able to return to China.

Johnny Hsiao, the main hero of *The Jing Affair* is mixed-race (a Taiwanese father and a Japanese-Portuguese mother) and a welcome change from the way Asian men were usually sidelined and portrayed as weak and effeminate. Another memorable character is CIA man Harry Retton – six foot three, thirty years in Asia, and probably the closest match to the author.

Two hilarious cameo appearances are made by characters Senators Oland and Dudd, both very much in the China lobby. Oland is no doubt a take on real-life politician William F. Knowland, a Republican senator from California but sometimes referred to as the "senator from Formosa" because of his strong support for CKS and the Nationalists. Likewise, Dudd is an obvious poke at Walter H. Judd, an influential Republican politician who had spent a decade in China working as a medical missionary.

Oland and Dudd – passing through on their way to Tokyo and delayed by plane engine trouble – are given the full red-carpet treatment. First there's a meeting with the senile president (described as the "Old Man" throughout the novel but a barely disguised Chiang Kai-shek), leaving them in awe. "That man is our greatest hope in Asia," Oland says to Dudd. Then they're off to one of the Matsu Islands to be witnesses to the massed ranks of the invasion force. Once on the ground, Oland tells his colleague Dudd, an ex-China missionary, to "talk with the men, find out how they feel about going home." His first two sallies draw a blank. "I'm afraid," he says a little ruefully to Oland, "either their Chinese is bad or mine has slipped." On his third attempt, Dudd finds a soldier who can understand Mandarin.

Clapping the boy on the shoulder, Dudd asked, "And how do you feel about going home, young man?"

A look of joy unbounded swept across the soldier's face. "When?" he cried.

"Very soon, now," Dudd answered with fatherly warmth. "By the way, son, just where is your *lao chia*, your ancestral home?"

"Oh, I am from Tainan, in south Taiwan," the boy replied.

A little later Dudd exclaims to Oland, "I can see it in those lowering faces, Walter. These boys are dedicated. They know evil when they see it. They'll go all the way."

Oland, preoccupied with thoughts of dinner, asks if they "shouldn't be getting back to Taipei? It's nearly six."

The identity of the author came to light with the publication of his daughter Danielle Flood's memoir *The Unquiet Daughter* (2016). D.J. Spencer was James (Jim) Flood, a long-time Foreign Service officer with the U.S. State Department (1951–1974) who had first come to Asia as a soldier in the Second World War and stayed on working as a reporter. Flood had a deep knowledge of Asia and was based in Taiwan around the time of the 1958 Second Taiwan Strait Crisis. Flood's daughter makes a compelling case in her memoir that her parents were the inspiration for the main characters in Graham Greene's acclaimed 1955 novel *The Quiet American*.

A few years after her parents had divorced, Danielle Flood learned that her biological father was not Jim Flood but an already married British intelligence officer in Saigon. It would take Danielle decades to get more out of her mother and extensive research to get to the bottom of the mystery. Her mother, who "was beautiful to the point of inconvenience," was twenty-four, pregnant, newly out of work and house, when Jim Flood, twenty-seven, married her and signed the birth register as Danielle's father.

* * *

The Jing Affair is an audacious book. Lampooning Chiang Kai-shek and Chiang Ching-kuo, and dedicated to the victims of Taiwan's White Terror, it spares no punches. The dangers of writing negatively about the Chiang family were empathetically shown in 1984 by the murder of the Chinese-American journalist Henry Liu in Daly City near San Francisco. Liu, a naturalized American journalist, had written a biography of CCK with salacious details of extramarital activities and illegitimate children, and also articles critical of the KMT. Wang Hsi-ling, director of Taiwan's national intelligence agency instructed the head of the Bamboo Union criminal gang to teach Liu "a lesson;" on October 15, 1984, two Bamboo Union gangsters turned up on bicycles in front of Henry Liu's house and shot him dead in his garage. They were quickly tracked down and the plot exposed. Among the gaffes was a phone call made by the killers to Taiwan's defense intelligence bureau to boast they had done the job, which was picked up by American intelligence. Henry Liu's murder created a political scandal with far-reaching consequences, straining Taiwan–American relations and in Taiwan itself causing demands for political reform.

The Henry Liu murder was also a huge boost for **The Soong Dynasty** (1985), a sensational expose of the KMT elite by Sterling Seagrave (1937–2017), the assassination a dramatic illustration of the KMT ties with organized crime, which was the central thread of the book. *The Soong Dynasty* chronicled the rise of the corrupt Soong family, with a particular focus on Soong Mei-ling (Madame Chiang Kai-shek) and her husband, the supreme leader of China from 1925, and later Taiwan until 1975. Seagrave portrays Chiang as thuggish yet cowardly, a puppet of the criminal Green Gang, a traitor ready to sell out to the Japanese – calling him "pathologically devious."

I'm embarrassed to think back to how easily I lapped it all up at the time and how the book colored my thinking for many years afterward. This huge bestseller was a mesmerizing story from a professional journalist with an enviable résumé.

Seagrave, however, is grossly unfair. This is how he describes the KMT's retreat: "Before 1938 was over, the Japanese had not only frightened Chiang and his regime into bolting from Nanking (and massacred 300,000 people thereby left undefended), but chased the Generalissimo unceremoniously out of Wuhan and five hundred miles farther up the Yangtze River."

This is simply untrue. Chiang's troops fought in Nanking, they fought before it fell, and they fought after it. The Battle of Shanghai, which preceded Nanking, was an epic, bloody three-month struggle in which the Nationalists lost some of their best troops. Seagrave doesn't mention it, or other battles in the early years. He doesn't mention the determined resistance in Nanjing, or the Battle of Wuhan that followed, where Nationalist casualties numbered hundreds of thousands and the Japanese army was badly hurt.

Writing in the *New York Times Book Review* (March 17, 1985), respected historian Jonathan Spence called the book "vigorously polemical, sharply biased and engrossing ... fast-paced and jammed with racy details and incident." He said Seagrave had greatly overstated the influence of the Soong family and the extent of criminal gang control over politics. The following year Donald G. Gillin (1930–2005) wrote a scathing twenty-four-page monograph in response to the book: *Falsifying China's History: The Case of Sterling Seagrave's The Soong Dynasty* (1986). Gillin was a China scholar and former head of the Asian Studies program at Vassar College, where he taught from 1968 until his retirement in 1992. He says *The Soong Dynasty* was "so biased, so unreliable, so riddled with errors, and so utterly lacking in historical perspective that much of it could be classified as fiction."

Gillin gives examples of selective quoting which misrepresented sources, omissions, and Seagrave's "biased, perjorative [sic] language" and his "ignoring unwanted material." He notes how Seagrave drew on accounts of China written by left-leaning journalists, with only selective and limited reference to more serious publications; an almost complete neglect of the mountains of materials at Stanford University's Hoover Institution; and the lack of reference to Chinese-language sources, even translated ones.

Seagrave said that he had to go into hiding following the publication of *The Soong Dynasty*. Much later he ratcheted this up a notch by claiming on multiple occasions that the murdered Henry Liu was a B-option target for assassins originally looking for him. In an interview on September 20, 2012, with the Red Ice Radio Podcast he says (around eight minutes into the program): "We've had a bunch of death threats. We hid out for a year off the west coast of Canada and just disappeared off the face of the earth for a while and kept a shotgun nearby. The guys who came looking to kill me, or us, couldn't find us, so they went down to San Francisco and they murdered a Chinese journalist named Henry Liu."

Seagrave made it to the respectable age of eighty, dying in 2017 in southern France, home for more than thirty years for him and his wife (and book collaborator), Peggy Sawyer Seagrave. An obituary from the website of his publisher, Verso, includes a 2011 email from Seagrave that describes how a "hired thug tried to murder" him on the narrow winding road up to their isolated house on a hill overlooking the Mediterranean. The incident involved Seagrave swerving to avoid hitting someone on the road, rolling down a steep hillside, and coming to consciousness with minor injuries twelve hours later in a hospital. In the email, Seagrave chides himself for making himself an easy target – living in and restoring a "thirteenth century Templar ruin on the shoulder of the mountain."

His secret address had been up on the Internet, his Amazon author's page reading: "They lived on a sailboat for ten years, then moved ashore to restore a 13th C stone wine-cave first built by the Knights Templar. It is surrounded by vineyards, with fine views of the Pyrenees and the Mediterranean." Not exactly deep cover.

With *The Generalissimo: Chiang Kai-shek and the Struggle for Modern China* (2009), by Jay Taylor, a thorough but sometimes hagiographic biography, the pendulum swung too much the other way, part of a tide of both Chinese and Western academics reassessing Chiang Kai-shek's legacy more favorably. For more on this and other important books on Chiang Kai-shek, see the upcoming *China in 100 Books*. For now, I will just note that there is still no complete, balanced biography of Chiang Kai-shek, and there is no book at all looking at his not inconsiderable thirty-year reign over Taiwan.

* * *

For a readable work about a political figure, it's hard to beat Peng Ming-min's *A Taste of Freedom: Memoirs of a Formosan Independence Leader* (1972), the moving autobiography of a reluctant hero and his journey from bookish youth to renowned scholar to political dissident. Understated but no less devastating, alongside the personal story it gives a wonderful sweep of Taiwanese history, ending with a moderate, reasonable call for Taiwan independence.

Peng was born into a prominent doctor's family in central Taiwan in 1923. He was a brilliant student and educated in the island's elite Japanese schools, where he was one of the few Formosans – and often reminded of this. Schooling became increasingly militaristic in the 1930s: "A fanatic principal and our military instructors inculcated in us a drill-master enthusiasm for war."

The following description of a teacher is typical of the odd gems the reader encounters in *A Taste of Freedom*:

We had one peculiar middle-aged military instructor named Tokunaga who was rather popular. He was straightforward, unprejudiced, and sometimes entertaining. If he thought a student was not acting briskly enough or seemed effeminate, he would rush forward and grab for the student's crotch "to see if he is really a man!" We missed him when he went off to the war, and were horrified later to hear that he had died on Guadalcanal, where, it was said, he had starved to death and had been eaten by his companions.

Peng moved to Japan to continue his studies, his heart set on studying French literature — against his parents' more sensible urging that he study medicine. He reached a compromise, selecting law and political science. Although he managed to avoid being drafted for military service, there was no escaping the war: he was badly injured in an air raid, losing an arm, and while recuperating, he witnessed the atomic bombing of Nagasaki.

His post-war return to Taiwan was bittersweet; the island's new masters were "unbelievably corrupt and greedy. For eighteen months they looted our island.... They were carpetbaggers, occupying enemy territory, and we were being treated as a conquered people." When matters erupted in 1947, Peng – despite his academic interest in politics – kept a safe distance and escaped punishment in the bloody crackdown and purges that followed.

Peng pursued his studies in Canada and France, and quickly established himself as an authority in the new field of international aviation law. Returning to Taiwan, he became a full professor aged only thirty-four, a young academic star attracting the attention of KMT leaders, who wanted to cultivate him as a model example of a local Taiwanese in the party elite. Not only did Peng refuse to become window-dressing as a token Taiwanese, he decided to fight back against the regime.

In 1964 Peng printed a manifesto calling for genuine democracy. Arrested for sedition and sentenced to eight years in prison, his international profile helped secure an early release. In 1970, while under house arrest and secret police surveillance, he made a daring escape to Sweden, where he was granted political asylum. With some help from George Kerr, Peng wrote *A Taste of Freedom*, which was originally published in 1972 and later translated into Chinese.

In 1992, after twenty-two years in exile, Peng Ming-min was finally able to return to Taiwan. He ran for president in 1996 in Taiwan's first direct presidential election, coming second to incumbent Lee Teng-hui.

Toward the end of *A Taste of Freedom*, Peng mentions being disturbed after his escape by those in the West who complemented their anti-KMT views not with pro-Taiwanese ones but with sympathy for the CCP's claims over the island.

I noted also at the same time, a new and rather unsettling tendency developing among some of the enlightened and liberal leaders in various countries. Appalled by the absurdities of the myths of the Nationalist Chinese government, which are certainly an affront to their reason, intelligence, and common sense, and eager to reject them, they sometimes tend to go to the opposite extreme and begin to embrace a new set of myths. These seem to be no more realistic and no more constructive than the old. These new myths are as follows: first, that Formosa has been, and therefore will always be, an integral and inalienable part of China; and second, that in order to bring to an end China's semicolonial status, in order that China may achieve recognition as a sovereign equal and regain her national self-respect, it is necessary to let her purely and simply annex Formosa.

He goes through these myths, debunking them, and suggests that they come from a deep and lingering guilt over Western mistreatment of China and the desire to atone for this guilt, plus the fascination and fear of the prospect of a rising powerful China. Despite Taiwan becoming a true democracy in the decades since Peng wrote that, the passage is relevant today.

When the international press ran the breaking news of Peng Meng-min's escape to Sweden, the KMT authorities were puzzled but not alarmed; they dismissed the story as a hoax, confident in the knowledge that Peng was safely under surveillance. Once it became obvious that Peng had indeed fled, they worsened the public relations disaster by saying he had only just now escaped, a fabrication that placed the escape three weeks after it had actually occurred (January 3, 1970). What lay behind these Keystone Cop antics?

The authorities had been certain Peng was still in the country because the agents from the Investigation Bureau assigned to watch and follow his every move had been submitting reports. They had supposedly been hot on Peng's trail around Taiwan during those weeks, in fact filing false expense vouchers for upmarket restaurants and hotels. In the interrogations that followed, the agents confessed that there had been stretches of weeks, even months, when they'd not seen Peng, and had fabricated reports to cover up their negligence and to claim expenses. Prison sentences and demotions ensued. None of this farce was publicly reported.

There were interrogations for activists too. The authorities suspected Hsieh Tsung-min (Peng's student and co-creator of the manifesto). He was arrested and tortured – beatings and sleep deprivation – for information related to Peng's escape. The interrogators told Hsieh that they knew Peng had flown out from an airbase near Taichung aboard a U.S. military plane; but Hsieh knew nothing of the escape plot and could not confirm the theory.

The KMT finally acknowledged Peng's escape, allowing the island's newspapers to run small stories. Blame was placed on the Americans, with the suggestion that Peng had received assistance from that useful, all-purpose bogeyman, the CIA.

The charge of CIA involvement seemed as plausible as any. It was believed by Mao Zedong and the CCP leadership, and it worried them. Thanks to declassified transcripts, we now know this was a subject of discussion during Henry Kissinger's secret trip to Beijing in July 1971 to lay the groundwork for President Nixon's historic visit to China in February 1972, the first stage of re-establishing relations with China. Mao's number two, Zhou Enlai, raised the question of how Peng had slipped out of the country: "Chiang Kai-shek is complaining greatly that it was CIA that allowed Peng Ming-min to escape from Taiwan." Kissinger assured him that as far as he knew the CIA had had nothing to do with the Peng case.

Kissinger made it clear to Zhou Enlai during his July 1971 trip that the Americans were willing to end their support for Taiwan, that they would switch diplomatic recognition from Taipei to Beijing in Nixon's second term. The Watergate scandal derailed Nixon from doing so, and it wasn't until 1979, under the Carter administration, that this happened. Neither Chiang Kai-shek nor Mao Zedong (deaths in 1975 and 1976, respectively) would live to see it.

During Nixon's week-long trip in 1972, he met with Mao just once, and although the meeting lasted a brief sixty-five minutes, the subject of Peng's escape once again came up. Mao feared

American support for the Taiwanese independence movement, and the Peng escape seemed like proof of their involvement. Zhou said: "Because you know even Chiang Kai-shek said that you let Peng Ming-min out." Kissinger denied it strongly, and promised that no American personnel or agency would help support the Taiwan independence movement.

"I endorse that commitment at this meeting today," said Nixon.

Zhou was still not placated: "I have received material to the effect that Peng Ming-min was able to escape with help from the Americans."

Nixon responded: "Chiang Kai-shek did not like it. You did not like it, either. Neither did we like it. We had nothing to do with it."

Kissinger added, "To the best of my knowledge that professor was probably able to leave because of help from American anti-Chiang Kai-shek left-wing groups."

In ***Fireproof Moth: A Missionary in Taiwan's White Terror*** (2011), former missionary to Taiwan Milo Thornberry (1937–2017) revealed in detail for the first time how he and his wife, Judith, organized the escape of Peng Ming-min. It's an uneven book; much of it is gripping, reading like a thriller, but its musings on religion and activism have less broad appeal.

Thornberry, who grew up in rural Texas, felt the call to service in 1955 as a seventeen-year-old. Before being assigned to missionary work in Asia (and not knowing it would be Taiwan) he began reading up on the region. *Thunder Out of China*, a scathing account of Nationalist corruption in World War II China by journalists Theodore White and Annalee Jacoby, made such a mark, Thornberry hoped he wouldn't be posted to Taiwan. He wanted to serve in Hong Kong, Singapore, or the Philippines, but it was Taiwan he was sent to. Before going in late 1965 he read – fresh off the presses – Kerr's explosive *Formosa Betrayed*.

Thornberry was in the Methodist church, a denomination with a proud China heritage. China had been a great achievement, with the influential Soong family the most famous adherents. Soong Mei-ling (Madame Chiang Kai-shek) was a Methodist; and three years after their marriage, Chiang Kai-shek was baptized as a Methodist. Methodists had not previously worked on the island, but Methodist missionaries and their organizations followed the Nationalists exodus to Taiwan. Given this church history, Thornberry administered to mainlanders more than Taiwanese, as well as fulfilling teaching duties at seminaries.

Thornberry found the political situation in Taiwan suffocating; he was unable to discuss politics and unable to follow news, whether local or international. The English-language KMT propaganda newspaper, the *China Post*, was "hardly better than nothing." He subscribed to *Time* magazine, which despite being pro-Chiang Kai-shek, was subject to government censorship, with some pages cut out. The less censored U.S. Armed Forces Radio and the *Stars and Stripes* newspaper were better sources of news.

The oddest example of censorship relates to the 1965 hit musical *The Sound of Music*. The Thornberrys went into the movie theater expecting a two-and-a-half-hour plus marathon but were out, he says, only forty-five minutes later, scratching their heads. The thought the movie "didn't make any sense at all" and wondered why it was receiving so many rave reviews in the United States. "We learned that the censors had removed all references to, scenes of, and songs about people escaping to the mountains." Even if that length is an exaggeration, it's still remarkable that such an innocent film would be censored (presumably done for unfavorable comparisons of martial law Taiwan with that of Nazi-ruled Austria).

After only a few months in Taiwan, the Thornberrys had a chance introduction to Peng, who became a regular visitor at their house over the coming years, "sometimes at strange hours" as evading lazy police surveillance favored night-time visits.

Thornberry was embarrassed by his fellow expats turning a blind eye to repression: "I couldn't understand how many missionaries, American students, U.S. military, and embassy personnel who heard the cries of the Taiwanese people could rationalize their inaction." He saw this as a quiet complicity in the fiction of "Free China" when most Taiwanese thought the country was neither "free" nor "China." There were, however, some likeminded foreigners, and with their assistance Thornberry set up an information-distribution network, handing news packets to interested foreigners, and using growing channels to distribute money to the families of political prisoners.

The idea for helping Peng out of the country was born in the summer of 1968, after Peng told them that an official had made a veiled threat. "You know, you could have an accident at any time and be killed." It couldn't be dismissed as mere bluster either, as through inside connections Peng had heard that there was indeed "a plan for me to have an 'accident.'"

Fearing for his friend's safety, Thornberry encouraged him to get out of the country, to which Peng agreed after some initial reluctance. It was easier said than done, of course, and the escape would take over a year of planning and preparation. Leaving on a fishing boat or a freighter was an obvious choice; but the Thornberrys and friends lacked the necessary connections to get Peng on a ship. Airports had too much security and would require documentation.

Inspiration came to Thornberry from a news magazine story concerning getting an East German into West Germany, and so the wheels were set in motion. The plan was simple: A foreigner would fly to Taipei, hand his passport to Thornberry, who would replace the photo with one of Peng, and then the Taiwanese dissident would use the passport to fly out. The foreigner would report his passport missing at his embassy and get temporary papers to leave the country.

It was simple but difficult, and requiring an extensive network and no leaks. Doctoring a passport requires expertise, and getting a well-known, one-armed figure through airport security presented formidable challenges. They also agreed it had to be done without the involvement of Taiwanese, for whom it could have meant "a death sentence." Foreigners, however, were on less dangerous ground; the Foreign Affairs Police normally dealt quietly with meddlesome foreigners by not renewing residency permits. The book's title, *Fireproof Moth*, comes from a U.S. State Department official comparing Americans in Taiwan to "fireproof moths," and it was a good description of how they could get close to the fire without getting burned, that is, engage in subversive activities without suffering the dire punishments that Taiwanese would be subject to.

A Japanese man called Abe Kenichi was found to fly in and hand over his passport. Peng, who would "go out disguised as a Japanese hippie musician," took pictures at a DIY passport photo booth and sent them to Japan, where supporters somehow managed to emboss the photos with a stamp so they matched the stamp in the Japanese passport. The embossed photographs were sent back to Taiwan.

Abe arrived on Friday afternoon. Time to switch the photos. Drawing on the information in the article about the escape from East Germany, Thornberry understood the photo needed to be split – removing the whole photo would tear the paper. So he had to split two photos and then glue one half to the other. Peng flew out on a Saturday night flight to Hong Kong and then traveled onward to Copenhagen and Stockholm.

Although the authorities never uncovered the Peng plot, Judith and Milo (and their two young children) were expelled for "unfriendly actions against the government of the ROC." They were given forty-eight hours to leave. No further explanation was coming. The U.S. embassy was unhelpful, unwilling to share what they knew. Ironically, while guilty of meddling in local politics and breaking numerous laws, the Thornberrys were expelled for something they hadn't done.

The KMT told the U.S. State Department – unofficially and without showing any proof – that the American missionary couple were involved in terrorist activities, specifically importing explosives, and involvement in two bombings.

The unproven charges would come to hurt Thornberry. His record flagged with "terrorist" accusations, he was unable to get visas to work in other countries – something he blamed on the State Department – and getting a new passport in 1990 required the help of two senators.

In 2003, the Thornberrys returned to Taiwan, invited to be honored for their work. After another trip in 2008, Milo decided he could finally write his memoir without endangering his Taiwanese friends.

* * *

Although the CIA might have been unfairly blamed for involvement in the secret extradition of Peng Ming-min, it was involved in numerous other cloak-and-dagger episodes, most notably an operation that brought Taiwan's secret nuclear weapons program to an end when it was only months away from readiness, and thus averting what could have been one of the great political crises of the late twentieth century.

Recent revelations from declassified material and Mandarin-language books by major participants sparked something of a book race to launch the first comprehensive English-language account of Taiwan's clandestine attempt to arm itself with nuclear bombs. The first title was *Crossing the Red Line: Consequences of Taiwan Emergence as a Nuclear Proliferant* (June 2018), by Taiwan-based journalist Alan Patterson, who worked closely with a former nuclear engineer, David Ho, whose 2015 Mandarin-language *Hedan MIT: yi ge shangwei jieshu de gushi* (*Nuclear Bomb MIT: "A" Bomb Made in Taiwan*) was the first insider account. Hot on the heels of Patterson's book was *Taiwan's Former Nuclear Weapons Program: Nuclear Weapons On-Demand* (November 2018), by David Albright and Andrea Stricker from the Institute for Science and International Security. The institute, a small D.C.-based non-profit NGO dedicated to decreasing the nuclear threat, was founded in 1993 by physicist David Albright.

In *Crossing the Red Line*, we learn how, on the morning of January 12, 1988, David Ho's superior, Colonel Chang Hsien-yi, did not show up for a scheduled work meeting. Neither was he at his house or any other likely location. It seemed as if he had vanished. The potential consequences of this brought panic to Taiwan's halls of power, for the missing man was deputy director of the Institute of Nuclear Research (INER), and he had compromising knowledge of Taiwan's secret nuclear program. It was bad timing for such an emergency. The very next day President Chiang Ching-kuo passed away at the age of seventy-seven. Would a hardliner succeed him? And what were the military's plans for the nuclear program, now, after so many years of undercover machinations, so close to completion?

Taipei's determined push for nuclear weapons went back to 1964, when the PRC conducted its first nuclear test. The ROC and the United States were aware of China's nuclear weapons program – much of the intelligence on it came from Taiwan's Black Cat Squadron of U-2 surveillance planes operating out of Taoyuan – but it had been thought a ready bomb was years away from completion. Taipei feared the possibility of a devastating nuclear attack on the island; at the very least, there was the danger that the threat of a nuclear conflagration might dissuade the Americans from fulfilling their pledge to defend Taiwan.

Albright and Stricker say that President Chiang Kai-shek and other ROC leaders "pressed for U.S. support for a Nationalist Chinese military strike to destroy China's nuclear installations." However, when it comes to Chiang asking to be unleashed, one can never be sure if he was serious; he might just have been positioning himself to be placated by U.S. concessions. Regardless of intent, his proposal was rejected.

Chiang initiated a secret program called the "Hsinchu Project," and put his son, Chiang Ching-kuo, in charge. Within the government, support for the program was not universal; the chief detractor, Dr. Wu Ta-you, a nuclear theoretical physicist and the country's top science adviser, was against developing nuclear weapons because of the exorbitant cost, the country's lack of scientific expertise, and the risk it carried of a preemptive PRC strike, which, in the worst-case scenario, would be a nuclear one. The KMT leaders thought otherwise and proceeded.

The mastermind behind Taiwan's nuclear program was Dr. Ernst David Bergmann (1903–1975), often referred to as the father of Israel's nuclear program. The German born and trained scientist, after helping Israel secretly develop nuclear weapons, resigned and continued his work as a private international contractor. He convinced President Chiang Kai-shek to follow Israel's example of developing nuclear weapons using a nuclear energy program as a cover. The Chung-Shan Institute of Science and Technology (CSIST) was established on Bergmann's recommendation. This large facility, located in Taoyuan County, undertakes research on a wide range of weaponry. Among its divisions was the Institute of Nuclear Research (INER), which sourced expertise, materials, and equipment from around the world – Israel, the United States, Germany,

Canada, South Africa, Japan, Norway, and France – the diversified sourcing aimed at keeping INER's real intentions under the radar. On Bergmann's advice, Taiwan acquired a research reactor from Canada that could produce plutonium suited to developing weapons. Construction at the Taoyuan INER facilities started in 1969, and the reactor went critical in January 1973. Taiwan also bought three nuclear power plants from the United States; construction of the new facilities for these began in 1971, and commissioning occurred from 1978 through the mid 1980s.

As the nuclear weapons program was taking shape, the political landscape was deteriorating. President Nixon's desire for American rapprochement with the PRC would come at Taiwan's expense. Nixon committed to removing U.S. nuclear bombs from Taiwan (completed in 1974) and to stopping the country from developing its own. The United States stepped up surveillance of INER's efforts, periodically stepping in to block suspicious purchases. The monitoring in Taiwan, however, was relatively ineffectual; before overseas inspection teams visited, they gave notice, which allowed for secret work at the facilities to be hidden.

U.S. president Jimmy Carter put his foot down soon after coming into office; in 1977 he gave Taipei a series of demands for American oversight. Taiwan's dependence on the United States meant the KMT had no choice but to accept the demands. Projects that had been uncovered were shut down; however, there were other undetected activities that continued.

In December 1978, President Carter publicly announced that the United States was switching diplomatic recognition from Taipei to Beijing, and as part of this all U.S. military personnel would be withdrawn from ROC territory. Around this time, the Chinese and Americans – sharing an interest in thwarting Taiwan's nuclear ambitions – started cooperating on intelligence. Albright and Stricker write: "Chinese and American agents would meet to discuss recent findings or developments at INER and CSIST at opera performances."

American infiltration often started by contacting and trying to recruit Taiwanese engineers or students when they were studying in or visiting the United States. David Ho's experience provides an example. In 1978 he entered Iowa State University to pursue a doctorate in nuclear engineering. Ho received a telephone call from a supposed businessman wanting to know about Taiwan's "economic and trade environment." Ho informed his military superiors, who told him to go along with the obviously bogus approach and see what happened. *Crossing the Red Line* details the clumsy recruitment attempts, including a fishing trip on a luxurious yacht, which ended with Ho escaping from a possible honey trap involving two bikini-clad blondes. Ho was later asked directly to become an informant by two American "Men in Black," a lucrative offer he declined.

This new world of espionage was not to Ho's liking, and he feared for his safety. Was he being paranoid? If so, it was understandable; two of his close Ohio university acquaintances died within six months. He didn't believe the official explanations and thought they had been murdered.

After completing his prize-winning doctoral work, Ho returned to Taiwan to do computer coding but soon needed to undertake a secret mission back in the United States. Because Taiwan's nuclear program was a clandestine one, there was no opportunity to test an actual nuclear bomb. Consequently, the Taiwanese needed to rely on computer simulation, which had its own challenges – among them, the need for a supercomputer. The United States had placed restrictions on selling supercomputers to Taiwan. To circumvent this, Ho went to the University of California, Berkeley, in 1983, ostensibly for postdoctoral research, and – with the help of a sympathetic professor – was able to access a supercomputer to run computer simulations.

A man who was successfully recruited by the CIA and would help bring down Taiwan's nuclear weapons program was Chang Hsien-yi, born in Hainan, China in 1943. He started working at CSIST in 1967, which sponsored his doctoral studies in nuclear engineering at the University of Tennessee from 1972 to 1976. Once back in Taiwan, he was a rising star, and in 1984, at the age of forty, was made a deputy director at INER. That same year he agreed to be an informant.

Chang Hsien-yi says the initial CIA approach was made in 1982 at a conference in the United States. The CIA angle was of safety for the people of Taiwan, which meshed with Chang's growing concerns about the dangers of acquiring weapons. Chang says he was not entrapped by the CIA, denying suspicions by David Ho that he was "seduced by women as blackmail to secure his cooperation."

Chang met his CIA handler every few months at a safe house near the Shilin Night Market in northern Taipei. As well as divulging the latest intelligence, Chang also handed over photos he'd taken of top-secret documents. Sometimes the CIA just wanted him to verify information. Among the topics discussed were systems readiness, procurements of materials and equipment, and future plans. For me, the most memorable intel he gave the CIA was of a project for nuclear weapon delivery. The Reagan administration had pressured Taiwan to abandon a ballistic missile program. Secretly developed by the CSIST – but not secretly enough – these Tian Ma ("Sky Horse") missiles would be capable of hitting Shanghai (680 kilometers due north). As Chang explained to his CIA contact, the solution to the missile-delivery problem came from the example of Japan's World War II kamikaze fighter pilots, many of whom flew out to their deaths from airfields in Taiwan. Taiwanese engineers were in the process of developing their own fighter, called the Indigenous Defense Fighter – itself a response to American reluctance to sell state-of-the-art planes – and this would be, with refitting, able to carry a nuclear bomb. An external fuel tank would be replaced by the bomb. The range would be limited – but it could reach Shanghai, one way. These would be no-return kamikaze missions flown by unmarried volunteers.

Armed with a surfeit of damning evidence to present to the KMT leadership, the Americans decided in late 1987 that it was time to act. They feared that an ailing Chiang Ching-kuo would be succeeded by a military strongman, one able to arm Taiwan with nukes in a few short months. Vice President Lee Teng-hui was in line to succeed. However, Lee, the first native Taiwanese to hold that position, lacked the power and prestige of Chiang. The Americans had believed President Chiang's assertions he did not want to fully develop nuclear weapons, only to have the capability to do so quickly. Would Hau Pei-tsun, the head of the military and a potential successor, be as compliant?

The U.S. government decided to get Chang – and his wife, two sons, and daughter – out of the country. First the CIA had Chang send his family away to Tokyo Disneyland on a vacation, telling them he would join them later. Chang – as a high-level military man needed permission to leave; he would sneak out of Kaohsiung International Airport to Hong Kong and then Seattle using a false passport. In Japan, Mrs. Chang was approached by a female agent who handed her a blindsiding letter from her husband; before this she had known nothing of his secret life as a spy. The letter contained instructions to proceed to Seattle, from where the entire family would travel onward to Washington, D.C., arriving on January 12, one day before Chiang Ching-kuo passed away and Lee Teng-hui was sworn in as president.

Within a week, the United States had presented Taiwan's leaders with a list of non-negotiable demands for the dismantlement of the country's nuclear weapons program. As Hau wrote in his diary, "considering Taiwan–US relations, we have to swallow the insult and let it go." Taiwan couldn't say no; apart from dependence on American military and economic ties, Taiwan had signed agreements that placed the country's nuclear power plants, which accounted for about a third of Taiwan's power supply, under U.S. leverage. A team of experts from the United States and the International Atomic Energy Agency (IAEA) descended on Taiwan's nuclear facilities and began their work. Taiwan would not be joining the nuclear weapons club.

Ending the clandestine program was a major achievement for American intelligence, a rare success that rewarded its careful, patient work. It was also a demonstration of the superiority of human intelligence over technology. The U.S. government could be criticized for allowing the weapons program to have gotten as far as it did, but all's well that ends well: the spy and his family were safely extracted; there was a fast, thorough crackdown on the nuclear facilities; and it was all done without embarrassing Taiwan or causing long-term damage to U.S.–Taiwan relations. The KMT deserves praise, too, for taking the loss on the chin and not extracting revenge.

After a month in a safe house, Chang was found employment at a nuclear research institute in Idaho. He retired in 2013 and set to making his side of his story public; the Mandarin-language book *Hedan! Jiandie? CIA: Zhang Xianyi fangwen jilu* (*Nuclear Weapons! Spy? CIA: Interview Record with Chang Hsien-yi*) was published in December 2016, and in Taiwan no less, a testament to the free press on the island.

David Ho was discharged about eight months after Chang's defection, and it was with some relief as he had developed doubts about Taiwan going nuclear. Despite having been a neighbor and close work associate of Chang's, there were no repercussions for him at all; he was not even asked about his colleague's defection, perhaps a result of Chiang Ching-kuo's death eclipsing events. Ho does, however, wonder if Chang was acting alone and suspects there was someone higher up protecting him; he finds it hard to believe Chang would otherwise have been promoted to deputy director at such a young age.

Although Ho initially felt anger at Chang's betrayal, his position changed over time. Patterson quotes Ho: "Chang Hsien-yi has generally been reviled in Taiwan as a traitor, but in hindsight, he may have been a hero who saved the island from a nuclear catastrophe." Albright and Stricker are unequivocal in their praise, saying "Chang has never been given the respect he deserves in Taiwan."

On balance, it seems a blessing that Taiwan didn't acquire nuclear weapons. Still, there are nagging doubts; I believe fears of a military coup were overblown, as were concerns of the military's reckless use of nuclear weapons. As for Taiwan's going nuclear causing a derailment of warming relations between Washington and Beijing – well, the CCP would achieve this itself with the Tiananmen crackdown in 1989. What did the Americans get for placating the CCP? We know all too well what they didn't get: reciprocal cooperation from China in stopping North Korea from going nuclear. And the question remains: would the PRC have been willing and able to launch a preemptive attack on Taiwan? I think not, though I'm glad this counterfactual wasn't put to the test.

Time will eventually render a verdict; if Taiwan one day finds itself under the PRC jackboot, the Taiwanese may well curse the Americans and the Taiwanese collaborators for disarming them. And time will also reveal more episodes from this fascinating saga.

Many secrets remain classified, many great stories remain to be written about it. I would love to see some novels exploring this shadowy Cold War history, and more non-fiction works.

Crossing the Red Line and *Taiwan's Former Nuclear Weapons Program* are a fantastic start to getting the story of Taiwan's nuclear weapons program out before an international audience. As well as being inherently fascinating, the story is important as a successful example of stopping proliferation, and also in letting Americans know that their leaders forced an ally – one trying to defend itself from a communist regime – to disarm.

I recommend reading both books; they complement each other – *Crossing the Red Line* is more loosely structured, speculative, and personal, whereas *Taiwan's Former Nuclear Weapons Program* is more comprehensive – and the overlap in material is actually a useful revision of a sometimes complicated story.

* * *

As we've seen in the last few books, the 1970s saw a humiliating diminishment of Taiwan on the international stage. The People's Republic of China was admitted to the United Nations in 1971, the ROC pulling out beforehand in protest. Nixon visited China in 1972, and the United States switched diplomatic recognition from Taipei to Beijing in 1979. The death of Chiang Kai-shek in 1975 finally brought to a close the Nationalist dream of recovering the mainland. During this period, an unexpected consolation came in the form of international baseball successes.

We saw earlier, in Morris' *Colonial Project, National Game*, how baseball was a part of Japan's "civilizing" mission. Now the sport was back at the forefront of national identity, a story told in Junwei Yu's **Playing in Isolation: A History of Baseball in Taiwan** (2007).

In one of the great sporting runs of all time, from 1971 to 1981 Taiwan's Little Leaguers went unbeaten at the annual championship in the American town of Williamsport, the twelve-year-old boys scoring an incredible thirty-one straight victories. A whole generation of Taiwanese grew up rooting for these schoolboy teams, including diehard fan author Junwei Yu, now a professor at the National Taiwan University of Sport.

Throughout the 1970s and 1980s, and even into the early 1990s, one of the most cherished collective Taiwanese experiences was staying up into the predawn hours each summer to watch live broadcasts of Taiwanese youths "crusading" at the three levels of Little League Baseball (LLB).

A pity then that the victories were tainted by rampant cheating (but more on that later). Let's go back in time to the arrival of the KMT in 1945 as the island's new masters. In spite of baseball's unfortunate associations with the Japanese era, it suffered only government neglect rather than persecution. Mainlanders much preferred soccer and basketball to baseball, and ROC teams had enjoyed regional success in those sports, so that's where the funding went. Baseball lacked prestige in KMT eyes and as such was less suitable for promoting the country.

The official indifference to baseball was arguably a blessing. Yu makes an impassioned case that baseball's golden era was the first two decades of KMT rule. "During this period baseball was a genuine pastime among the public, who enjoyed it with deep passion and affection. The unlinking of baseball, state, and market ironically helped Taiwanese baseball grow in a more robust and normal way, as people organized teams freely and voluntarily."

Baseball provided a welcome venue for the Taiwanese language. At the time, the KMT prohibited its use at school, and Taiwanese-language radio and television broadcasting was extremely limited. The Taiwanese language was, however, allowed in baseball, a rare public area where it could be spoken freely. Interestingly, baseball jargon even today is an interesting hybrid of Taiwanese, Mandarin, Japanese, and English.

Taiwanese baseball jargon contains numerous words that came from Japanese, which in turn came from English; so we have *pitcha*, *kyatcha*, *homuran* (pitcher, catcher, home run), and so on. These linguistic borrowings from the West via Japanese extend to many areas, including daily sustenance: bread and beer (*phang*, from the Japanese *pan*, taken from Portuguese; and *bilu*, from the Japanese *biiru*, in turn a loanword from the Dutch *bier*).

Morris relates some amusing cross-cultural interactions from the 1950s, when Taiwanese playing against teams from the American Seventh Fleet stationed in Taiwan, "would purposely lose so that the Americans would be in such a good mood that they would give their superior equipment to their valiant but lesser Taiwanese rivals." Lin Huawei, a youth player who went on to coach the national team in the 1990s, told the author that "one of his fondest and most transformative childhood baseball memories was drinking his first Coca-Cola at a game sponsored by American troops at the field across the street from his Tainan home."

Nineteen sixty-eight was a landmark year for Taiwanese baseball. The Hongye (Maple Leafs) – an elementary school baseball team, named after Hongye, a little village of Bunun Aboriginals in southeastern Taiwan – scored a 3–0 home series victory over a champion Japanese team. The victories were an absolute sensation, in part because this was the first student contest between Taiwan and Japan, and also because live television coverage brought a new dimension to the games.

Alas, the glory was based on deception. Nine of the eleven Maple Leaf team were overage and playing with false names (and forged documents) provided by their coach, school principal, and head administrator. When the fraud was uncovered, the authorities handled the prosecution as discreetly as they could; court proceedings were held at night, and the three defendants were given suspended two-year sentences.

In a way, the sins of the fathers seem to have been visited upon the sons. The Hongye players weren't able to translate fame into educational or work opportunities. Many of the boys ended up poor, overly fond of the bottle, and in an early grave. When Junwei Yu wrote *Playing in Isolation* (published in 2007), seven out of the thirteen Hongye team members were already dead, a shocking mortality rate for a cohort then in their fifties.

A year after the Maple Leaf victories, Taiwan took part in the Little League Series held in Williamsport, Pennsylvania. The Taichung Golden Dragons won the championship, the first of many much-needed boosts to national morale.

And the Little League Baseball cheating I alluded to earlier? LLB was supposed to be a fun competition based on community teams drawing players from a population of no more than fifteen thousand people. What Taiwan did was bring the best players together to form what were in effect national all-star teams (by drawing on a population of fifteen million, that translates to cheating by a factor of one thousand times). Another rule violation related to practice hours. The Taiwanese kids were practicing baseball full-time, as much as nine hours a day.

After its Little League success, Taiwan soon starting attending the next age-group LLB championships: the Senior League (ages thirteen–sixteen) in Gary, Indiana, and the Big League (ages sixteen–eighteen) in Fort Lauderdale, Florida. Once again, these were virtually national teams and they dominated year after year.

Yu brings up an interesting point about the LLB competitions. Though they were billed back in Taiwan as world tournaments, the truth was that for the older leagues, the real action was happening in another competition, the IBA, where Taiwan won only one championship. The IBA was dominated by Cuba and the United States. Taiwan sent their top teams to the weaker LLB and the national runner-up to the real world series, the IBA, which received less publicity and was not broadcast on the island. Yu explains that the government and media upsold the LLB by adding a "world" and calling it the *Shijie Shaobang Lianmeng* (World Little League Baseball).

A new chapter in Taiwanese baseball began in 1989 with the formation of the Chinese Professional Baseball League (CPBL). To raise standards and add some international flavor, foreign players were hired. They were mostly American and Dominican players, and initially there was a limit of four imports per team.

Morris describes in *Colonial Project, National Game* how the foreign players were given "Chinese" names that were often blatant products placement. Two were named after noodle dishes, luckier ones after beer. These names were not even half-clever transliterations based on similar sounds between the player and product names. Here are some examples for beer: Ravelo Manzanillo (*Baiwei* – Chinese for Budweiser), Steve Stoole (*Meile* – Miller), and Jose Gonzalez (*Meilehei* – Miller Dark).

Pitcher Jose Cano became known as "Ah Q." Readers familiar with twentieth-century Chinese literature will recognize Ah Q as the protagonist in Lu Xun's 1921 landmark novella *The True Story of Ah Q*. Don't think too much, as the Taiwanese say; the nickname was just a fun food reference, a Taiwanese word play on *khiu* ("Q") for chewiness associated with Uni-President food products. (In Taiwan chewiness is considered a positive quality and you'll sometimes see the English letter Q on food packaging and food stall signs.)

The professional league has brought its share of shame upon the game, chiefly in the form of match-fixing scandals. Yu blames the lack of genuine interest in baseball (and other sports) on old

Confucian ideas prizing academics over athletics. He's not optimistic about returning to a purer amateur baseball. Although this may all seem rather depressing, it actually makes for gripping reading.

9

Taiwan after Dark

WHILE it might be an exaggeration to say Taipei was ever a notorious den of sin, the expectation for a young man going there during the decades of the Cold War was that he would be led astray by temptations of the flesh. This was especially true when Taipei became a popular R&R destination for American troops during the Vietnam War.

A product of these times is **Taipei After Dark** (1967), a "travelogue" describing the seedy side of the city, "blatant sex capital of Asia, where vice is legal and the price is right" as screamed on the cover. The breathless shill on the blurb gives travel highlights:

- the brothels of Wan Hua, where 75 cents buys the best prostitutes in the world
- the Stella Beauty Parlor, where extraordinary services are offered for everything but a haircut

- Peitou, a hot springs resort which features the most exotic "bath" in town

Whether you prefer the gigolos, the young homosexuals who work the hotels, or group sex, you'll find them all – in all combinations – on this idyllic island of delight.

The breathless depiction of Taipei as a banquet of fleshly vice carries over from the blurb to the text, although the content is more suggestive than graphic. Harris was a frequent visitor to Taipei – and a fan of its carnal offerings – so we get some good first-hand accounts, and the insights offered by his expat friends help raise *Taipei After Dark* above the merely puerile. There's Harry, "a laconic American newspaperman," who explains how the KMT's red-carpet welcome for sympathetic voices attracts a steady stream of media and political "small-timers from America." One of the tricks of these junketeers is to register at a top hotel in the downtown area but to actually stay in Beitou, where it is easier to partake of the resort's skilled prostitutes.

Another expat, a German social worker based in Wanhua, tells Harris that the prostitution in that district "is a distortion of the traditional Taiwanese foster parent system." Girls, who come "mostly from little towns past the mountains along the east coast," are taken in and raised for the trade, sold to brothels for five hundred dollars for a two-year period.

Harris calls Wanhua "the lowest of the city's brothel areas … a place where anything, be it heroin or a young boy, can be obtained." Its alleyways are teeming with young women soliciting passersby from shack doorways. And Harris allows himself to be dragged in for a casual quickie. "She may have been only a temporary two-year whore but she knew her business."

This strikes a callous note coming directly after the long description of the girls' circumstances. As does his casual reference elsewhere to getting teenagers "very likely under the legal age of eighteen" who he and Harry pick up "from a canal bank." In an act of chivalry, however, they don't bargain the girls down from the asking price of four dollars for the night.

Speaking of legalities, the history of prostitution law in Taiwan is complicated, with the occupation's status oscillating between complete illegality and limited legality whereby certain districts or licensed establishments could offer services. Harris' visits – and those of the next few authors – were made during a time of laxity.

The man behind the book was Fred (Frederick K.) Poole, a Bangkok-based American journalist looking to supplement the money he made writing for Time Life. He said decades later that he did his "own research, even in the middle of the night," and that the book was "mostly based on truth." *Taipei After Dark*, which was written under the pen name Andrew Harris, was part of an "After Dark" series on the world's flesh pots; Poole also penned the editions for Bangkok and Manila. At the other extreme, he was writing for school children – producing a series of books on Southeast Asian countries that was aimed at the lucrative school library market. His biography of Mao Zedong and a Vietnam War novel appear to have sold few copies. Thus are often the realities of making a dollar from writing: textbooks and trash to pay the bills.

Another hack who wrote about the sleazy side of the Far East was Irish journalist turned full-time writer Sean O'Callaghan (1918–2000) whose long-forgotten titles include one featuring a chapter on Taipei. The book in question is ***The Yellow Slave Trade*** (1968), a voyeuristic though not X-rated "investigation" of prostitution in East Asia. The author has himself as a Philip Marlowe hard-boiled knight walking the mean streets, "investigations which covered thousands of miles and took me eighteen months to complete." He gets up close and personal with the working girls but is too much of a gentleman to ever sample the merchandise (or at least tell us about it).

The short chapter "The Room Girls of Taiwan" describes O'Callaghan's stopover in Taipei on his way from Hong Kong to Japan. The title comes from his claim that "Taiwan is the only country in the East where hotels supply room girls to guests who require their services." He says it was standard practice except for the leading Grand Hotel.

The level of research behind the book is hinted at by the author's first morning in Taiwan. He awakes in a drunken daze, a moment of confusion as he realizes he's in a hotel. He can recall a boozy send-off in Hong Kong, and then hitting the bars of Taipei once he'd landed but nothing afterward. And then there's the mystery woman in his room.

> I shook the girl awake. "Who the hell are you?" I asked.
> "I am your room girl," she answered.

The pretty "girl" (who the author estimates to be about twenty-four) explains in good English that when he checked in after coming from the airport and was asked if he wanted a room girl, he had chosen her.

The author's intrepid investigations into the evils of the flesh trade have to take a backseat, as he finds three hundred American dollars worth of yen missing from his wallet. Initially suspecting his room girl, he is persuaded that he was ripped off at a bar. He can't recall the bar, but she does. After a pleasant afternoon sightseeing (she's good company, "witty and highly intelligent") and learning from her about the room service trade, he goes back to the bar.

He finds the previous night's drinking buddies, tough American soldiers, who help persuade the manager to return the money. The next day, deciding that discretion is the better part of valor, the author catches a plane to Tokyo.

* * *

One American writer visiting Taipei in the late 1960s thought his hotel sufficiently memorable to pen a 149-page travelogue account with it at the center. John Ball's **Dragon Hotel** (1969) is among the oddest Taiwan books you're likely to come across. An affectionate tribute to Taiwan, it's well enough written yet supremely lightweight. So little happens in this portrait of Taipei that the author's warning at the start seems borderline insane: "This book is not a novel. What you will read in the following pages is real and happened just as it is set down here."

It's not as if the author was a wallflower on his first trip abroad, or even to Taipei. John Dudley Ball (1911–1988) knew travel and adventure well; he was a commercial pilot before the Second World War and served as a navigator in the Army Air Transport Command 1942–1945, flying "the Hump," the supply route from India over the eastern end of the Himalayas to Chiang Kai-shek's forces in southwest China. By the time Ball got to Taiwan in 1968 he had been a journalist, a movie critic, a public relations director, and was now a major mystery writer. His 1965 mystery *In the Heat of the Night*, notable for featuring a black police detective called Virgil Tibbs, had won the Edgar Allan Poe award for Best First Novel and been made into a Hollywood film that won the Academy Award for Best Picture of 1967.

Dragon Hotel begins with an early-morning flight from Okinawa's Kadena Air Base to the American side of Taipei's Songshan Airport. Ball was a guest of the U.S. Navy, working on an unspecified writing project. His flight was early and there was nobody at the airport to meet him. After waiting a while he was approached by a local man who handed him a card. "I am Mr. Kung," he announced. "I am manager of the most useful and practical hotel in Taipei."

A sales pitch followed, with feminine companionship a major selling point. "Before you are unpacked very specially-selected Chinese girl friend will be awaited for you. Satisfaction guaranteed always Dragon Hotel. English by all personnel speaked." Of the girls, Mr. Kung effused: "Beautiful always. Of very good character, also health card."

Ball called his hosts and learned that they had booked a room for him at the Taipei Foreign Correspondents' Club. He taxied there and checked in, finding: "An intimate place which offers a sitting room equipped with a cheerful fireplace, a small bar, and, insofar as I could discover, only one bathroom." There was a noisy party that night, and it didn't help that the shared toilet was next to his room with only a thin wall between.

Come morning Ball decided to move somewhere nicer; he could go to the First Hotel, where he had stayed on a previous trip, or perhaps treat himself to some luxury at the Ambassador. However, he chose to give the Dragon Hotel a try. Before long, he was pulling up in front of the five-story hotel at 40 Changchun Road, Mr. Kung and the staff greeting him as if they had expected his arrival at any moment.

The first morning at the Dragon he went to the resort area of Beitou to have a Japanese-style "hotsie" bath, which he explained fondly from many previous experiences in Japan involves a young woman washing you from head to toe. The staff at the Dragon gave Ball a note in Chinese to help him find a place. Ball didn't get what he wanted but ended up with a massage from a blind nineteen-year-old masseuse. On leaving the establishment he found out from the receptionist that his Chinese note read: "I desire a girl. Please get me a very good one." Ball was furious; he had shown the note to a family on the train from Taipei to Beitou and other people on the way there. He complained to the confused Dragon Hotel staff, who explained that they thought he wanted a girl. Early on in the book there's a lot of this kind of exasperation from the author at the constant soliciting, whether it's him during his first days at the Dragon, or recalling his previous trip to Taipei, when he was brought a succession of girls to his room, or pedicab drivers pestering him with, "You want to see skivvy movie, mister?" "Two girls do very funny show." Or, "Girl, best looking." You can't help wondering whether the author doth protest too much and his fondness for Taipei and the Dragon Hotel stemmed from the fact he was banging whores like a drum the whole time he was there.

The Beitou misadventure is one of many mildly amusing encounters with the staff, some cultural but mostly language missteps, few of which rise to the hilarious but most of which are culturally insensitive by today's standards. For an author lauded for breaking racial barriers by making a black detective his star protagonist – against his publisher's recommendations – he seems rather deaf to the mockery of the natives in Taiwan.

Or perhaps we've become too sensitive to making fun of mangled English. Does the following make you grimace or grin? A hotel clerk tells Ball: "Can get you fine pletty girl fliend can now come make you much happiness." For me it's more groan than chortle, but it depends on each specific usage. When the clerk produces the woeful textbook he's learning English from, it's amusing to read sentences from it such as: "It is with overwhellming (sic) honour that I make greeting to you by my insufficient self." Ball says it was painful seeing language "being raped" like that, so he rewrote the sentence as, "How do you do?" and then went about writing further corrections in the rest of the textbook.

His eagerness soon saw him roped into holding a free English class for the staff, but he was compensated by having as a student the gorgeous Miss Lin – "a rare and striking beauty" he guessed to be twenty-four. The smitten Ball spent time with her outside of the class; it was an unconsummated, innocent yet transactional relationship of an older man happily giving favors in exchange for the company of a young beauty, something that seems less sordid when across a cultural divide. In Ball's words, "There are some women with whom a brief moment of even such restrained intimacy is something to be valued."

Ball finishes his book with a few pages of sentimental flourish; though admitting it may have been undiplomatic of him to desert the Foreign Correspondents' Club for the Dragon Hotel, he says he "would not have missed the experience for anything." And again the reader scratches his head at his unexplained sentimentality. We aren't even given an indication of the length of his stay there – perhaps a couple of weeks, but he never says. What a mysteriously plodding account, suitable background for a police procedural, well, if dead bodies and actions were sprinkled through it and we were reading through the dry bits for clues.

Still, the book may appeal to anyone who was out East in the 1970s and before, and it has some good local period color that would be useful for novelists; nuggets like the incessant horn blowing by drivers, or the cost of a ride for three people on the Wulai push-car railway (NT$50, though they'll try for more from a foreigner). Then there's the poverty; describing the suburbs of Taipei: "areas largely of wretchedness: of very substandard dwellings, ragged children, and of a forced acceptance of the whole situation by those who lived there."

The Cold War martial law atmosphere is obvious, from the traffic policemen – "starched, sharply tailored khaki uniforms, spit-shined combat boots, white helmet liners, and with 45-caliber pistols holstered at the hip," to "huge billboards depicting in comic-book style the treacherous activity of spies and saboteurs and the heroic undertakings of the nation's servicemen." And the presence of U.S. military and the oversized impact of their spending power is apparent: "For perhaps a mile and a half down from the Grand Hotel there is an almost unbroken double row of curio shops, hotels, airline offices, and compounds devoted to the American military forces."

* * *

For a no-need-to-read-between-the-lines account of libertine adventures in Taiwan, nothing comes close to Daniel Reid's astounding memoir, **Shots from the Hip: Sex, Drugs and the Tao** (2019). It's a spinning carousel of anecdotes, musings, and insights that leaves you shaking your head in shock and smiling with vicarious enjoyment, and perhaps with a feeling of regret that your own youth wasn't more misspent.

Reid, who lived in Taipei from 1973 to 1989, is a prolific writer on Chinese philosophy, medicine, and food. He has also written travel books on East Asia. By number of titles – more than thirty – and copies sold, he is the most successful Taiwan expat writer.

Reid was born in San Francisco in 1948, coming of age in the right place at the right place to enjoy what he regards fondly as "America's most exceptional moment, the Late Sixties." As a student at Berkeley, he threw himself into the heady mix of sex, drugs, and rock and roll, especially the first two. His love affair with traditional Chinese culture came as a wave of LSD-inspired clarity during an introductory lecture on China in his senior year. After a gap year, most of it spent on the hippy trail in India with his older brother (and funded by making several marijuana drug runs from California to New York), he completed a master's degree in Chinese language and civilization. Midway through his course he used the summer vacation to visit Taiwan and road test his language skills; he had a great time and decided to live there after graduation.

His sixteen-year Taiwan adventure began when he returned in 1973, a twenty-four-year-old "refugee … in search for a new place to call home after the collapse of the short-lived Late Sixties Dynasty in America and the rise of corporate culture there."

And then he got a corporate job. His father, a senior executive with Trans World Airlines, visited Taiwan and used his connections to get Reid a position at the Hilton Hotel in Taipei, which was owned by the airline. The hotel was brand new, the tallest building in Taiwan at the time, and the first international five-star hotel in the country. Located on the southern side of Taipei Main Station, it's still there today, though run as the Caesar Park Hotel since 2000.

After a year at the Hilton, Reid moved on to a managerial position at the American Club in China, another oasis of luxury in Taipei, this time one geared for the American expat elite. This disconnect between Reid's self-professed leftist anarchist, anti-corporate views and his advantageous personal choices reminds me of the first time I read one of his books, a travel guide to Taiwan containing words of praise for right-wing dictator Chiang Kai-shek, and I was left wondering how much the author believed what he had written and how much was convenience. It's hard to respect a man if his seemingly strident beliefs are so pliable that they never translate into a personal cost in the real world. Thankfully, such doubts, which threatened to sour me on *Shots from the Hip*, were placated when I read with reassuring delight how Reid had taken financial hits on a point of principle, and such a minor point at that: Romanization in his books. Hanyu Pinyin versus Yale to be exact.

Hanyu Pinyin is a system of Romanization developed in China in the 1950s, and has for decades been the most commonly used system worldwide. Reid favors another system called Yale, named after the university where it was developed in the early 1940s, because he regards it as closest to English pronunciation. A good example is the Romanization for that mysterious circulating life force: "qi" in Hanyu Pinyin, "ch'i" in Wade-Giles, and – easiest for an English speaker – "chi" in Yale.

Reid learned the Yale system at the Monterey Institute while doing his master's, and has remained loyal to it, still using it in all his books. "I have twice refused to sign contracts with publishers who insist I change all the Yale spellings in my manuscripts to the 'official' pinyin spelling, insisting they agree to keep the Yale spellings in the text before I sign the contract."

Taiwan was, for an amorous young Western man like Reid, an absolute paradise, and his life in Taipei was "a nightly carnival of wine, women, and sensual pleasure." Not someone given to doing things by half, he threw himself headlong into this "garden of carnal delight," and admits to becoming "obsessed with having sex with Chinese women." He says there is something special about the women in Taiwan, possessing as they do a traditional Chinese "insight into the true nature of men and consummate skill in dealing with male sexual drive."

After about two and a half years in the high-end-hospitality trade, Reid decided he had had enough of regular work. He quit his job and devoted his time to exploring traditional Chinese martial and medical arts under accomplished masters, including one of the all-time martial arts greats, Hung Yi-hsiang, with whom Reid studied *qigong*, a kind of stationary, deep-breathing tai chi.

Reid's journey as a writer began in 1978 with a knock at the door of his house in Beitou (a pleasant northern Taipei suburb where he lived during his entire sixteen years). Two American editors from Hong Kong, one of them Fred Poole, the author of *Taipei After Dark*, were in town looking for someone to write a chapter on Taipei nightlife for a regional guidebook. This was Reid's first paid writing gig, and it led to numerous article assignments on travel and culture for magazines, and then various book projects, including ones on travel and food for a newly opening China.

He was commissioned to write the first international travel guide on Taiwan, *Insight Guide: Taiwan* (1984). A few years later, he and Canadian photographer Ian Lloyd took a chance self-publishing a bilingual pictorial coffee table book showcasing Taiwan's natural and cultural beauty: *Reflections of Taiwan* (1987). To cover the production costs of the first print run of twenty thousand copies, Reid tried to pre-sell the books, utilizing all his impressive contacts with government departments, hotels, and travel agencies. He had orders for the entire lot in just two weeks. Reid's share of the profit from book sales was US$20,000! For those not familiar with the typically miniscule amounts of money in publishing, let me assure you that represents a notable success.

Reid's first work on traditional health practices was *Chinese Herbal Medicine* (1983). The book had its origins in a back injury. Reid took a friend's recommendation to seek treatment at a small private clinic with a traditional Chinese medicine practitioner. Dr Huang Bo-wen didn't cut the most commanding presence, dressed as he was in slippers and crumpled clothes and chain smoking "Long Life" cigarettes. He used *tui-na* (literally "push and grasp"), which is like acupuncture with pressure massaging rather than needles, and then applied a balm of herbal paste. Reid made a fast recovery and was so impressed that he returned to the clinic and asked Dr Huang if he could be a part-time apprentice in order to learn the basics of Chinese medicine. Thus began a friendship and a two-year period of informal training, and a solid beginning to Reid's journey into traditional Chinese medicine.

Now we come to the culmination of Reid's Taiwan adventure, *The Tao of Health, Sex, and Longevity: A Modern Practical Guide to the Ancient Way* (1989). I remember buying a copy in the mid-1990s from the Caves Bookstore on Zhongshan North Road in Taipei. It was jaw-dropping: a portal into a bizarre parallel world; reading it, you felt like a Gulliver cast upon a strange shore. The book revealed a new way of seeing the world through the simple yet beguilingly mysterious force of Tao, and gave practical ways to implement "the way" in your own life; there were sections on Chinese medicine, breathing exercises, meditation, and – most remarkable of all – esoteric Taoist sexual disciplines carrying the promise of becoming a sex god. Intermingled with traditional Chinese wisdom were Western New Age elements such as fasting, colonic irrigation, and eating raw food.

What to make of it all? There was at the core of Reid's text some admirable commonsense: taking responsibility for one's own well being, and viewing health holistically and consequently emphasizing the treatment of root problems rather than symptoms. But, for a skeptic such as myself, there was also an awful lot of unscientific and unhistorical nonsense — highly readable nonsense admittedly, but still nonsense. Legendary characters such as the Yellow Emperor, China's mythical civilizational founding figure, are presented as real, their magical feats recounted with a straight face and no qualification. For instance, we are told the Yellow Emperor "kept a harem of 1,200 women with whom he coupled frequently" and "discovered the secret of immortality through the subtle blending of male and female essence during sexual intercourse."

Reid rehashes old slanders against Tang dynasty ruler Empress Wu Zetian. We are to believe that China's first female ruler was a nymphomaniac who so overengaged her favorite palace stud that he died from exhaustion, and that she, aided by special elixirs concocted from "tiger's blood and fresh semen milked from her consorts," remained sexually active until a year before her death at the age of eighty-one. There's no analysis, no attempt to sift kernels of truth; instead, there's an admonition against discounting "the Empress Wu's story as an eccentric fable (which it is not)." And then there's the mention of a Taoist adept who lived to the age of 256, which is the kind of incredible tale that inspired Robert W. Smith and Donn Draeger to come up with the Gilbey hoax.

Some of the practical medical advice is equally eyebrow-raising. For a severe cold he recommends a "3-day therapeutic fast with twice-daily colonic irrigation," which seems a case of the cure being worse than the disease.

However, the book is a great insight into traditional Chinese thinking, and it's fantastic fun, especially the chapters related to the bedroom arts. While Reid was doing research on Taoist sex practices for the book, he came across a method known as "contact without leakage," in other words copulation without completion by the male. The Chinese have long considered ejaculation highly debilitating for men, and related cautionary tales have been a mainstay of Chinese folktales and literature through the ages, most commonly seen in stories about ghosts and fox spirits taking the form of beautiful maidens in order to seduce men and steal their precious bodily fluids. Although Reid was skeptical about the practice of semen retention, he tried it and found it easier than expected, and immensely beneficial for his sex life and general health.

Thirty years after its debut, *The Tao of Health, Sex, and Longevity*, which has been published in eight languages, remains Reid's top seller, though *Shots from the Hip* deserves to take that crown. It's an exceptional work: unvarnished, beautifully written, thought-provoking, and, yes, sometimes infuriating.

In 1989 Reid left Taiwan to live in Thailand. *Shots from the Hip* covers Reid's earliest days in Thailand, but for his adventures since then, you'll need to read the sequel, *Shots from the Hip: Energy, Light, and Luminous Space* (2020).

* * *

Given that sex sells, I'm a little surprised by the paucity of titles on the subject. As with the majority of books on Taiwan, most entries in this field are academic works. There's *Governing Sex, Building the Nation: The Politics of Prostitution in Postcolonial Taiwan 1945–1979* (2015) from the sneakily named Cambridge Scholars Publishing (there is no link between the publisher and Cambridge University). Turning to a more prestigious press, Routledge has published *Japanese Adult Videos in Taiwan* (2014). According to the blurb: "Based on extensive original research on how Japanese adult videos are consumed in Taiwan, it presents a rich picture of how Japanese adult videos are transformed into something Taiwanese, and how they are incorporated into both male and female Taiwanese sexual culture." I think I'll pass on that.

Another Routledge title, *Perverse Taiwan* (2016), is a collection of essays looking at queer culture in Taiwan. It opens with editors Howard Chiang and Yin Wang explaining that the book "argues for a revisionist account of what we call 'perverse Taiwan' by reframing its genealogical roots in distinct historical periods, by redefining its nested positionalities along different axes of global epistemological renditions, and by refiguring its cultural modes of embodiment amidst the ever-shifting intersections of social and temporal coordinates." That's a hell of a sentence, and likely as far as the general reader gets into the book.

There's a lot of this unnecessarily painful writing in academic publishing – so many trees sacrificed for publications that will largely go unread and uncited, priced for a shrinking, captive university library market. There are solutions to getting academic publishing a wider readership: obvious ones like producing books with low prices and engaging writing, and more innovative approaches, such as making the e-book available for free. The University of California Press, for example, has an open-access imprint called Luminos whereby digital editions of books are made available for free and paperbacks for about US$35. The downsides are that the authors need to contribute US$7,500 to the publishing costs (this in theory is expected to come "either from their home institution and/or another independent funding source") and they get no royalties on their work; you read that correctly – no royalties at all, and the only payment is from the author to Luminos. However, with regard to the royalties, the dirty secret of academic publishing is that, outside of a tiny minority of prescribed course textbooks, the typical annual royalty earnings on a title is so small it's hardly worth the hassle of processing it. Luminos currently has three titles covering Taiwan, including *Outcasts of Empire: Japan's Rule on Taiwan's "Savage Border," 1874–1945* (2017), by Paul D. Barclay.

A book that provides a possible alternative model for academic publishing is **Going Down to the Sea: Chinese Sex Workers Abroad** (2014), by Ko-lin Chin, a professor of criminal justice at Rutgers University. The solution: produce two versions from the same research, one for the academy and a spinoff book for the regular reader. This is what Chin did. His research findings of the sex trade were published in an academic book, *Selling Sex Overseas: Chinese Women and the Realities of Prostitution and Global Sex Trafficking*, co-authored with James O. Finckenauer. Chin, however, wanted to publish a book with more general appeal, one that gave voice to the women, with them telling their stories in their own words. He also wanted to give a behind-the-scenes look at ethnographic fieldwork on a sensitive issue. *Going Down to the Sea* is that book. The title refers to a Chinese euphemism (*xiahai*) for the sex trade.

Chin's research was directed at an important question: To what extent is the international flesh trade the result of nefarious criminals using deceit, threats, and violence to control women, and how much of it involves women voluntarily choosing to join the profession and stay in it?

His focus was on Chinese prostitutes working overseas. Between 2006 and 2008, Chin traveled to nine cities in Asia and the United States, interviewing a total of 149 female Chinese sex workers. Although it sounds like difficult, even dangerous, fieldwork, it was relatively sedate considering some of Chin's previous studies. Among the subjects he has researched and written about are the drug trade in the Golden Triangle and Taiwanese gangsters, the latter leading to the excellent *Heijin: Organized Crime, Business, and Politics in Taiwan* (2003). Finding and talking to prostitutes was easy in comparison. Chin paid the prostitutes for their time and reassured them about not revealing their true identities.

Of the 149 women interviewed, Chin chose eighteen to profile in the book, two of whom were prostitutes in Taiwan. As Chin explains, the sex trade in Taiwan is dominated by Chinese women ("mainland sisters") who have come in on fake marriages — and so it was with the two cases profiled.

We meet twenty-eight-year-old Mi Mi in Taichung City, the daughter of dirt-poor farmers in Hunan Province. She voluntarily went to the city of Dongguan to work in the sex industry when she was eighteen. She had spent time in Shanghai and Hong Kong (from which she was deported), and was now in Taiwan for the second time. Her first visit for six months in 2005 was on a fake marriage to a Taiwanese man. She was now doing "outcall" work. This usually involves being sent by a "company" (a pimp) with a *mafu* ("jockey" or driver) to a "store" (an apartment) provided by a middleman who had typically found the customer.

The actual interview with Mi Mi was something of an ordeal. It's nine in the evening and Mi Mi has already completed seven sessions. The last customer paid for four sessions, an expensive US$460 (each session, forty-five minutes, costing US$115). Mi Mi agrees to be interviewed, but the pimp's phone rings. A client is lined up – could the author wait until after the session. And so Chin heads off with the pimp, driver, and Mi Mi. Half an hour later they're at an apartment building, where the "store" operator has a rented apartment. Mi Mi is quick: she's back in twenty-five minutes and hands over the equivalent of US$62, which is what the store operator has given her. The calls keep coming in to the pimp from middlemen. He sends out drivers and women; and there's more work for Mi Mi too. And still more, until finally, after the twelfth session – an inebriated guy at a motel – they get down to the interview at five in the morning. As he did with the other women interviewees, Chin aimed to put Mi Mi at ease by making the interview seem like an informal chat: he did not ask for a real name, took no pictures, and used no recording devices; he didn't even carry pen and paper, instead writing the details down post-session.

Chin's second interviewee is a thirty-two-year-old from Shanxi, again from a poor rural family. She had been working as a nightclub hostess in China but was frustrated by her low earnings (US$360 a month). Then she met someone who said there was easy money to be made in Taiwan. And thus began, in 1997, the first of six trips to Taiwan in ten years, flying in as the wife of a Taiwanese citizen the first four times and smuggled in by boat the last two (because of tighter airport security). Being smuggled in cost her US$6,250 – the same as getting a fake marriage and coming by plane.

Both women earned a little under US$40 per session with a customer. Although they didn't consider themselves cheated, they thought the amount they received – about a third of what a customer paid – was unfairly low. There were just too many people taking a cut: the pimp, the person finding the client and supplying the apartment, the driver, and the agent who had arranged the trip to Taiwan (despite getting reimbursed for the initial cost, they still took a small cut of each session). Neither prostitute saved much money – in Mi Mi's case, having a mah-jong gambling habit didn't help matters. Sadly, both had very little to show for their years of hard work.

Looking at the all the Chinese sex workers' experiences, several main points come through. Chin says "the vast majority of them were not deceived, coerced, or forced into the sex trade abroad." Yet even though none of the women in Taiwan would be considered trafficking victims under a strict definition of the term, their plight was still serious: arriving under debt, being "owned" by agents, and often being financially exploited.

The findings of the research behind *Going Down to the Sea* raise an interesting dilemma. Cracking down on the trafficking of sex workers in some ways makes the situation worse for the women because it increases their expenses (in getting travel documents, paying off connections, doing jail time, etc.) and puts them under greater control of the pimps and agents.

10

Rich and Free

MARTIAL LAW ended in July 1987. Later that year family members were allowed to visit China; old KMT soldiers finally reunited with their families after a separation of four decades. Investment in China would soon follow. Over the next few years restrictions on movies, music, books, the media, and the Taiwanese language were relaxed. A cultural and political renaissance had begun. Chiang Ching-kuo died on January 13, 1988, and was succeeded as president by Taiwan-born Lee Teng-hui, who pushed through reforms of democratization and localization. All this was against the dynamism of a booming economy, since the mid-sixties the fastest growing in the world. Taiwan had become rich in a single generation and now it was free: wild, exhilarating days lay ahead.

* * *

A novel that beautifully captures the post-martial law years is *Heaven Lake* (2004), by John Dalton. Describing a young American missionary's experiences in Taiwan, it's part a coming-of-age tale and part a travelogue through China – a thoughtful story about faith, loneliness, and love.

Heaven Lake has an interesting origin. It was 1989 in the Taiwanese backwater city of Touliu (Douliu), Yunlin County. American John Dalton had moved to Taiwan several months earlier to teach English. One evening after work, Dalton and a few of his fellow expat teachers were eating at a restaurant. A local Taiwanese businessman approached them with an intriguing story and a strange offer. While on a recent business trip to China – investment once more possible after a four-decade freeze – the man had met, fallen deeply in love with, and proposed to "the most beautiful woman in China." She and her family had accepted his proposal. However, the bureaucratic obstacles to a cross-strait marriage meant it would be many years before she'd be able to come to Taiwan. And thus an offer was made: ten thousand U.S. dollars for any foreigner willing to travel to China, marry the beauty, bring her back to Taiwan, and then immediately divorce her. Dalton didn't give the proposition any serious consideration (even in 1989 dollars, the amount was hardly worth the moral compromise), but the proposal did stick in his mind and a decade later would form the framework for his debut novel.

In *Heaven Lake*, recent college graduate Vincent leaves the small Midwest town of Red Bud, Illinois, to serve as a missionary in the city of Douliu. When approached with the fake marriage proposal that the author himself had heard, Vincent angrily turns it down. Circumstances, however, change; and Vincent eventually finds himself on an epic overland journey from Hong Kong to Xinjiang in China's far northwest to marry the beautiful Kai-ling.

Making the protagonist a missionary rather than an English teacher was a wise choice. While an English teacher can immerse himself in the culture or keep it at an arm's length to the extent that he wishes, the missionary can't. The "Jesus teacher" has to engage the local people yet not go native. And being a young missionary is especially fraught with tension; apart from having to repress sexual desires, there's the contradiction of giving moral guidance when personally knowing so little about life, so little about the culture.

Vincent's early days in Douliu are overwhelming. He struggles to makes sense of the strangeness of the place and people.

There then began a time, several weeks' worth of uncharted days, when Vincent roamed the various quarters of Touliu, its labyrinthlike open markets, its unruly business district, both its shabbier and more privileged residential neighborhoods where the homes were crannied together and forked by slim, winding alleyways. He was trying to form an articulate opinion of the town, one he could set to paper and pass on to his parents and a few longtime acquaintances at St. Mark's Church in Red Bud. The shape of that opinion, though, proved to be something of a problem. Yes, the buildings were all formed of pearl-gray concrete rather than wood or brick. Yes, the traffic was unreasonably loud. But these were only the obvious differences. The real difference, Vincent believed, had something to do with the climate itself. Call it a variation of latitude, maybe, a subtle inflection in the atmosphere. Familiar objects seemed to weigh a few ounces less here. Odors were sharper. The air – how to describe it? – was oddly textured, foreign, its foreignness most noticeable in the scattered, coppery light of sunrise and dusk.

The paragraph above is a good example of the lovely writing in *Heaven Lake*. You don't write a passage like this in a day or even a week. It's the result of layered hard work and inspiration over a long period of time. Most writers would trade their daily target of five hundred words for a line like, "Familiar objects seemed to weigh a few ounces less here." As well as being well crafted, the writing is accurate in its descriptions. I should know – I used to live just down the road from Douliu, missing the author by a year.

After arriving in Douliu, Vincent shares a house with Alec, a moody Scot with a fondness for marijuana. Alec is a seasoned traveler and the kind of affable deadbeat who in those days (the novel is set in 1989–1990) could drift in and out of Taiwan as they pleased, picking up lucrative teaching work and then suddenly departing to travel around Asia for months. This was possible because there weren't many foreigners in Taiwan at that time, especially in places like Douliu: "[Vincent's] presence in Touliu's markets and restaurants caused a stir. Children squealed in surprise and called out 'American' or 'outsider.'"

Vincent moves into a vacant house that he turns into a ministry building. He offers free English lessons followed by Bible study, and also takes on some English classes around town to earn some money. These include a class of adoring girls at a high school; yes, the weakness of human flesh will be sorely revealed.

As an interesting aside (an infuriating one, actually) regarding the remuneration for teaching, Dalton mentions that Vincent was paid NT$500 an hour (about US$16 an hour at current rates) for one of his classes. Damn, that's not much less than what foreign teachers in Taiwan earn now, three decades later. And given the drop in currency and purchasing power, in real terms that's easily double what more qualified teachers are earning today.

By the end of the book, Vincent has – through his various trials – learned a lot about himself and about life. In a sentence reminiscent of a closing passage in Somerset Maugham's *Of Human Bondage*, Dalton writes:

But he rose the next morning anyway, rose sluggishly and thick-tongued and with an abiding conviction that whatever his present life was leading to, it was not so much a wealth of sustained happiness or pinnacle of accomplishment as a circuitous and impossible striving toward a destination that couldn't be reached.

I won't go into details about the characters or plot for fear of spoiling the narrative. This is one of the books I especially want you to read rather than just read about. It takes its time with some old-fashioned pacing but rewards the patient reader. Instead of plot, we can turn to a few aspects of the writing of the book. After four years in Taiwan, Dalton returned to the United States and began work on his novel. The writing was an eight-year struggle. On his website he describes how, by the summer of 1996 he had nearly 280 pages done. A close rereading of the novel set off alarm bells: "foolishly, I'd begun the book with eighty pages set in Red Bud, Illinois and another thirty in a Taipei parish – all pages designed to convince the reader that my protagonist, Vincent, was serious about his vocation. But good writers could accomplish the same thing in a few paragraphs or short scenes. And much of the rest of the novel was functional but not really good." Dalton cut the first 110 pages and started over, straining to make his writer tighter and deeper.

And so I kept on. I taught. I waited tables. I lived my life. I continued to work on my book. In 1998 I reached the half-way point. By then I'd been working on the book five years. Friends and family, who'd once been encouraging, now, out of concern or embarrassment, avoided the topic of my novel.

He finished it in 2002. His agent sent the novel to a dozen publishers; five were interested, and a week later he had a signed contract. Redemption! Despite the struggles, Dalton says he never considered giving up. *Heaven Lake* was published in 2004 by Scribner, achieving some critical and commercial success in the United States.

Of course, good sales (and the bonus of US$5,000 for winning the Sue Kaufman Prize for First Fiction) look less rosy when divided by eight years plus of work (such mathematic cruelty is best avoided). Dalton makes his living as an associate professor, teaching creative writing in St. Louis, where he lives with his Taiwanese wife (they met during his time in Douliu) and two daughters.

Heaven Lake remains obscure among Taiwan's expat community, something I hope this entry can help rectify.

* * *

In choosing works to include for *Taiwan in 100 Books*, I deliberately included some where the country was not the author's main focus. I did this partly because these books are generally unknown, even to hardcore Taiwan bibliophiles. But mainly because they offer different perspectives – sometimes ill-informed yet with a welcome candor. There's a selection bias for straight Taiwan books; the author has undoubtedly invested years of his life in the country, probably likes it (why else spend a year or more writing a book about it?), and can expect to face negative or positive consequences depending on what he writes. The casual observer, however, who includes Taiwan as a chapter among other destinations, has less investment in the country and the book's reception there. This gives authors a certain freedom and their opinions a freshness.

Such a book is **Fight for the Tiger: One Man's Battle to Save the Wild Tiger from Extinction** (1995), by Michael Day. A book on tiger conservation in Asia seems an unlikely entry, but the relevant chapters perfectly capture the wild late years of Taiwan's economic miracle, when the island was newly free and awash in money for the first time.

The author's chance encounter with a tiger on a camping trip in southern Thailand in 1990 proved life changing for the Englishman, who was then in his late thirties. He gave up his job running an advertising agency and threw himself into tiger conservation. Day began collecting evidence of the illegal trade in tigers, with his first covert filming operation taking him to Taiwan in May 1991. He tells the story with a lot of dash. Although making himself the hero of his own tale is self-serving to some extent, he does seem to have been a larger-than-life figure: a tall, well dressed, brash rabble-rouser who would attack not only wildlife traffickers but also governments and even the conservation establishment, such as the World Wildlife Fund. His tiger crusade took him to Thailand, Taiwan, China, and Russia. For his Taipei episode, however, the hero of the story is a young woman.

Flying from Hong Kong to Taipei, Day befriends a "stunningly attractive" Taiwanese woman called Rebecca Chen, thinking for unexplained reasons that he will have less chance of being pulled over by customs if it appears they're traveling together. He upgrades her standby ticket to business class and they get to know each other. She works for a courier and freight company in Taipei, is in her late twenties, and lives at home.

Exploring the city from the Cosmos Hotel in downtown Taipei near the main train station, Day finds Taipei a crowded, polluted, traffic-snarled mess: "a city under siege" from a "relentless onslaught of construction." This was during the building of the MRT (Mass Rapid Transit), which opened in 1996. "The ground shook with continuous pounding of pile-drivers, and huge mechanical diggers prodding the ground."

Day reconnects with Chen a few days later, and they go to Dihua Street, an old part of the city with shops selling dried food-stuffs, including the body parts of wild animals in open view. Day tells Chen about his mission and she agrees to help him with his undercover filming. What bravery and trust! The author compares this to an English girl colluding "with a Chinese undercover agent looking into fox-hunting or hare-coursing in the wilds of Suffolk."

Day and Chen head to Snake Alley – a sleazy market in the red-light district of Wanhua specializing in aphrodisiacs like snake and turtle blood – for a test run. He's trying out his two spy cameras, one in a shoulder-bag and another in a hat, the lens at the front disguised as a piece of a gaudy ornament. The hat camera has cables from the hat down to the battery and recorder around his waist. Day and Chen are both role-playing: Day graying up as a sugar daddy and she the bimbo. Chen, wearing "bright red hot-pants and low-cut blouse," was the perfect distraction while he covertly filmed snakes being skinned alive and turtles decapitated.

After a week in Taipei, Day had already found eleven Chinese medicine shops with "tiger bone openly on sale in the front window." This was actually illegal thanks to a recent law, the ROC Wildlife Protection Law of 1989, which had banned the trade in endangered wildlife. Yes, things had been worse. In the mid-1980s public tiger slaughters took place around the country, including in a village not far from where I'm writing this. Tigers were butchered in public and the parts – meat, bones, blood, head, tail, tongue, and penis – auctioned off to the large crowds gathered around. More than just being out in the open, these were promoted spectacles, with advertisements in local newspapers, trucks with loudspeakers, and so on. These events stopped after outrage from conservation groups.

The trade in tigers continued but was now mostly underground, and Day was determined to get video proof. To do this, he was going to play the part of a wealthy American – fake Rolex, showy ring, and other trappings, Texan drawl – who was looking to buy a present of a tiger cub for his gold-digging girlfriend.

Chen finds a lead, and they set off for a poodle parlor near Dinghao Market (today an expensive area known for brand-name clothes). The pet store is a front for smuggled wildlife. Once in the windowless back rooms they see various animals and are offered a baby orangutan for NT$150,000 (about US$5,000), and a clouded leopard and a black panther for US$3,800, "including the cages and delivery." From the store they are driven southeast of the city to meet a man who has tigers. In a scrapyard with cages, there are seven tigers, an aged chimp, an enormous orangutan, and an American mountain lion – all the animals in poor condition. "I was looking at an illegal tiger farm," amazingly "in full view of a suburban neighbourhood."

Day returned to Taiwan in December 1991. This time information led him to the south of the island. Once again accompanied by Chen, he arrives by train at Kaohsiung. In the station restroom he gets into costume (moustache, spectacles, graying hair, and his hat with the camera), posing as a "big game-hunter from Texas" looking to find, on behalf of an associate, a supplier of tiger skins and also tiger bone wine for the U.S. market.

They're picked up by a Mercedes and taken to meet an illegal wildlife importer of sinister demeanor called Mr. Chan, who casually throws a cellophane bag across the desk and asks Day to identify the contents, which look "like a sun-dried sponge." Day admits he doesn't know what they are. "Human placenta," collected from "Chinese hospitals and dried with great skill. Highly nutritious," Chan explains. Next, Chan shows him a tiger femur, and arranges for his customers to be taken to a warehouse. As Day enters, he flicks on his video camera. The warehouse seems to be full of contraband from

China – mushrooms, seeds, and other dried goods. Day is shown and gets valuable footage of wildlife products: a bag of tiger bones, four skins – three tigers and a leopard – poorly cured, and shown the remains of a tiger (a rib cage, a skull, and a reassembled skeleton to show the bones are legit), said to be from Thailand.

This was the highlight of Day's two-week trip. Before leaving, however, icing on the cake was a visit to a restaurant in Taichung called "Bu Jung Bao," which was "an opulent new karaoke bar built like a pyramid." The restaurant's house specialty is tiger-penis soup, and good footage was obtained.

Michael Day's undercover work in Taiwan, and later China and Siberia, helped establish him in the conservation field. In 1992 he and his wife founded a charity called the Tiger Trust. The same year he returned to Taipei with a film crew for Yorkshire television; the resulting award-winning documentary would air in 1993.

Day contributed to bringing heat onto Taiwan at a time when the country was "gaining a reputation in some circles as the environmental cesspool of the world." It was a long rap sheet: as well as tigers, ivory, and rhino horn, there was the trade in orangutans and exotic birds, dolphin slaughter, and drift-net fishing. In 1994 the United States imposed trade sanctions on Taiwan, punishment for the nation's poor efforts in trying to halt the sale of products from endangered species, in particular tiger bones and rhinoceros horns. The sanctions were on wildlife products, coral, shell jewelry, butterflies, and snake- and crocodile-skin shoes, belts, and purses. Sales of these items were worth a mere US$25 million or so a year, a pittance compared to regular trade. This, however, was an embarrassing loss of face for Taiwan – the first time the United States had imposed such sanctions. The government and civil groups in Taiwan worked hard to turn things around. Education and punitive legislation alongside cultural shifts mean that Taiwan is no longer the environmental cesspit it once was.

Michael Day and his Tiger Trust had less of a happy ending. In 1996, a year after the release of *Fight for the Tiger*, Day came under criticism by various environmental groups for mismanagement of funds, something Day brushed off as rival organizations' ulterior motives. Whatever the case, he dropped out of the public eye soon after that, and when I asked around various tiger groups in 2002 for leads on what he was doing I drew a blank.

* * *

When I first arrived in Taiwan, a few years after Michael Day's visits, there were more stray dogs and cats than pet ones. It was clearly not a nation of animal lovers, with two exceptions: pigeons and fish were popular. The often-blue pigeon houses atop the block-house architecture were a feature of the skyline, the owners on roofs waving poles with flags suspiciously like low-tech communist agents signaling to invasion forces. The birds were racing pigeons, which were keenly bet upon. Fish could be seen in ponds, in aquariums in both homes and businesses (and seafood restaurants); I soon learned this was due to ideas of good luck; water is good *feng shui*, and fish are lucky (because *yu*, the Mandarin word for "fish," sounds like the word for "abundance").

Another Taiwan-related book on an endangered species is **The Dragon Behind the Glass: A True Story of Power, Obsession, and the World's Most Coveted Fish** (2016). American journalist Emily Voigt goes on the trail of the Asian arowana or "dragon fish," with Taiwan among fifteen countries visited (how many books do you need to sell in order to repay such travel expenses?). Although Taiwan is not a big part of Voigt's investigative journey, the episode is so classically Taiwanese that it's worth retelling here.

The Asian arowana comes in various colors, with the star Super Red found only in a remote area of Borneo. Discovered by Indonesian loggers cutting their way into the rainforests of the island's interior, it was smuggled to Taiwan in the early 1980s, "where it became the object of a virtual cult." From there, the craze spread to Japan and further afield in Asia, becoming an "example of a uniquely modern paradox – the mass-produced endangered species." Fish farms in Southeast Asia cater to regional demand; but because arowana are an endangered species in the wild, international regulations restrict the trade and importation of these fish, and they are barred from entry into the United States.

The Asian arowana, photograph by Marcel Burkhard

The author speculates on several possible explanations as to what sparked the craze; was the status-symbol fish "Taiwan thumbing its nose at the Chinese Community Party," which then still saw pet ownership as decadent? A celebration of its Chinese culture? Or did they just love fish?

Voigt makes the typical outsider's error of framing everything in Taiwan as related to China and to ancient Chinese heritage. I believe the appeal of the dragon fish was luck (a quadruple whammy of auspiciousness: dragon, red, fish, and water), especially for gamblers, a not insignificant chunk of the population. There was also the appeal of something new and expensive at a time when decades of thrift was giving way to outrageous consumption; this was a time of crazes – dragon fish were not unusual in this regard – when there was a lot of new money looking for a home. Among the animal-related crazes was one around 1989, when hundreds to a thousand orangutan infants were smuggled into the country from Borneo. The inspiration for this was the broadcasting on Taiwanese television of an American drama in which the lead family had a pet orangutan. All too predictably the craze led to an epidemic of psychologically damaged adult primates being abandoned.

The Dragon Behind the Glass sees Voigt track down hunters, breeders, collectors, sellers, smugglers, and the wild fish itself. It's Voigt's desire to speak to an elite collector that takes her to Taiwan. She gets picked up at the airport and tags along with two Taiwanese from a local fish magazine, *AquaZoo*. They arrive at a new mansion-style house on the outskirts of Chiayi City. Voigt approaches the door, spies an aviary with a pair of Taiwan blue magpies, the national bird of Taiwan, noting that it's illegal to keep them as a pet.

She is greeted by the collector Su Wen Hung and his "profoundly white teeth." Su is the "so-called toothbrush-bristle tycoon," president of a manufacturing company for plastics machinery and plastic filaments, things like the bristles on toothbrushes. One of Voigt's companions explains that "he also makes the hair of the Barbie."

Arowana (dragon fish) have been bred for appealing traits such as brighter colors or a lack of, with the rare albino fetching the highest prices; and Su owns the only albino arowana in Taiwan, for which he paid US$150,000. Voigt finds the toothbrush-bristle tycoon a far from loquacious interviewee, with "less to say about his arowana than I'd heard aquarists tell me about their $2 guppies." It turns out that Su is no fish nut – he just likes collecting rare and precious things, such as Harley-Davidson motorcycles, prize-winning pigeons, and champion German shepherds. And the $150,000 price tag for the fish was "no big deal" – he has a dog that cost four times as much.

* * *

For a more heartening look at wildlife in Taiwan, let's turn to the *Birdwatcher's Guide to the Taipei Region* (2004), published by the Taipei City Government's Department of Information. Taiwan is home to more than six hundred bird species, including fifteen endemic species and dozens of endemic subspecies. The greater Taipei region, with its mix of river, coastal, mountain, and lowland habitats, is surprisingly rich in birdlife. The bird-watching guide provides illustrations, detailed route descriptions, and maps for seventeen major bird-watching areas. We visit parks in the heart of the city like the Taipei Botanical Garden, where there's a good chance of seeing the memorably ugly Malaysian night heron, common urban birds such as the Japanese white-eyes, and a few escaped domesticated birds. Further afield we explore Wulai in the mountains south of the city and the Guandu wetlands near the mouth of the Danshui River, where you'll find common birds like the gorgeous river kingfisher and, in winter, numerous migratory birds, including, if you're especially lucky, the endangered black-faced spoonbill.

The birding guide was one of a series of excellent publications produced by the Taipei government in the early 2000s. Though obviously accentuating the positive, these books were lovely productions: inexpensive, informative, beautifully illustrated, and practical. My favorite is the outstanding *Private Prayers and Public Parades: Exploring the Religious Life of Taipei* (2002), by Mark Caltonhill. It's an excellent introduction to contemporary religious practices. Caltonhill says in the preface that he wrote the book that he himself wished to read but had not been able to find: an accessible guidebook to local customs. He covers the major religious elements – the triumvirate of Confucianism, Daoism, and Buddhism, plus ancestor worship – as they are manifested in daily life. We learn about divination, religious festivals, the major deities and patron deities, and a bewitching variety of other topics.

A good example of the nuggets of information found in the book is the explanation for the "wealth-beckoning cats." These small cat figurines with one raised paw, seen next to cash registers in shops across the country, are a legacy of the period of Japanese rule. "Known as *maneki-neko* in Japanese, they are mostly yellow (money-making) or white (lucky), though black-colored (warding off evil) cats also exist." Caltonhill outlines various old folktales explaining the origins of the cat. The one best known in Taipei involves a dissolute young man who brings his family to the brink of ruin through reckless gambling but is saved by his devoted and pious cat, Tama. The gambler reforms his ways, restores the family business, and in gratitude has a statue made of the cat.

Another Taipei City Department of Information publication is *Reflections on Taipei: Expat Residents Look at Their Second Home* (2003), by Rick Charette. In their own words, fifteen long-term residents share their experiences and opinions. The format used is unfortunate; with each expat answering the same questions – first impressions, changes seen, and so on – there's inevitably a lot of repetition. The book's standout contribution is from Father Jean

Lefeuvre (1922–2010), a French Jesuit priest and scholar, who moved to Taiwan in 1953 after being forced out of China by the Communists. Drawing on his fifty years' experience, Fr. Lefeuvre gives penetrating insights on society in *Reflections on Taipei*. There is, he says, "a deep-rooted Chinese sense of 'democracy,'" where "Everybody has their own ideas, everybody has their right to express it, everybody has the duty to listen to and clearly demonstrate respect for the opinion of everybody else." He talks of the strength of the family, and the bond between mothers and sons: "the deep, fundamental bond with the mother is often an obstacle to a man being able to develop a healthy relationship with his wife."

As well as doing pastoral work, Fr Lefeure was a world authority on oracular and bronze inscriptions, and as a founding member of the Taipei Ricci Institute oversaw and was an important contributor to *Le Grand Ricci*, one of the great book projects of the twentieth century. The Chinese–French dictionary, published in 2001 after five decades of work by a team of Jesuit scholars, is the most comprehensive dictionary of Chinese in a modern Western language. It consists of seven volumes of more than 1,200 pages each.

* * *

Another monumental reference book, though in this case the work of an individual, is Ralf Knapp's *Ferns and Fern Allies of Taiwan* (2011). Yes, it's more a book to be admired than read, and I admit not having done much of the latter. My admiration, however, runs deep. I know from firsthand experience the demanding amounts of time and money involved in such a project. (In my storage room in old files and boxes lies an abandoned book on the snakes of Taiwan, which I was working on with herpetologist Gerrut Norval.)

German engineer Ralf Knapp, having married a Taiwanese woman whom he met in Austria, moved to Taiwan in 1998 to work for a German company. He ended up staying longer than his initial three-year contract, and his interest in plants became a specialized passion for Taiwan's ferns. From around 2003 he threw himself into searching out and cataloging Taiwan's more than seven hundred species of ferns. Knapp's research took him all over Taiwan, from tropical to alpine habitats, and on many occasions into dangerously steep mountainous terrain. Straying off the beaten track brought other dangers too; he twice contracted the notoriously painful scrub typhus.

After seven years of intense fern-hunting weekends and vacations, Knapp had ample material for a comprehensive guide. Of course, having sufficient material and transforming it into a printed book are different matters. Knapp was unable to find a publisher; a thousand-page manuscript on Taiwan's ferns, with more than 4,700 color photographs, and from an unknown, uncredentialed author – these were not exactly winning ingredients for a bidding war between big-name publishers. Rescue came from the Dr. Cecilia Koo Botanic Conservation Center (KBCC), a plant conservatory in southern Taiwan's Pingtung County. This private foundation did not have their own publishing arm, but, recognizing the importance of Knapp's work, decided to set one up – KBCC Press – in order to handle it. The resulting 2.2 kilogram behemoth, *Ferns and Fern Allies of Taiwan*, was well received, and KBCC Press has moved forward with other English-language titles, including *The Wild Orchids of Taiwan* (2014) and two supplements to Knapp's 2011 fern book.

* * *

Let's turn from the uber-niche interest of ferns to the merely niche hobby of trains. Taiwan is a superb destination for rail fans: there's the bullet train, Taipei's showcase MRT, the scenic East Coast railway, the busy main trunk western line, quaint branch lines, and the magnificent Alishan narrow-gauge forestry railway, which climbs a stunning two thousand meters.

During the mid-1990s I lived in a small town in central Taiwan on the main western rail line. Trains meant much-anticipated visits to nearby cities. I have especially fond memories of lazy rides on the slow, rattling *putongche* trains (long since replaced by the silver commuter electric trains). The antiquated carriages had old-school windows that you could slide up for a pleasant breeze and an unobstructed view of the rice fields rolling by. Whatever the class of train, arriving at a station always had a touch of magic to it. Leaving the countryside, you'd quickly ease past rows of grimy city back walls and disembark at stations that – with their Japanese colonial-era architecture, quaint topiary, and railway staff in old-fashioned uniforms – were a taste of pre-KMT Formosa. And then, finally stepping out from the shade of the station, you were hit with all the color and bustle of modern main-street Taiwan.

Long underrepresented on the Taiwan bookshelf, there are now four railway titles: *Rails to the Mines: Taiwan's Forgotten Railways* (1978), by Charles S. Small; *Narrow Gauge Railways of Taiwan: Sugar, Shays and Toil* (2018), by Michael Reilly, de facto British ambassador to Taiwan 2005–2009; and, best of all, two volumes by Loren Aandahl, *The Taiwan Railway: 1966–1970* (2011) and *The Taiwan Railway: 1971–2002* (2012).

Aandahl (an American with a Norwegian surname) began his Taiwan adventure wearing nappies, arriving in the city of Hsinchu with his Lutheran missionary parents in 1955 at the age of eighteen months. Hsinchu would be his home for the next sixteen years. Among Loren's earliest childhood memories are countless hours spent watching trains at a railway crossing near his home. It was a fascination that he never grew out of. When he attended boarding school at Taichung's Morrison Academy from 1959 to 1970 the highlight was the fortnightly train trip between school and home. During his high school years, he acquired a camera and began taking pictures of the railway. The resulting pictures, along with others taken on family trips around the island, are the heart of *The Taiwan Railway: 1966–1970*. His photographs are a rare record of the railways during a time of strict martial law, when photography of strategic infrastructure was prohibited. Taking these pictures involved daring and guile. Although Loren could – being a foreigner – get away with more than Taiwanese citizens, he still had run-ins with the authorities.

In 1970 Loren moved to the United States to attend college. Working in the aviation industry in the ensuing decades meant cheap flights for frequent visits back to Taiwan, where he continued to ride the rails and document the evolution of the country's railways. Pictures from these later trips – supplemented by ones from fellow former residents – were compiled to produce *The Taiwan Railway: 1971–2002*. Both largely pictorial, the two volumes were self-published and beautifully printed in Taiwan. They are books for both hardcore train-spotters and then others like me, who, while not knowing their *angle cocks* from their *hoop tablets*, have some emotional attachment to Taiwan's railways. I take my hat off to the author's passion and hard work.

* * *

In the years before the Internet shrank the world, foreign residents in Taiwan and the region had a tougher but richer experience, and an enormous amount of opportunity. Such were Dennis Rea's years of musical high adventure between 1989 and 1992, described in **Live at the Forbidden City: Musical Encounters in China and Taiwan** (2006, 2016).

When American Dennis Rea first arrived in China in January 1989, the thirty-one-year-old Seattle-based musician was just tagging along. His fiancée, Anne Joiner, had landed a job teaching English at a university in Chengdu, the capital of Sichuan Province. Rea also obtained an English-teaching job at the school and the couple lived together on campus.

Rea was in some ways like a time traveler from the future or a Gulliver from a strange land, guitar in hand, bearing the dubious gifts of progressive rock and free jazz. Before long he would go from obscurity to accidental rock demigod. Rea became involved in the burgeoning music scene. Local musicians were hungry to learn about Western music and Rea found himself in great demand as a guitar teacher and performer. During his fifteen-month stay in China he was invited to increasingly large concerts and to high-profile radio and television appearances, played with some of the biggest stars in China, and recorded a best-selling album. China was virgin territory in those days – the first major Western pop group to visit was George Michael's Wham! in 1985.

After Rea's year at the university was up, he moved to the southern Taiwanese city of Tainan, where he taught English, only this time earning as much in a day as he had in a month in Chengdu. As well as playing in various bands in Tainan, he organized two tours of China (one with a Taiwan expat band and another with musicians from Seattle).

In Tainan, his band Identity Crisis played at pubs and other venues, and sometimes more lucratively at the city's night markets. Rea is dismissive of the music scene in Taiwan, which he says consisted of "shallow, escapist pop" and local bands playing cover versions of Western hits "like the inescapable 'Hotel California,' seemingly Taiwan's unofficial national anthem." He had expected more from a country shaking off decades of repression and music censorship. As in China, "Richard Clayderman had blanketed Taiwan with his vapid pianism," and "the hottest act going was the Little Tiger Team, a sickeningly cute trio of adolescent boys." The handful of edgy Taiwanese rock bands failed to capture a large audience.

Despite the bubblegum pop and the seemingly peaceful society, Rea found a hard edge to Taiwan. He was shocked by the violence around him; "to this day I've never accounted as much foul play as I did in my three short years in Taiwan. Kidnapping, burglary, extortion, and underworld violence were commonplace at the time." And close to home. A mother of children they taught was killed in a burglary; an acquaintance's brother was roasted alive in a basement bar, gasoline poured and set alight by a gangster; one of his young students was apparently beaten to death by his father; a male Canadian teacher was kidnapped; and a female American teacher was drugged and raped.

For a spirited defense of Taiwan's Mandopop, you can read Marc L. Moskowitz's *Cries of Joy, Songs of Sorrow* (2009). In this academic but readable book, Moskowitz (author of *The Haunting Fetus*, which we encountered earlier) argues convincingly that Taiwan's pop music has more depth to it than most Westerners appreciate, and that the dominance of Taiwanese music in China's music market (much diminished in the decade since the book was published) was a remarkable achievement, the infiltration not only shaping Chinese music but having an immense influence on popular culture.

* * *

One band bringing memorable color to the Taiwan music scene is the Muddy Basin Ramblers, formed in 2002, the name a reference to the rainy weather of the Taipei basin. The Ramblers' playlist runs across a broad swath of old-time American music – bluegrass, blues, jazz, and hillbilly swing. One of the six core band members is T.C. Lin, who plays the trumpet and washtub bass, and who is also an accomplished photographer, filmmaker, and writer. His ***Barbarian at the Gate: From the American Suburbs to the Taiwanese Army*** (2014), published under the name T.C. Locke, is the unique account of a how a white American came to do military service in the ROC Army in the 1990s and what he experienced.

Military service is for many Taiwanese males the most memorable experience of their lives, a difficult rite of passage into manhood – of becoming a *guolairen*, someone who has "been through it." Traditionally remembered with horror and nostalgia, compulsory military service has in recent years been softened and shortened, down to four months and possibly to be phased out completely. When Locke was drafted in 1996, compulsory military service was for two years.

Locke had fallen in love with Taiwan during a year of language study in 1988–1989. He decided to make the island his home and, with some difficulty, acquired Taiwanese citizenship in 1994. A couple of years later, he received in the mail an order from the draft board to present himself at a government office in Hsinchu. It was an unexpected and unwanted shock, one that meant dropping his "wonderful new life" for the next two years. He started worrying about being able to handle it, recalling all too vividly the horror stories his male Taiwanese friends had spun.

Army veterans had told of being forced to spend hours lying on the parade ground under the fierce summer sun, suffocating inside heavy quilts, while men who had served in the navy told stories of ship decks covered in rats, which were collected by aboriginal sailors to be traded for extra leave time, and unpopular sailors being thrown overboard in the dead of night. A former infantry soldier had described his company being made to complete rounds of physical training with bars of soap in their mouths, being allowed to stop only if the soap not only remained in place, but also showed no teeth marks.

Like the majority of draftees, Locke served in the army. Basic training at boot camp – and service afterward – was tougher than most readers will expect; it was physically demanding, the discipline strict, and with shouting hard-ass sergeants from central casting. Although the conscripts might have been civilians only yesterday, they were trained with a seriousness indicating possible deployment, which was not entirely impossible given the political situation. In the run-up to Taiwan's first presidential election, in March 1996, China was threatening invasion and "testing" missiles in the seas around Taiwan. Locke says, "The base was on alert most of the time, and our drill sergeants were often called out at night for extra guard duty, making them even crankier during the daytime."

T.C. on guard duty

Military life was a daunting challenge for the perennial outsider, the soft-spoken introvert needing to conform to military life in a setting – where, as the only Westerner – he was to be the ultimate odd-man-out. However, although boot camp was hard, Locke was pleasantly surprised to find himself as just one of the men and not treated like an outsider. "None of the soldiers ever tried to speak to me in English; no one ever assumed that I didn't speak

Chinese, used idiotic sign language or spoke extra slow and overly loud, staring intently at me as they did so to 'help' me understand them. In most respects, I'd been treated exactly the same as any other recruit."

Locke served the rest of his two years at a mountain base in Miaoli County, his assignments ranging from guard duty at gates (hence the title), to running a karaoke bar for officers, to slaughtering diseased pigs.

Over time he developed a deeper sense of belonging and acceptance than he ever had before. "I'd finally reached an acceptable balance between my American upbringing and my current Taiwanese life. I'd never be fully Taiwanese, nor would I ever be fully American." But he was fine with it.

Among the things he learned in the military was conversational Taiwanese (though "riddled with various swear words"). Locke makes an important observation about the difference between the use of Mandarin and Taiwanese.

Throughout my time in the army, Taiwanese, as opposed to Mandarin Chinese, held a special purpose for certain types of communication. Mandarin was the "official" language for orders and everything "above the table." But Taiwanese – which is not actually from Taiwan originally but rather from China's Fujian Province, where the language is known as Minnan – was a *si-di-xia* or "under the table" language, used for more intimate, personal communication. At formation, when someone wanted to say something unofficial or off-the-record to an officer, they used Taiwanese, the connotation of which was "Hey, this is what I honestly feel," as opposed to the "this is the official version" feeling of Mandarin.

Another deep insight he shares relates to the less legalistic, rules-based nature of doing things the local way:

> Life in the Taiwanese military, or in Taiwanese society for that matter, was never about following strict rules and definitions; it was about doing what had to be done with a minimum of trouble for everyone involved. The rules, not unlike the tones in the Chinese language itself, were merely a rough guide at best. It was this system that had kept everything going despite enormous setbacks, kept society operating in circumstances under which it had every right to fall apart.

An earlier version of Locke's conscription memoir came out in Chinese in 2003 under the title "Taiwan mantou – Meiguo bing" ("Taiwanese Steamed Bun, American Soldier"). The "mantou" in the title is a colloquial reference to doing military service. Locke explains:

> *Mantou* is a ubiquitous type of steamed bread many people in Taiwan eat for breakfast and a staple of the average institutional diet. If a soldier ate one of these a day for two years, by the time he had eaten 730, constituting a proverbial "mountain of *mantou*," he would then be finished with his service. So "counting *mantou*" denotes spending time in the military. Not coincidentally, it is also used for prison sentences.

* * *

The Third Cross-Strait Crisis of 1995–1996 may have abated, but the year 1997 was not a good one for Taiwan; a decade after the lifting of martial law, a wave of violent crime – amplified in the public imagination by a new freewheeling media – had Taiwanese deeply concerned about civil order. The nadir came with the remarkable case of Chen Chin-hsing, an eight-month crime saga that gripped the country. The life-and-death climax of this tragedy involved an expat family from South Africa and was played out live on national television. The father, a former parachute brigade commander, and then South African military attaché to Taiwan, McGill Alexander, tells what happened in **Hostage in Taipei: A True Story of Forgiveness and Hope** (2000).

The book opens on the evening of November 18, 1997, with Alexander just home from the embassy and settling down to relax in the living room, when a disheveled stranger suddenly appeared, one arm around his twelve-year-old daughter Christine's neck and a pistol pointed at her head. The family – Alexander, wife Anne, daughters Christine and twenty-two-year-old Melanie, and adopted infant son Zachary – had been taken hostage by a man they had seen in "wanted" posters: Taiwan's most notorious criminal, Chen Chin-hsing.

Seven months earlier, on April 14, Chen and two accomplices, Lin and Kao, had kidnapped sixteen-year-old Pai Hsiao-yen, the daughter (and only child) of a celebrity singer and television personality named Pai Ping-ping. The mother was a household name and presence – a former teen singer and actress, and now a middle-aged TV host. After abducting the girl on her way to school in Taipei County, the kidnappers demanded US$5 million and sent a severed finger to show their seriousness. Chen and his accomplices failed to turn up at a series of drop-off points, fearing that Pai had been tailed by police or media. In anger, the kidnappers beat the girl, so badly, in fact, that she died from internal bleeding. This did not stop them from still trying to collect the ransom.

On April 25, police converged on Chen Chin-hsing's apartment in Sanchong, Taipei, but he managed to escape. The next day police closed in on him again. He escaped in a firefight, and a massive manhunt was launched west of Taipei. On April 28, Pai Hsiao-yen's naked, battered corpse was found in a drainage ditch on the outskirts of Taiwan. She'd been dumped there about ten days earlier.

The month of May proved frustrating for the police. Mounting public anger at the epidemic of violent crime and police impotence was expressed in mass demonstrations. Six months earlier the nation had been shocked by the still unsolved, execution-style killing of the Taoyuan County magistrate and seven associates. Later that month (November) the murdered, naked body of feminist politician Peng Wan-ru was found outside an abandoned warehouse on the outskirts of Kaohsiung. Last seen getting into a yellow taxi, she had been raped and stabbed more than thirty times. This was another unsolved crime.

After laying low for months, the fugitive Chen and two accomplices kidnapped a businessman in the Taipei suburb of Beitou, managed to extort NT$4 million (US$130,000), and disappeared. Days later, the trio robbed a house in Taipei. Public pressure mounted and the police further ratcheted up their efforts. On August 19 a tip-off enabled the police to corner Chen's two accomplices in a dead-end alley in central Taipei. Two hundred police secured the area. A shootout left one policeman dead and another seriously wounded; one of the wanted men, Lin, shot himself in the head rather than be taken alive. The other, Kao, managed to slip through the cordon. And once again the police were under the media glare.

After a period of quiet, Chen's crime spree resumed, first with the rape of a female high school student. (Chen would later be accused of eighteen rapes and admit to more, though he had lost count and couldn't be sure.) Then on October 23, at a plastic surgery clinic on Taipei's Roosevelt Road, three corpses were found: the surgeon, his wife, and a nurse, murdered, and the nurse raped beforehand. Kao had had eyelid surgery and they'd stabbed and shot the three to leave no witnesses behind.

Kao was spotted ten days later in the Taipei suburb of Shilin but, an exchange of gunfire and chase notwithstanding, got away; and the ensuing large-scale manhunt came up empty. The police eventually caught Kao on November 17 in a brothel; he died in a firefight, but as with Lin it was from him taking his own life, not from a police bullet.

Chen would make his final dramatic move the following day. His wife had been given a twelve-year sentence as an accomplice in the kidnapping and murder of Pai Hsiao-yen. He insisted on their innocence and thought he might be able to push for their release if he had some foreign hostages. After taking the Alexander family hostage, Chen called the police, who arrived in force, the media hot on their heels. McGill Alexander says that the police were trigger happy, opening fire on the house, he and the other family members shouting for them to stop. The next police move was to storm the house; but the attempt was stymied. Alexander was accidently shot in the leg by Chen, and daughter Melanie was hit in the wrist and back. Chen allowed them to leave for hospital treatment – unarmed police chief Hou You-yi personally coming in and taking the two wounded family members out.

Struggling through the media scrums to the waiting ambulances proved an infuriating ordeal. The media, from the very beginning of the case had behaved badly – by interfering in the ransom drop-offs, publishing a photograph of the naked corpse of Pai Hsiao-yen, giving Chen a sympathetic platform as a Robin Hood figure, and more. Alexander doesn't hold back, comparing them to "a pack of African wild dogs." That's not a throwaway line either; one chapter is titled "Wild Dogs."

The standoff continued, all watched live on television throughout Taiwan, including telephone conversations between Chen and TV stations. With government promises to reexamine his wife's sentence, Chen eventually gave himself up.

The twenty-hour ordeal makes for a gripping narrative, though appreciation of the heavy Christian focus that permeates *Hostage in Taipei* will vary depending on how you see such things. The Alexanders believe their hostage taking happened for a reason; it was as an avenue for Chen to find Christ and be saved. Chen found God during his incarceration (he was executed by firing squad on October 6, 1999). He had been moved by the Alexanders, their faith and praying, and their forgiveness. Gill and his wife corresponded with Chen and visited him in prison to present him with a Bible. The conversion of Chen is given as a positive ending to the story, a wicked man turning to God. However, even the author admits that it is difficult to be sure whether Chen, "showman and a manipulator of the media *par excellence*," was sincere.

* * *

Chen Chin-hsing's deadly rampage is obviously one of the inspirations behind Alvin Lu's atmospheric thriller **The Hell Screens** (2000), a beautifully written, wonderfully paranoid vision of late 1990s Taipei. In the novel, Chinese-American Cheng-Ming is obsessed with a serial rapist-murderer known as the Taxi Driver Killer, or simply K, who is terrorizing Taipei. The police are constantly closing in on the killer but are never quite able to catch him. Like real-life killer Chen Chin-hsing, K is in frequent communication with the media (mailing letters to the press), scorning his pursuers and taking pleasure in his infamy.

Despite a confusing plot of blurred times, places, and personalities, *The Hell Screens* is a powerful work with some of the best writing I've seen in a Taiwan novel. The prose is eerie, hypnotic, immersive, strange, challenging. Here's a passage with protagonist Cheng-Ming in a taxi moving through the streets of Taipei:

Under stoplights amid the flooding, we were snarled with other vehicles. Red neon turned the sidewalks into scenes of carnage soaking the dark earth. I read electric signs fixed to buildings by metal scaffolding, their downpour of characters suggesting a world of gardens, bamboos, phoenixes, and willow trees, a book of poetry come unraveled and its pages lit on fire. Still, I could not read them as anything other than pictures.

As the cab sunk into richer fog, the driver turned on the air conditioning to bring a clean chill over the car's interior. Outside, on the sidewalk by a temple spouting incense smoke from artificial waterfalls, blind masseuses in makeshift plastic-sheet ponchos set up aluminum chairs, offering salvation to the teeming, suffering backs lined up before them. On the other side of the street, candy-colored lights of betel nut stands swirled, illuminating the rain in seductive colors. We circumvented the city's dense inner neighborhoods by turning onto a newly built highway that traced the outskirts along the river. Through the fogged windows, the river was only a wash of green and gray that rose so that it was difficult to separate water and shore and it seemed that we were about to be swallowed by the waves.

11

LOST GIRLS AND
HAPPY RENUNIFICATIONS

THE 1997 Chen Chin-hsing case might well have been an abject nadir for the fourth estate, but at least they would redeem themselves the following year with an international adoption drama, the subject of *Kartya's Story* (1999). Written by adoptive mother Nola Wunderle, it was republished in 2013 in an updated version with the more accurate title of **Lost Daughter: A Daughter's Suffering, a Mother's Unconditional Love, an Extraordinary Story of Hope and Survival.**

It's 1981 in Melbourne, Australia. Nola and Othmar Wunderle, already parents to two boys and an adopted girl, are waiting at the airport for their fourth child, nine-month-old Kartya. The only time they've "seen" her is a photo taken about five months previously. This long-anticipated meeting is bittersweet; instead of the happy, plump baby in the photo, she's now a scrawny, sickly, screaming baby who avoids eye contact and has scars and discoloration around her wrists and ankles, indicating she had been tied up and neglected. The Wunderles are left wondering what the backstory is: all they know is that according to the adoption papers, she is Lin Mei-li, third daughter of Lin Ah-hua, with no father named.

One day in 1982 Nola Wunderle received, out of the blue, a telephone call from Taiwan. It was a journalist from the *United Daily News* newspaper, asking about the adoption and reaction to the news. What news? The lawyer involved in Kartya's adoption had been charged with offenses related to illegally sending children overseas for adoption. Nola assured the journalist all the paperwork was in order, the baby willingly given up by the mother. In the coming days the Taiwan story made the international press, with headlines such as "45 Detained over Baby Trade Racket," "Babies Sold for Adoption, Say Police," and "Interpol to Help Stolen Babies' Natural Parents." A Taipei-based ring of doctors, midwives, and lawyers were being investigated for involvement in buying and selling about sixty-four babies for adoption. The Wunderles heard nothing more from the media and were not contacted by the authorities, so assumed everything was okay and that Kartya's adoption was not under scrutiny.

Raising Kartya proved difficult. She was a moody, rebellious child, a troubled teen who skipped school, took drugs, and periodically ran away from home. For despairing mother Nola, it seemed that the root cause was Kartya's identity issues, and she became convinced that finding the birth mother was a matter of life and death.

Nola tracked down an Australian journalist in Taipei named Ian Hyslop. He and his Taiwanese wife, Kathy, were moved by the story and agreed to help. Good news came through in a fax: Hyslop explained they'd helped track down the mother's residence; she was out but he would soon speak to her. Elation turned to despair when the next fax message arrived. Hyslop had talked to Lin Ah-hua, but she was not the birth mother. She had lent her name for the paperwork but didn't know the real birth mother. It was a terrible blow; the seventeen-year-old Kartya reacted badly, temporarily running away from home and going back on heroin.

The good news, Hyslop said, was that the Taiwan media and authorities would try their best to find Kartya's mother. As part of the publicity-driven search, Nola and Kartya flew into Chiang Kai-shek International Airport on June 5, 1998. Despite it being close to midnight when they exited customs, they found dozens of reporters awaiting them, the first taste of a media frenzy. Taiwan television gave the story huge coverage, and multiple women came forward as possible mothers. While awaiting the results of DNA tests, Nola and Kartya were shown around the island, people young and old recognizing Kartya from the coverage. A little over a week after arriving, there was a match, and – in the early hours of the morning, so as to elude media scrutiny – an emotional meeting of birth mother and daughter took place. Before the reunion, the police told Kartya what they had learned about her abandonment. The birth mother had been unmarried, with Kartya her second daughter. Her deadbeat partner sold Kartya (for about NT$36,000) without the mother knowing. The horrified mother tried to get the baby back but couldn't, and left her boyfriend, who died at the age of thirty-two from alcoholism.

After the reunion, Kartya stayed on with her new family; but things didn't go well – her drinking, and anti-social, moody behavior causing problems. She moved back to Australia, resumed taking drugs, and became a single mother. It was not a Hollywood ending, but, as the subtitle says, a story of survival, which is something.

* * *

Thirteen years later, the Taiwanese media once again lent a helping hand in reuniting a daughter with her family. This time the case didn't involve the adoption of a baby but the sale of a seven-year-old girl into indentured servitude, a story told in *My Name Is Also Freedom: The Shari Ho Story* (2018), by Melodie Fox and Shari Ho.

Ho, from the Paiwan tribe of southern Taiwan, first came to public attention in November 2011, when CNN broadcast a report on modern-day slavery. It featured a young woman in California who had been sold in the mid-1980s by her impoverished parents to a wealthy family in Taipei who later emigrated to California. After twenty years of unpaid drudgery and ill-treatment she had managed to escape and seek assistance. The CNN story created a media storm in Taiwan; Ho became a household name, and it wasn't long before her family members were found.

After seeing media reports about the case, a young woman came forward claiming to be a younger sister (this would in time be confirmed) and the seventy-one-year-old mother was soon in the spotlight, expressing a wish to see her daughter once again, a hope given special urgency as she was suffering from oral cancer. Not surprisingly, considering Taiwanese sensitivity to overseas news coverage of the country – and what could be worse than the taint of slavery – the government and China Airlines stepped in to pay for and organize a trip to reunite Ho with her family in Taitung.

Ho's sad story was the product of her father's alcoholism; he was abusive at home and unable to hold down a job. His drinking would lead to an early grave – riding while heavily intoxicated, he died in a motorcycle accident in 1994. Although recollections of her childhood are mostly hazy, one of Ho's vivid memories is of a baby sister being sold to a couple (luckily, she would be treated as a real daughter, not indentured labor).

In 1985 the father took Ho, the second of six girls, to various factories, hoping to sell her, but he was told she was too small. With the help of a broker, he found a prospective buyer – a rich old woman in Taipei who needed help with housework – willing to pay NT$10,000 (about US$320) for the girl.

The Old Lady – she is never referred to by name – was a cruel woman of about seventy, who treated Ho harshly from the very beginning, constantly berating the girl and sometimes administering beatings. Ho was never allowed to attend school, never taught to read or write. She started work before dawn and seldom went to bed before midnight.

In 2002 the Old Lady's family emigrated to the United States and Ho went with them. The move actually made things harder; before she had taken care of one person, but in the States that was widened to the Old Lady, a bigger house, the "Daughter" and her husband, and also cleaning the Daughter's store. At the store, however, she struck up a clandestine relationship of shared smiles and a few cordial words with a good Samaritan who sensed something was wrong and helped rescue Ho in 2005.

The police and the Human Trafficking Task Force became involved. There was a court case, but – as with many parts of the memoir – the details are unclear, leaving us wondering what happened. Author Melodie Fox tells Shari Ho's story with great sympathy, though perhaps sometimes this has meant not pushing for or presenting difficult questions. Writing an autobiography (the book is in the first person) for a survivor of horrendous abuse is obviously a challenging task. You have a shy, traumatized speaker periodically breaking into tears, illiterate and unskilled in communication, and not entirely comfortable in English (or Chinese for that matter), no written records to supplement memories, and you want to write the book in the subject's voice, not your own.

My Name Is Also Freedom has a strong Christian flavor. Thankfully, this never takes the form of denigrating heathen Taiwan, which would actually be difficult given that Ho's family and the Old Lady were also Christians, the latter being a regular church attendee. The tone of the book is not accusatory toward Taiwan, Shari's family, or the Paiwan community.

At the same time that Shari Ho's book came out, the publisher Sherry Ward released a companion title, **Finding Freedom Was Just the Beginning** (2018), which is her "behind-the-scenes look" at the making of *My Name Is Also Freedom*. The subtitle "God's Hand in the Journey" gives a good indication of the heavy religious content of this short work. I read it to see if any of the unanswered questions I had from the first book would be addressed.

Sherry Ward runs a company called Square Tree Publishing, which provides services for people wanting to go the self-publishing route. She was feeling frustrated about the books she was working on not being the right match for her values, when, meeting Shari at a women's conference at her church, she decided a book on Ho's story would be the meaningful project she was craving.

Ho was cautious about doing a book and it took a while for her to agree. The project got going in early 2015, when Melodie Fox, Ward's friend and a content editor for her publishing company, began getting Ho's experiences down on paper. It was a three-and-a-half-year adventure. Any publisher or author will understand Ward's sentiments when she admits there were "many nights of crying out to God, 'When God ... when ... when will the book be done?'"

She says the book took so long to write because of Fox's time-consuming research – more than forty interviews with Ho and those involved with her story – and her determination to get it right. Part of this thoroughness involved a trip by the Square Tree team – Ho, Ward, Fox, and a translator – to Taiwan in January 2018. This trip makes up the bulk of *Finding Freedom Was Just the Beginning*.

Ho took her companions to places from her old life in Taipei: it was a way to put the past behind her and also useful for Fox in her writing. They went to shops and markets, the apartment where she had lived, and to a park, where Ho showed them her favorite tree. It was an old one whose upper foliage had been cut in a boxy shape. For Ward, this was a match with Square Tree Publishing, bringing the author to new tears at God's providential hand.

The book has a lot of looking for the hand of God, a relentless joining of dots to find his workings, and no more so than when they visit Elim, a Christian bookstore and publisher in Taipei. Ward wanted to talk about a possible translation of the yet unfinished book. During the discussion Elim president Elder Huang related in tearful testimony a traumatic experience from his college days: visiting an aboriginal village on the East Coast, he had been an impotent witness to a girl being sold for money and liquor. Unable to do anything to help that girl then, now was his chance, and he promised to take on the book.

After that meeting, Ward went into a prayer room at the Elim bookstore, where a Taiwanese lady pointed out the resemblance of the Square Tree Publishing logo to the sign of Asher, the eighth tribe of Judah, for which they sometimes prayed. The author, overcome at this and several other coincidences showing God's omnipresence, remarks in awe, "God is HUGE!"

As an agnostic I'm not the target audience, so I can't complain about the amount of religious content, but I wish it were accompanied by the application of the idiom, "God is in the detail." Alas, the book falls short in answering basic journalistic questions of *who*, *what*, *when*, *where*, and *why*, and reading it feels like having a conversation with someone in a witness-protection program. For example, we learn that, "The original contract for her indentured servitude was for a set amount of time," but there are no further details.

My criticisms aside, Ward is to be commended for publishing Shari Ho's story; it's a reminder to be vigilant to human trafficking and the suffering of those around us, and more specifically, it tells of the lingering desperate poverty among certain communities in Taiwan as late as the 1980s. Even in her small district of Dawu Township, Shari Ho was just one of many young women sold. It was a nationwide phenomenon; in fact, the sale of aboriginal girls into prostitution was so serious a problem in the 1980s that the fight to end it would lead to criminalizing prostitution.

* * *

A better written and more uplifting memoir of a Taiwanese girl given away by her parents is journalist Mei-ling Hopgood's **Lucky Girl** (2010). Mei-ling was adopted in 1974 from Taitung, in the then relatively remote southeast, by an American couple from Michigan. She had a happy childhood, with two adopted boys from South Korea as playmates and adoring parents, and felt little desire to trace her roots. Mei-ling assumed she had escaped poverty and was grateful.

The go-between who had made the adoption happen was a young American nun from Detroit (a relative of a friend of the Hopgoods) called Sister Maureen Sinnott. Sister Maureen had arrived in Taiwan in 1967, and, after two years in Hsinchu studying Mandarin with fellow nuns and priests, served as a midwife in St. Mary's Hospital in Taitung. (You might recall that this is the hospital to which Barry Martinson donated the royalties from his book *Song of Orchid Island*.)

Sister Maureen was contacted by the Hopgoods, who asked about the possibility of adopting a child. And, indeed, there was a father – with five girls already and unable to afford another – looking to give away a newly born sixth girl.

Clearing the bureaucratic hurdles took about eight months, during which time Maureen took care of the baby. The girl was given the name Mei-ling (Maureen's Chinese name). Maureen kept up occasional correspondence with the Hopgoods through the years, and spoke with Mei-ling when she was in her early twenties. Maureen asked if she should make enquiries about the family. Mei-ling didn't sound enthusiastic, so the nun didn't follow up. Later Mei-ling asked Maureen if she had written to the hospital. Maureen took the question as a request to write; she did so and learned that both parents were from Kinmen, the father a farmer and the mother a housewife, aged 59 and 54 respectively. Mei-ling had eight siblings: six sisters in Taiwan and one adopted brother, and a sister given up for adoption to a couple in Switzerland. The family was delighted to be reconnected and asked Mei-ling to come for Chinese New Year (February 1997). In fact, they were scarily keen, bombarding her with letters, email messages, faxes, and phone calls, with little concern shown for social niceties, such as when requesting she buy and bring some large-sized clothing for her "fat brother" and fish oil for her birth father's digestive problems. Unfiltered but also generous, the father repeatedly offered to pay for Mei-ling's airfare to Taiwan. She decided to go at the end of March 1997, paying her own way but accepting the ticket fare for Sister Maureen, who came along for moral support and translation help.

The entire family, whom the author refers to as the Wangs, were waiting for Mei-ling at the airport. It was an overwhelming reunion, a loving embrace by a large, noisy family. Despite the language barrier she quickly bonded with her sisters, though wasn't quite sure what to make of her blustery father and docile mother.

Mei-ling was impressed by how developed Taiwan was and also how middle-class her sisters were; they were all educated and working:

what struck me most was the realization that my siblings were not merely the children of a poor farming family, as I had believed. If I had an image of my birth family at all in my head, it had been in black and white and dismal. They would be gaunt, wearing ragged clothes and probably standing in some barren field with a shabby, straw-roofed hut at their backs, a stereotypical portrait of third-world poverty. I mean, that was why they had given me up for adoption, right?

The family *had* been poor; but that was not the entire story. Between that 1997 reunion and the publication of *Lucky Girl* in 2010, Mei-ling made several further trips back to Taiwan, gradually learning more about her family, quite a lot of it rather dark and related to her biological father's determination to have sons. The father was one of nine sons, six of whom had died in childhood. In his mind, the survival of the family required a male heir to support and care for the parents in old age, to carry the family name and bloodline, and to worship the ancestral line.

In 1965 Mrs. Wang had given birth to a boy. Unfortunately, he was sickly and had a cleft palate. The mother believed the father knocking a hole in a house wall had somehow injured the baby; according to this widely held superstition, house repairs during pregnancy can cause deformities. The facial defect could have been remedied with surgery, if they'd been able to afford it. Within a few days of his birth, the boy was dead. The grandmother and father, deciding the child would face a miserable life and thus was better off dead, laid the boy on a bed and withheld nourishment.

When the family moved from Kinmen to Taitung in 1972, they met an impoverished couple who, unable to feed their baby son, gave him to the Wangs. Misfortune struck again in the form of a severe fever, which seems to have caused some mental retardation. The quest for a worthy male heir continued; but the mother kept producing girls: Mei-ling in 1973 and then another girl, who would also be adopted, this time by a couple in Switzerland.

The book is full of further revelations, including the father bringing a mistress into the house. Although Mei-ling was disgusted by his behavior, she also found her birth mother's submissiveness disheartening. And Mei-ling wondered about the role of the grandmother. This woman, who "bore nine boys – three of whom survived" ... "had the final say behind so many key decisions: when to give and not to give a child away, when to adopt one."

The question of keeping or giving away a girl was a mixture of harsh practicalities and superstition. The grandmother insisted the family keep the fourth daughter as she had a red mark on her head like a successful Chinese emperor: the girl would likely bring luck to the family. Similarly, the youngest girl, born three years after Mei-ling, was kept, because she was born in the auspicious year of the dragon.

Mei-ling Hopgood writes with great humor, passion, and fairness. *Lucky Girl* is by far the best Taiwan adoption story available in English; it's fascinating material, satisfying in terms of narrative arc and the mysteries solved, and it's very well written. Unlike most adoption memoirs it's a story that will appeal to all readers. And despite some darkness, it's a heart-warming book: Mei-ling reuniting with her family is not just gaining a new family and culture but a look at the possible life she might have had. She comes away from it more appreciative than ever of how lucky she was. The book is dedicated to her adoptive parents: *For Rollie and Chris.*

* * *

Lucky Girl was an inspiration for another Taiwan adoption book, Marijane Huang's **Beyond Two Worlds: A Taiwanese-American Adoptee's Memoir and Search for Identity** (2017).

Four-month-old Marijane was adopted from a Taipei orphanage in 1966 by an American military family based in Okinawa, the father with the U.S. Air Force (a B-24 pilot in the European theater during the Second World War) and the mother a nurse.

Marijane grew up in Louisiana, where she was often the only Asian face, believing she was of Vietnamese and Japanese ethnicity and with little interest in her birth parents or identity (though coincidentally or not marrying an American of Vietnamese-Japanese heritage).

After her adoptive mother died in 2008, Marijane, then forty-two, saw for the first time her adoption papers. She was shocked to learn that her biological parents were in fact Chinese (from Guangxi Province), the mother thirty-nine and the father fifty-five at the time of her birth. She'd been given up for adoption because the family was too poor.

The revelation compelled her to investigate her roots. Marijane figured that her parents would already be dead but also that there would be family members who knew something. Internet searches led nowhere and she felt like giving up. In 2009 she met Mei-ling Hopgood at a book signing for her memoir *Lucky Girl*. Though Hopgood couldn't help with specific practical leads, Huang gained renewed determination from meeting Hopgood.

Even with the help of an adoption agency social worker originally from Taiwan, it was a long, frustrating path. However, in 2011 she made contact with her siblings: two older sisters and an older brother. Marijane flew to Taipei in early 2012 for a reunion, her siblings delighted to see their long-lost sister (and their comfortable lives a dramatic illustration of Taiwan's progress during the decades).

Although of likely interest to adoptees, *Beyond Two Worlds* lacks the drama and interest of *Lucky Girl*. There really isn't enough material for a book: a two-week visit to Taiwan, no living parents, and very little family history explained. It would have made sense to compensate by giving background information on adoption in Taiwan, but this is not explored.

* * *

The legalization of abortion in 1985 and the concurrent rise in sexual freedom – though one not matched with sexual education – as well as a desire for smaller families led to a dramatic increase in the number of abortions, both by unmarried mothers looking to end an inconvenient pregnancy and married women terminating an unwanted girl. In the 1990s at least thirty percent of all pregnancies in Taiwan ended in abortions. In response to this, there emerged religious services for the appeasement of the spirits of these aborted fetuses. This is the subject of a fascinating academic title from the University of Hawai'i Press, *The Haunting Fetus: Abortion, Sexuality, and the Spirit World in Taiwan* (2001), by Marc L. Moskowitz.

Moskowitz, now a professor of anthropology at the University of South Carolina, lived in Taiwan from 1994 to 1999. He was studying Mandarin in Taipei and preparing for a dissertation on family planning when, eighteen months into his stay, he heard a chance mention of the belief in "the haunting fetus." He had found himself a new dissertation topic: "Fetus-Spirits: New Ghosts in Modern Taiwan."

The Haunting Fetus doesn't read like an academic book that started life as a doctoral dissertation. Moskowitz avoids jargon, and he has a talent for writing; it's no surprise that his undergraduate degree was in English literature. He handles a delicate, gruesome subject with sensitivity, empathy, and – where appropriate – humor.

Moskowitz interviewed dozens of women and also some men who had direct experience with fetus ghosts, and various Buddhist and Taoist masters – ranging from the sincere to the comically dubious.

Fetus spirits are considered potentially malevolent; if they should seek revenge, they're capable of inflicting sickness, injury, and even death. They almost never remain in fetus form as spirits, typically appearing as if physically one to five years old but mentally more mature, and are often believed to be omniscient.

They appear in dreams to women or are cited as a reason for a woman's misfortune by religious practitioners. The author even met women who had been approached on the street by strangers or by taxi drivers claiming to have the "third eye" (i.e., the ability to see ghosts) and telling them that they could see a fetus ghost following them. Help was offered, at a price.

To appease or exorcise fetus ghosts, various services are available, ranging from individuals operating at home to large temples dedicated almost exclusively to this purpose. Moskowitz visited the largest such temple, Dragon Lake Temple in Miaoli County. The temple, founded in 1975 by a retired school teacher was a mix of Taoist, Buddhist, Confucian, and folk religion components, typical of the syncretic nature of religion in Taiwan. The appeasement process took three years at an annual fee of NT$1200 (US$35). Worshippers were given a red contract, "essentially a legal petition to the gods and fetus ghosts," which stated the person's guilt, apology, and commitment to appease the fetus ghost for three years. This legalist element is a central part of Chinese religion (temples are in many ways representations of heavenly court, with statues of deities presiding as court officials). Prayers were made, incense and ghost money burned, and the worshippers received a fetus ghost statue, about a foot high and made of solid metal. The contract was sometimes read aloud in front of the statue. Attendance at Dragon Lake Temple was also required at special ceremonies twice a year.

Moskowitz says the temple contained 16,400 fetus ghost statues and averaged 5,400 new fetus ghost cases each year. Appeasement on a massive scale, efficient and reasonably priced, profitable but not a rip-off. Other temples and practitioners the author investigated were more expensive.

Moskowitz concludes that fetus appeasement is sometimes financially exploitative but provides psychological comfort in helping alleviate parents of guilt.

The practice of commercial fetus ghost appeasement is not as ancient as one tends to expect of Asian superstitious practices. It seems to have appeared in the 1970s and grew rapidly in the 1980s, inspired by a phenomenon in Japan, where it peaked from the mid-1970s to the mid-1980s. (Taiwan tends to follow Japanese and American trends, and also Korean ones these days.) Religious entrepreneurs introduced it to Taiwan. It was an attractive moneymaker for fortune-tellers, spirit mediums, and exorcists. Aborted fetuses were so common they were an easy target to blame for any problem. And a fetus ghost was easier to blame than a regular adult ghost, because unborn children receive no funeral.

Appeasing fetuses, however, was a not entirely imported practice; it had been done previous to the 1970s but less frequently and with much greater secrecy. The practice ties in with some old beliefs, such as prohibitions against premarital sex and most notably the Buddhist precept against the taking of life. However, as the author notes, making offerings to the spirits of a younger generation goes against Confucianism veneration of one's elders and ancestors.

The author saves the oddest aspect of fetus-ghost practices for the last chapter: "Blood-Drinking Fetus Demons: Greed, Loathing, and Vengeance through Sorcery in Taiwan." This is basically the black magic "raising" of fetus demons and setting them against one's enemies.

* * *

Another book that covers a religious fashion – this time Tibetan Buddhism in the 1990s – is *Searching for Buddha's Tooth: Personal Stories of Tibetan Culture* (2005), the debut work of talented Tibetan writer Tsering N. Khortsa, who developed his craft in Taiwan, including several years writing for the *Taipei Times* (under the name Tsering Namgyal). The book has ruminations on Tibetan exile, Buddhism, and literature. Tsering is part of the Tibetan diaspora – born in India, his father having fled communist rule in Tibet. The author first came to Taiwan in 1989 as a student on a Taiwan government scholarship, and material on Taiwan accounts for about one third of the book.

Searching for Buddha's Tooth opens with the 1999 arrival to much fanfare of a religious relic, a Buddha's tooth, which was likely a fake, and then a second relic a few months later. Tsering describes the Taiwanese fascination – often shallow – with Tibetan Buddhism; there are amusing anecdotes of Tibetan monks being asked for stock tips and romance advice.

The author highlights the parallels between the Tibetan and Taiwanese political situations, and the irony of the KMT's Tibet policy. The Chinese Nationalists and the Tibetans shared a mutual enemy and the common exile experience of recreating and holding onto their identities and the dream of returning. Thus, the KMT and Tibetans could have been useful allies. Instead, the KMT chose to maintain the fantasy that they had rights to Tibet (and the independent country of Mongolia for that matter). Good relations with the Dalai Lama's government-in-exile at Dharamsala would need to wait until the 1990s, culminating – to China's phlegmatic outrage – with the Dalai Lama's first historic visit to Taiwan in 1997. On a second visit in 2001, the author had the privilege of an audience with His Holiness.

12

Twenty-first Century Taiwan

WHEN setting an English-language novel in Taiwan, the writer is faced early on with a fundamental choice: will the main character or characters be outsiders or locals, or perhaps a Taiwanese-American to bridge the gap? Having a foreign main character allows for the readers – typically outsiders – to identify more closely. This also allows a parallel discovery of local customs by the protagonist and reader.

A rare case of going completely native is Joe Henley's superb *Bu San Bu Si: A Taiwan Punk Tale* (2017), a gritty journey into the underground music scene in Taipei. The novel has an all-local cast of characters (with the exception of a minor Filipino one); no need for a foreign guide, no cultural tourism — it throws you in for a full-on Taiwanese experience, crediting the reader with enough brains, life experience, and shared humanity to make sense of it all.

Of course, there's a world of difference between choosing a local perspective and being able to write one. Joe Henley, a Canadian freelance writer from Saskatchewan who came to Taipei after graduating from journalism school in 2005, is able to do so. Alongside writing ability, he has – as a metal/punk musician and a journalist covering the music scene in Taiwan – a surplus of hands-on experience.

The novel's forward matter contains an explanation of the title:

Bu san bu si, "Not three, not four." A Mandarin phrase used to describe someone who behaves in a strange and traditionally unacceptable way. An idiom reserved for punks, lowlifes, and gangsters — the so-called dregs of society.

Such is Xiao Hei, the novel's central character, a talented yet lazy young musician. He's looking for shortcuts to the incompatible mix of punk street-cred and the glamorous trappings of fame. Xiao Hei is bass guitarist in a four-man band called Resistant Strain, "a bunch of nobodies in a scene full of more nobodies," playing in dives "where everyone knew everyone and no one was anyone."

One of just two regular venues for Resistant Strain is Jackie's Bar, run by gangster Jackie.

Jackie's Bar was one of just a few places left standing where bands could play, one of fewer still that didn't make bands pay to play. At Jackie's everything was straight up. You played, you got fifty percent of the door. No bullshit. No gripes. Some of the swankier clubs in town had a minimum attendance they made the bands cover themselves. If a certain number of bodies didn't come through the door, the difference came out of the band's pocket at the end of the night. Whether it came willingly or by force, that was up to the players. But they always paid. Resistant Strain had played one show at one of those pay-to-play joints, a place called Brick City. At the end of the night the owner had come up to Xiao Hei with his hair slicked back and his hand out, demanding twenty thousand *kuai*. He never got the cash. What he did get was a slug in the nose and a few well-placed kicks in the ribs once he was on the ground.

Hard-nosed Jackie has a soft spot for Xiao Hei and is something of a father figure to the young man. Xiao Hei lives with his mother; his father ran off with another woman soon after Xiao Hei was born.

[Jackie liked Xiao Hei] because he played with heart. Xiao Hei wasn't flashy. He had skill, but not the kind he had to flaunt. Pretty good on the back-up vocals, too. And Resistant Strain wasn't like so many of the other bands who aped Western trends so faithfully that they might as well have been playing note-for-note renditions of a composite of the worst aspects of radio-friendly rock and pop. The Strain took Motörhead speed metal and topped it with a sneering teenage indolence that you either let society wrest away from you by the time you hit twenty-one or held onto forever, for better or for worse. Born to lose. Live to win. Part of him hoped they would hold on. Another part of him hoped they would wise up and go to business school or take up a trade.

They don't wise up. And Xiao Hei, in particular, is going to get an education the hard way.

* * *

Another novel that takes us into the gangster underworld is Francie Lin's **The Foreigner** (2008). The market response to the novel is a mystery. The book is little known despite winning an award and coming from a major publisher, Picador, which even went to the expense of doing an audio version – extremely rare for a Taiwan book. When I first came upon the novel, I was intrigued by the disconnect between the stellar critical reviews and the mediocre Amazon ones. Was the award basically a participation trophy? Some keyboard exploration ensued. What Lin had won was an Edgar Award for the category of Best First Novel by an American Writer; you may recall that *Dragon Hotel* author John Ball also won this award. The Edgars are bestowed – without an accompanying monetary prize – by the Mystery Writers of America organization, which isn't too shabby; so, in short, they're prestigious but cash-strapped. As for the discrepancy between critical and popular reviews, my black-hearted nepotism detectors went off when I read that author Francie Lin was a reviewer herself in her role as associate editor of a literary magazine and had reviewed books for the *Los Angeles Times*. It was time to read the novel.

The plot is as follows: the death of Emerson Chang's controlling mother sets the financial analyst and forty-year-old virgin on a journey from San Francisco to Taipei. He's in Taiwan to scatter his mother's ashes and settle her estate and re-establish contact with his wayward younger brother, Little P (P for Peter), whom he has not seen in a decade.

Emerson hardly recognizes Little P on meeting him; he's "lean, wolfish" and with stitches, bruises, and injuries suggesting a violent life. Little P works at their uncle's KTV parlor. An innocent though he is, when Emerson meets Little P's thuggish associates – Poison and Big One – he suspects his brother is involved in nefarious activities. As he learns more, family secrets unravel; soon he's in over his head and facing mortal danger.

The Foreigner, on top of covering the standard writing checklist points – plot, sub-plots to keep us guessing, characters, evocative descriptions (reflecting the author's time spent in Taiwan on a Fulbright Fellowship, gathering material for her novel) and so on – has two elements that stood out for me: the Chinese mother–son dynamic, and also having an Asian-American as foreigner in his own "homeland" (Emerson speaks neither Chinese nor Taiwanese, and is a cultural illiterate).

Although the story is interesting and well told, I came away surprised that *The Foreigner* had won an Edgar Award. The protagonist is just a little too much of a wimp, a little too naïve and ignorant of Taiwanese culture and language to be wholly convincing; and with a pure Emerson pitted against his bad brother, the story gets overly Old Testament at times.

Returning to the mystery of the novel's underperformance and poor customer reviews, I think there are three reasons: readers coming to it with high expectations because of the Edgar and positive newspaper reviews; readers' difficulty in relating to such a straight-laced forty-year-old virgin; and the novel not being a neat genre match – with its elements of self-discovery and family relations, it doesn't fall easily into the mystery, thriller, or crime slots. Also, the cash-less Edgar Award – which carries the expectation of "mystery" – seems to have created certain expectations. All in all, a novel worth reading, but we still await a great mystery set in Taiwan.

* * *

I believe every country should have its own English-language fictional detective series. And it doesn't matter if the protagonist is a private investigator, a police detective, or an amateur sleuth; as long as there are dead bodies and intrepid investigators on the trail of the killers.

With Japan we're spoiled for choice; offerings include James Melville's thirteen-book series featuring Superintendent Tetsuo

Otani of the Kobe Police Force. China has the Judge Dee series by Robert van Gulik, and others. Tibet is the setting for Eliot Pattison's Inspector Shan series. Even Laos has the twelve-book Dr. Siri Paiboun series by Colin Cotterill, chronicling the cases of an elderly physician and national coroner in the 1970s.

It's a shame Taiwan doesn't have anything to compare. I'm hopeful, though, that someone will take up the challenge. Detective stories often sell well, and, given their built-in audience for sequels, require less promotional slog. They also offer opportunities for film and television adaptations. At the moment, the Taiwanese crime bookshelf is limited to a single series, Ed Lin's three Taipei Night Market books – **Ghost Month** (2014), *Incensed* (2016), and *99 Ways to Die* (2018) – featuring young food vendor Jing-nan, who repeatedly finds himself drawn into crime cases.

Ghost Month incorporates several quintessential Taiwanese elements: religious superstitions, gangsters, night markets, and betel-nut girls. As the title indicates, the story is set during "ghost month," the seventh month of the Chinese calendar (typically falling in August) and a time when the dead roam the world of the living. The spirits – euphemistically referred to as "good brothers" rather than "ghosts" – are placated with offerings of food and ghost money. Superstitious in spite of its modernity, Taiwan takes the month seriously; house sales fall, weddings are avoided, and grandparents warn against going swimming because of the water ghosts.

The protagonist of *Ghost Month*, Jing-nan, runs a food stand in a Taipei night market. In Taiwan, some of these markets are weekly affairs – such as in the town I call home, where one comes to life every Saturday evening in front of a Taoist temple just twenty meters from my house. In some cities, however, larger night markets operate every day. The Shilin Night Market, where twenty-five-year-old Jing-nan has his food stand, is Taipei's biggest and best known.

Though *Ghost Month* has tremendous local color and is a likeable enough, it opens with what I think is an impossible plot premise. When Jing-nan sees a television news story about a scantily clad betel-nut girl who has been shot dead, he realizes she is his wife-to-be, Julia, whom he's not seen for seven years. Yes, seven years. Jing-nan and Julia were high school sweethearts. On graduation they both headed to study in the United States, but on opposite coasts — Jing-nan at UCLA and Julia at NYU. They agreed not to contact each other until Jing-nan was ready to marry her, and he would appear unannounced, a knight on a white horse carrying her off to be wed. Jing-nan returned to Taiwan after learning that his father had cancer; compounding matters, his mother died in a car accident on the way to the airport to pick him up. Jing-nan's dying father asked him to take over the family food stall at the Shilin Night Market. Jing-nan also inherited his grandfather's old gambling debt to the wrong kind of people. Years go by and Jing-nan was never in a position to marry Julia. And with her death it's too late. But he will get to the bottom of the murder despite being warned off by the CIA and gangster heat.

As I read on through the novel, the words "seven years" kept echoing in my thoughts. It's just implausible that, in the first place, the couple would agree to an excruciating open-ended arrangement and not contact one another through the years, and, second, that Jing-nan had not a single piece of news on Julia during that time from old classmates or mutual family acquaintances.

Jing-nan's food stand consists of "five solid tables set up with sturdy chairs, all under a roof," selling grilled meat on skewers and a spicy stew of intestines. He calls the stand Unknown Pleasures after the English post-punk band Joy Division's 1979 debut album. Jing-nan is a big fan, and there are numerous mentions of the band throughout the novel.

The character of Jing-nan is quite Westernized considering his brief stay in the United States. In some ways he's playing the role of tour guide for readers. *Ghost Month* is packed with digestible cultural, historical, and political information on Taiwan, which makes it a good choice for visitors and new arrivals to Taiwan. There's even an extensive glossary at the end of the book. The explanations do inevitably slow the pace of the narrative, especially in the first half; but I presume the author is writing primarily to a North American audience and sees them as a justifiable compromise.

Ghost Month presents Taiwan as a more dangerous place than residents will recognize; this is reasonable for a crime mystery, and there is actually a lot more happening behind the scenes than most people think. Author Ed Lin incorporates his background reading into the story. (In the glossary he recommends Ko-lin Chin's *Heijin: Organized Crime, Business, and Politics in Taiwan*, which he says "will leave you slack-jawed.") We learn about the *jiaotou*s – pseudo-gangsters rather than real ones, local enforcers who oversee a few blocks: "Most of their money comes from running the local temple – a major source of tax-free income – and bars and nightclubs."

Taiwan has larger, organized gangs (triads, if you will) such as the Bamboo Union and the Four Seas. These are relatively new, the two mentioned formed in the mid 1950s by mainlander youth. For the gang in *Ghost Month*, Lin has taken the precaution of an invented name: Black Sea.

From two-bit gangsters to food vendors to real estate developers, Lin presents a whole cross-section of society. Helping out at the Unknown Pleasures stand are an aborigine and an old mainlander, and a friendly fellow vendor is a Hakka. The novel emphasizes the ethnic divide between *benshengren* (native Taiwanese) and *waishengren* (mainlanders who came over with the KMT); although useful to readers imagining a monolithic Taiwanese population, the focus on this is slightly dated. The *benshengren-waishengren* dynamic probably reflects in part author Lin's family background, a first-generation American to a Taiwanese father and a mother from northern China (whose father was a KMT officer), with the homeland frozen, or lagging, in time to some extent, and the diaspora more polarized than the people in the home country.

Lin came to *Ghost Month* having written a crime mystery series about a Chinese-American policeman in New York's Chinatown of the 1970s. *Incensed* (2016), the second in Lin's Taipei Night Market series and a sequel to *Ghost Month*, is set during the Mid-Autumn Festival (Moon Festival), with Jing-nan looking after a troubled teenage girl as a favor for his gangster uncle. It has similar weaknesses and pleasures as the earlier novel; the mystery element could be stronger, but Jing-nan and his buddies are engaging characters and the local color is informative.

The night market is an excellent choice of fiction setting as it embodies so much of the national character and flavor: the neon, noise, good-natured bustle, and tolerant crowds rubbing shoulders without aggression; the vendors' entrepreneurial spirit; and the love of food and snacking. Yes, above all, night markets are about tasty snacks: stinky tofu, pig blood rice cakes, barbecued squid, oyster omelets, mini hot pots, pepper pork buns, and on and on.

* * *

The topic of food has long been a publishing industry staple around the world. For Taiwan, the standout English-language book success in recent years – other than the perennial chart-topping Lonely Planet travel guide – has been Cathy Erway's ***The Food of Taiwan: Recipes from the Beautiful Island*** (2015). Normally I would read such a bestseller right away, if not from interest, then at least from curiosity; but it took me three years to get around to doing so because Taiwanese food coverage is something to which I possess a knee-jerk hostility. Perhaps it's all those inane Facebook pictures, or it could be the local media's embarrassing fixation with and tourist authorities' would-be promotional material on the wonders of Taiwanese cuisine churned out the in the mistaken idea that the prime attraction for visitors is stuffing one's face with greasy night market snacks or bland regional dishes. The emphasis on local specialties is particularly annoying; anyone for Chiayi's square biscuits, Tainan's *danzi* noodles, Taichung's sun cookies, Penghu's brown sugar cake, or Changhua's *ba-wan* (basically a large dumpling with a gelatinous wrapping)? I'm nearly always underwhelmed when I try these starch-filled specialties: confirmation of my theory, which I mentioned earlier in this book, that if a food is sufficiently tasty it will spread. And it's always struck me that an overemphasis on the food of a place reveals a lack of interest and knowledge in other elements like history, flora and fauna, and art.

The Food of Taiwan, however, does a great job of going beyond the wok and bowl and incorporating Taiwan's history and culture. It is also in small part a memoir, as the author relates her family's connection with Taiwan and her own discovery of Taiwan and its cuisine. Erway is a well-known food blogger (Not Eating Out in New York) and the author of *The Art of Eating In* (2010), which describes her two-year abstinence from restaurants. She was born in the United States to a Taiwanese mother and an American father, her parents having met in Taipei in the 1970s. A first-generation American such as Erway would typically have spent several school vacations in Taiwan visiting relatives and learning Chinese, but her case was slightly different. Her mother's side of the family didn't have deep roots on the island, Erway's grandparents having immigrated to Taiwan from Hunan Province in 1948. And a few decades later, all her Taiwanese relatives – her grandparents and an uncle and aunt – had moved to the United States.

Erway did, however, decide to spend the 2004 spring semester of her last year in college in Taipei studying Chinese, and this is when her love affair with Taiwanese food began. It was both an exciting new experience and a kind of homecoming:

The world of Taiwan – and especially its food – became three-dimensional to me almost from the moment I stepped off the plane. Suddenly, all the foods that I had grown up eating made so much sense to me. All the aromas and tastes were so much richer. And they were so varied! While I could recall my mother making stir-fries with slivered pork and vegetables as a go-to dinner routine at home, in Taiwan I got to taste the tender, gelatinous strips of pork belly and crisp, herbal Chinese celery tossed rapidly together in a smoking-hot wok. The Taiwanese fried chicken, its crackly, seasoned crust served atop rice and a drizzle of sauce, was something that I'd never encountered at home. Salty, soothing eggs dyed from a warm bath of soy sauce–based broth that I snacked on frequently as a child were available everywhere in Taiwan, in all different shades and sizes. One slurp of a beef noodle soup's broth was practically enough protein for the day, so dense and satisfying it was – yet also so reminiscent of my mother's weekend favorite red-braised beef stews.

The Food of Taiwan has a long but interesting introduction; as well as her own personal story, there are sections on the history of the island, its people, the land, and agriculture. The food section starts with a useful primer on common ingredients: chili bean sauce, dried shiitake mushrooms, crushed peanut powder, dried baby shrimp, five-spice powder, rice wine, and so on. Then there are extensive recipe sections, including some of my favorites common dishes: beef noodles, peppery pork buns, and three-cup chicken. Whether you try any of the recipes or not, they're still informative, helping you match the ingredients and cooking methods with the final tastes you encounter; the "secret sauce" behind the food, so to speak.

Erway explains that she chose to focus on dishes for which ingredients – or substitutes – can be found in the United States. She describes but does not give a recipe for stinky tofu, which is a dish Taiwanese themselves don't attempt to make in their own kitchens. As Erway says: "no one would want to stink up their entire home for weeks or months to make it."

Interspersed among the recipes are interesting tidbits of background information. In the case of beef noodles, we learn:

> It's widely believed that this hallmark of Taiwanese cuisine was created within the military villages set up to accommodate the influx of mainlanders at the middle of the twentieth century. There is nowhere else a noodle soup quite like it, although the dish has conspicuous influences from Sichuan province — chili bean sauce and Sichuan peppercorns. Some call it Taiwan's "national dish," while others argue that Danzai Noodle Soup ... is more representative of older, more traditional Taiwanese cuisine.

The recipes are laid out in easy-to-follow steps. However, it's difficult to predict how much success you'll have in replicating them back home. My own attempts to cook Taiwanese food for family members during trips back to New Zealand have not covered me in glory. I think it takes a bit of trial and error, such as getting a feeling for the flavors and saltiness of the soy sauce and rice wine used.

Practice will make edible, though, and through your experimentation you'll likely find a few shortcuts. The recipes could be stripped down if you're just cooking an everyday meal as opposed to, say, trying to impress a girlfriend's parents. The list of ingredients for beef noodles, for example, other than the obvious beef and noodles, is vegetable or peanut oil, ginger, garlic, scallions, red chilies, a plum tomato, sugar, chili bean sauce, rice wine, light soy sauce, dark soy sauce, Sichuan peppercorns, five-spice powder, anise, baby bok choy (or a leafy green vegetable substitute).

The Food of Taiwan is lushly illustrated, with food pictures, of course, but also ones of scenery and daily life by photographer Pete Lee. More than just a cookbook, it would make a nice souvenir of one's visit or residency on the island.

* * *

For a more detailed backgrounder of food in Taiwan, the must-read book is *A Culinary History of Taipei: Beyond Pork and Ponlai* (2018), by Steven Crook and Katy Hui-wen Hung. Englishman Steven Crook, who has called Taiwan home since 1991, has a good claim, along with Richard Saunders and J. Michael Cole, to being the leading expat writer; his previous titles include *Keeping Up With the War God: Taiwan, As It Seemed to Me* (2001), *Dos and Don'ts in Taiwan* (2010), and *Taiwan: The Bradt Travel Guide* (2011, 2014, 2019).

The book is really about the food of Taiwan; the "Taipei" in the title is so it fits in with the publisher Rowman & Littlefield's series "Big City Food Biographies" and its focus on metropolises celebrated as culinary destinations. The Taipei book has the honor of being the first series entry for an Asian city.

The "ponlai" in the subtitle refers to a strain of rice developed in Taiwan during the Japanese colonial period, stickier than the *indica* rice cultivated previously and quicker growing, often allowing for an extra annual crop.

A Culinary History of Taipei goes through the evolution of numerous ingredients and dishes, and the process of food production from farm to plate. I was especially interested to read about beef, my favorite meat and something a couple of my in-laws won't eat. "The popularity in recent decades of beef is striking because, just a few generations ago, the consumption of bovine meat was anathema to Taiwanese of Han descent. This taboo has its roots in ancient China, where laws prohibited ordinary people from killing cattle." Oxen were seen as loyal co-workers that helped generations of Taiwanese farmers wring a living from the land.

> A traditionally minded Taiwanese farmer is no more likely to feast on a bovine than his British counterpart is to eat his sheepdog.
>
> Literature and folk songs from the eighteenth and nineteenth centuries celebrate cattle that are admirably loyal to their masters, even saving their lives by warning of impending earthquakes or other disasters. Eating an animal after it has labored in your service would be to invite karmic retribution; in those stories where an ox is butchered for food, the farmer often suffers nightmares in which the animal takes revenge on him.

The prohibition slackened during Japanese colonial rule and then further with urbanization. Helping the rise of beef noodles as an iconic Taiwanese dish were ingredients made more readily available by the U.S. presence on the island: "Some of the meat consumed in these places was American and arrived on the island in cans intended for US military mess halls. Another American contribution came in the form of donated and subsidized flour."

As well as expected food influences from China, Japan, and the United States, there are a few unlikely beginnings revealed. I would never have expected a Russian connection behind the pineapple cake, now the go-to food gift and souvenir. The authors explain that the modern pineapple cake was developed in the early 1950s by a Russian baker at Astoria Confectionary and Café, founded in 1949 by six White Russians who had fled the Communist capture of Shanghai, and a local partner, eighteen-year-old Archibald Chien. Astoria was a pioneering Western-style bakery, instrumental in either bringing to Taiwan, or popularizing, birthday cakes, chocolate cake, donuts, Western-style fruit cakes (with a local twist of using longans), and fruit jams. The Russian origins of the café and its goodies were played down as the Soviet Union was an arch-enemy. Still, the bakers could take comfort knowing that two of their regular patrons were president-in-waiting Chiang Ching-kuo and his Belarussian wife. Located in downtown Taipei just off "Book Street" and still there today, the Astoria was popular with local writers, poets, and artists, including Pai Hsien-yung, author of seminal works, *Taipei People* (1971) and *Crystal Boys* (1983), both of which are available in English translations.

* * *

Moving from these food books with general appeal, let's turn to a super-niche title: **Taiwan: A Travel Guide for Vegans** (2015, 2018), by New Zealander Jessie Duffield. Traditional vegetarianism in Taiwan stems from religious precepts and differs in various ways from its Western counterpart. Meat and seafood are off the menu – though not eggs and dairy products – but also some pungent vegetables like garlic and onions, which are considered too stimulating to the senses.

Duffield does a good job of dispelling some myths about vegetarianism in Taiwan. First of all, there aren't as many vegetarians as normally assumed. Some self-described vegetarians are really only part-timers, forgoing meat on the first and fifteenth day of each lunar month. Second, a shop sign swastika is, Duffield says, only a partial aid for visitors. The ancient symbol (which Hitler reversed) is associated with Buddhism and vegetarian restaurants: find a reversed swastika and you've found yourself vegetarian food. However, looking for a swastika is not the best way to go about finding vegetarian restaurants because "only a small proportion of vegetarian restaurants actually use it, and some non-vegetarian restaurants also use it to advertise that they (apparently) serve some vegetarian food." He explains that it's better to look for the more common signs featuring Chinese words for "vegetarian:" 素食 (sùshí) or 蔬食 (shūshí).

Another myth is that fake meat is vegan. The fake meat – worth trying even by the carnivorous just to experience the ingenuity behind creating such tasty substitutes – sometimes contains dairy products, egg, and even meat products – i.e. fake fake meat.

Duffield asserts that Taiwan is "one of Asia's most under-rated tourist destinations," with great scenery (away from the ugly urban areas), culture, and people who are "exceptionally friendly and welcoming to visitors." The country is also good value: "infrastructure almost comparable to Japan and prices almost comparable to Thailand."

Duffield's travel recommendations include Bao'an Temple (over the better known Longshan Temple, "whose famous courtyard is used more by photographers than worshipers"); the Xiaocukeng Ancient Trail, which goes from the old mining town of Jiufen over a mountain to Houtong; and Lion Head Mountain in Hsinchu County, an area of temples in the mountains that offers a combination of Buddhism and hiking.

No prizes for guessing that *Taiwan: A Travel Guide for Vegans*, currently available only as an e-book, was self-published; a commercial publisher wouldn't invest in such a narrow market slice. It's obviously a labor of love, the detail and the practical usefulness of the descriptions showing that the author has – as he states early on – visited everywhere he mentions in the guide. This kind of field research is expensive; there are accommodation and transport costs and, of course, numerous restaurant bills, with the author sometimes eating a restaurant meal for the benefit of the guide when a snack or packed lunch would have sufficed. For niche books like this, especially reasonably priced ones such as Duffield's three-dollar vegan guide, the author is in effect heavily subsidizing each purchase.

* * *

A weakness of the English-language corpus for Taiwan is the lack of diversity in the pool of authors. I'm thinking here not about nationality or ethnicity so much as employment. The two tribes overrepresented are academics and English teachers. There's not even much diversity within each tribe. Take for example the sameness of English teachers who've written a book on Taiwan; the average teacher is a single male from the Anglosphere who arrived in Taiwan in his mid-twenties to mid-thirties, liberal arts degree in hand, a fondness for travel and beer, found life agreeable enough, married a Taiwanese (often a student or teaching colleague), and settled down. These men may have moved a little from straight teaching into editing or picked up sideline income streams, but take the "John Smith is a writer based in Taipei" bylines with a pinch of salt; it's safe to wager Mr. Smith's earnings from writing make it more hobby than paid occupation.

Not surprisingly, the most common kind of book written by English teachers have been memoirs about their life in Taiwan, though the degree of classroom action included varies considerably. Most titles have been self-published. The only exception (if we're not counting Janet McGovern, author of *Among the Headhunters of Formosa*, as an English teacher) I'm aware of is Samuel Joshua Brown's *Vignettes of Taiwan* (2006), which in part helped him embark on the journey to impoverished vagrancy – better known as being a travel writer.

Admittedly there's not much quality competition, but the pick of recent memoirs that contain material on teaching is Ken Berglund's ***An American Teacher in Taiwan*** (2012). He worked in Taiwan from 2004 to 2008, first in Hsinchu for a large chain school called Hess, and then in Taichung for another chain called Kojen. Both these schools were private ones known as "buxibans" (usually translated as "cram schools"), which range from small independent schools with a few classrooms to nationwide chains, and are where most Western foreigners work. The majority of students are elementary and junior high school students, so classes are in the late afternoons and evenings, and on Saturdays. Some buxibans offer a variety of subjects (math, chemistry, etc.), while others specialize in English. All of them are private businesses and as such education usually takes a back seat to making money. Berglund has a negative opinion of teaching at cram schools, describing it as "basically just glorified babysitting."

An American Teacher in Taiwan gives greatest coverage to the intense early period of Berglund's stay, successfully conveying the author's disorientation and stress of landing on his feet. It's easy to forget how overwhelming the first days of your new life in Asia can be; the crushing language barrier makes simple things like ordering a meal an ordeal, and the "easy to find" work that people so casually mentioned can prove elusive. Holed up in a shabby hotel, and then a shabby hostel as you count your rapidly shrinking finances, you ask yourself, "God, what am I doing here?" My first trip to Taiwan was such an ill-fated foray; a week in Taipei was enough for me. (Six months later I came back for a position in small-town Taiwan.)

With admirable honesty, Berglund says he moved to Taiwan because his life in the United States was going nowhere; he had just gotten a divorce and loathed his job. A friend with Taiwan experience kept telling Berglund that he should teach English there. The author took a worthless distance teaching course (which gave him a certificate despite not completing a single hour's experience of real teaching); and he managed to convince a friend, David, to go with him. Berglund arrived in Taipei without a job lined up and just two thousand dollars to his name. He and David stayed at the Happy Family Hostel ("a piece of shit"). He recalls lying in his bottom bunk bed, staring up at the wood board under the top bed; messages were scrawled on it, one of which stood out: "It has come to this."

The first week in Taipei was especially difficult. On the first day they were looking for an American-style restaurant and ended up in a place called "BBQ Party," (perhaps not the best choice, seeing as David is a vegetarian, but they were footsore and hungry). The pair were perplexed, not only that they had to grill the food by themselves but also by the huge quantity they had mistakenly ordered. Enormous plate after enormous plate of meat, seafood, and vegetables were brought out to the bewildered newbies. They were completely vanquished, yet still more plates of food came, which they had to wave away, much to the amusement of the other customers.

On the following day, the two Americans were shaken down at a hostess bar: "For the second day in a row, we had spent a fortune and made ourselves look like fools. If we kept having days like this, our money would be gone in about a week." What on earth were these cash-strapped newbies doing in a hostess bar on just their second day you may well ask. They had been wandering around the streets of Taipei when two women invited them into a bar. Though Berglund is a light drinker and David a teetotaler, they decided to go in. After ordering a Taiwan Beer and a Pepsi, they were joined at their table by six friendly women who chatted with them and turned on a karaoke machine.

English teaching jobs proved harder to come by than they had expected, and they soon gave up hope of finding work in Taipei. Through a recruiter, Berglund landed a position in the small northern town of Toufen, but promptly lost the job when the school asked for a second demo. He eventually secured employment with a large school chain called Hess in the city of Hsinchu, and David ended up in a one-horse town called Lunbei in Yunlin County. Now even more so than then, inexperienced newbie teachers typically do a year or two "apprenticeship" in the boonies before leaving for the larger cities.

Berglund packed a lot into the years that followed. He found a girlfriend, who soon became a wife, and they had two children. He kept a blog about his Taiwan experiences, and readers encouraged him to write a book, which he says he did as "an honest attempt to help other people who were thinking of moving to and teaching in Taiwan." Berglund is of the generation of writers who cut their teeth on blogs. I never thought I would say this, but I miss the Golden Age of blogs – that decade before the ascendency of smartphones and Facebook; at the time, I thought blogs were all too often self-obsessed and amateur, but I didn't know they'd be largely replaced by something much worse.

Berglund is very blunt in *An American Teacher in Taiwan* – about himself, other people, and assessments of various facets of the country. On driving he says, "Taiwanese people have a reputation for being very friendly people. For the most part, it's true, as long as you're not on the road. On the road, they become an entirely different beast." In an earlier section he quantifies it: "90% of Taiwanese drivers drive like total selfish assholes." That's true as a general point but obviously overstated; and yet, tone down the phrasing to "drive with little consideration for fellow road users" and it's not far off the mark.

The traffic might be bad, but the good news is that white geeks can get laid: "Geeks of America, rejoice! For here is a country you can go to and date a beautiful woman. No longer will you have to download porn from the Internet. You can go to Taiwan and get a real, live girl! It doesn't matter what you look like."

On Taiwan's healthcare system, which is a government-run, single-payer, universal health insurance scheme with coverage that includes dental care and prescription drugs, he writes: "Taiwan has great, inexpensive health care, and because of this, EVERYONE wants to see the doctor for EVERYTHING. If you have a cold, go see the doctor. If you scrape your knee, go see the doctor. If you are coughing, go see the doctor."

In 2008 Berglund and his family moved to Austin, Texas. He chronicled this in two follow-up books, *From Taiwan to Texas: Life in Mid-America* and *The Reluctant Austinite*. He also wrote some fiction, and in a dream come true for every ESL teacher who has ever put pen to paper, had a massive bestseller. His horror tale *Small Town Evil* (2013) was an Amazon sensation, selling more than a quarter of a million copies! To my knowledge, that makes him the all-time most successful former Taiwan teacher-turned-writer.

* * *

Another foreigner who experienced a hard landing is the unnamed fictional protagonist in *A Taipei Mutt* (2002, 2017), written by Eric Mader, a longtime American resident in Taiwan. To describe this engrossing, fearless novel as unusual doesn't even come close.

A Taipei Mutt starts out with a twenty-nine-year-old American man, the narrator of the tale, arriving in Taipei to work as an English teacher. The first Taipei impressions will be familiar to many readers: the wearying but exciting shock of chaotic traffic, the stifling heat and humidity, the linguistic confusion. However, not many of us have found ourselves, just hours in the city, flirting with a gorgeous customer in a bank queue, and – jet lag be damned – being whisked off to her apartment.

The woman is a classic East Asian beauty: smooth milk-white skin, long black hair, and sultry dark eyes. Unfortunately for him, she is also a witch. As their lovemaking reaches a crescendo, he finds himself transformed into a dog — a Scotch terrier mutt, to be exact.

Our mutt manages to escape and begins a precarious existence as a stray dog, scavenging and begging for scraps, and thus giving us a dog's-eye view of the city. He can still think and talk like a man, though he has an increasingly acute sense of smell. The novel has some terrific passages conveying the heightened perceptions. When he enters Taipei Zoo at night, he feels a sense of terror and menace:

> Mingled with the smell of dung and oppression was something else too, an element that, in my canine sensorium, induced much of the terror. There was in the zoo the smell of an almost infinite tedium. The smell of unrelenting fatigue and the sweat of idleness.

After lengthy discussions with various zoo animals, the mutt leaves the zoo on a mission to reverse the magic that changed him into a dog. He hopes by repeating the circumstances of his transformation (that is, fornication with a human woman) he will change back to a man. Giving urgency to this endeavor is his race against the clock as he feels his mind becoming ever-more canine.

A book like *A Taipei Mutt* could easily lose steam when the novelty of the premise fades, but the story has an especially strong second half. Though his content matter is sometimes a challenge, Mader can certainly write, earning himself get-out-of-jail cards where weaker writers would flounder. Take, for example, a scene when the mutt is lust-struck on seeing a teenage girl with traffic-slowing sex appeal and very little clothing. Canine desire, he says, comparing it to the human variety, "hits like slow lightning ... stronger, more complete, more able to unhinge the mind...."

> Her scent was devastating. My dog's nose had latched onto it even as I strode up, and now I was completely awash in it. It poured down around me like electric nectar as she knelt at the bus stop petting my head and back.

"Electric nectar" – what a terrific phrase! Veteran *Taipei Times* reviewer Bradley Winterton is a fan of the quirky novel, writing in 2003: "It's the sort of book that could overnight easily become a local cult item." This hasn't happened, but then again – what *has* become a cult item?

* * *

Eric Mader works as an English teacher. No surprise there, or that he would choose to avoid it as a subject of his writing. Alas, is the work so dull we need to imagine ourselves transformed into beasts? As I mentioned previously, the expat employment situation in Taiwan is depressingly predictable; the great majority of Western residents are English teachers, with a few engineers and missionaries thrown into the mix, and not much else. I've got nothing against the much-maligned English teacher – sure, there are some losers, but on the whole they're an interesting group, usually equipped with the language skills and free time to explore their interests.

Moreover, let me put a positive spin on the situation and say that the lack of foreigners in a range of professions means there is enormous opportunity for prospective writers to pen an account of such experiences. We need more variety – books like *Barbarian at the Gate* (T. C. Locke's experience of serving in the ROC army), journalist memoir *Welcome Home, Master*, and American musician Scott Ezell's ***A Far Corner: Life and Art with the Open Circle Tribe***, published in 2015 by the University of Nebraska Press.

Like many long-term expats in Taiwan, Ezell's first encounter with the country was incidental. He came in 1992, on a friend's recommendation, to study Chinese, an interest that sprang from his love of the Tang dynasty poets, polymath bohemians like Li Bai who celebrated and lived contemplative yet enjoyable lives of nature, wine, and the rejection of material ambition. Ezell says he "arrived in Taiwan with visions of Taoist recluses drinking wine in bamboo groves and Zen monks cutting cats in half to prove that the world is an illusion." Of course, what he found was something rather different: the noisy, materialistic frenzy of a Little Dragon in a headlong rush of development.

In 2002, after a decade in Taipei studying and working as a translator and musician, he did what many expats in the big cities dream about doing (but almost never do); he left Taipei and moved to the East Coast, to the coastal village of Dulan in a rural coastal area a little north of Taitung City. Ezell would soon find his own Taoist-like band of bohemians, a group of aboriginal artists, predominantly of the Ami tribe, who informally went by the name of the Open Circle Tribe.

Early on, he finds himself on the beach: "I did not realize it at the time, but sitting around a fire, passing *mijiu*, songs, and a guitar around a circle of friends would essentially comprise my social life for the coming two and a half years I lived in Dulan."

His aboriginal artist friends were musicians and wood carvers (typically of driftwood and, rather disappointingly, using chain-saws). Ezell's main art form was musical composition, his biggest project being a 2003 album, *Ocean Hieroglyphics*, recorded away from chainsaws in his remote house, where he set up an old-school analog recording studio.

Scott Ezell, as well as being a musician and artist, is a poet. I'm biased against modern poetry – it's a generally lazy, self-indulgent form – but I have to admit that Ezell's poetic leanings enrich his prose. *A Far Corner* is full of memorable phrasing. Here's an example of Ezell's magnificent descriptive powers:

July, the gut and groin of summer, the days sticky and thick with heat. Ducking out of the sun became a movement both primary and unconscious, an instinct like dodging a blow or swatting at the whine of a mosquito by your ear. The mountains that were sharp green in spring became drab and muted, as if their color was a blade hammered dull by heat. The ocean sank into a brooding blue, its currents and movements retreated beneath the surface, leaving a skin like old paint to absorb the crash and roar of the sun. The air hazed and thickened, the smell of decomposition climbing through like vines, rising up from the soil, from wilting leaves. Flowers shriveled, leaving seed pods that rattled as I moved through the brush up on the mountain. The sky yawned, blank and empty, a bored god, butane blue....

His descriptions of aboriginal music and singers are also moving, though, for my tastes, a touch too romanticized: "His voice evoked the hills and ravines of Dulan, the undulating bluffs along the coast, the texture of the sea breaking blue-green over stones. The Amis songs had a rhythm and pulse that belonged to this place, passed down breath by breath through generations."

Ezell is masterly when he's describing mundane things such as a mom-and-pop supermarket.

His store was a yowling chaos, with ten times too many things crammed on dusty shelves with no apparent organization, a mayhem of mercantile accumulation.... On a butcher's block by the cash register, slabs of pork lay for sale beneath a mesh dome, the wood scarred and concave from decades of chopping meat. A mechanical fly whisk turned above, a bit of plastic twine tied to a length of rotating coat hanger.

Scott Ezell's time in Dulan reached a climax at a big concert at an old sugar factory that had been turned into an arts and culture center. Undercover cops claimed Ezell had violated the terms of his visa by playing music in a public venue. Ezell's residence visa was sponsored by a record company, but it did not specifically include a right to perform music in public. Now, if this applied to only paid musical performances, that would be one thing – however, unpaid performances were also technically illegal according to the interpretation. Of course, only someone with malignant intentions would try to enforce it; Ezell says this was the case, a local police officer with a grudge against foreigners.

Ezell's residence permit was cancelled and he was given two weeks to leave the country. A Taiwanese lawyer friend, Roger Wang, fought his case, and the musical community and the English-language press made a lot of noise. (As an aside, Ezell says that the case never made it into the Chinese-language newspapers.) Ezell managed to get a stay on the cancellation of his residence visa until the legal case had been settled. Although he was likely to win it, he chose not to stay and fight. Living under a cloud of deportation, and being barred from playing music at the sugar factory or elsewhere in public would remove much of his fun. In addition, Ezell feared the police might hassle his friends to get at him, so he decided to leave Taiwan.

A Far Corner deserves to become a Taiwan classic. So far it has largely slipped under the radar, but hope springs eternal in the world of words.

* * *

Another underappreciated gem from someone who is not an English teacher is **Welcome Home, Master: Covering East Asia in the Twilight of Old Media** (2015), where we follow an American free-lancer on the Taiwan beat. Journalism major and newbie reporter Jonathan Adams decided to base himself in Taipei, arriving in the summer heat of 2004 and staying until 2011. He'd been told Taiwan was an under-appreciated and under-reported story in East Asia, and a good place to live. On a more practical level, the only job offer he had got was for a position in Taipei.

While stringing for *Newsweek* and other publications, Adams worked as a "copy-monkey" at Taiwan's leading English-language newspaper, the *Taipei Times*. His fellow expat colleagues were doing a good job of perpetuating the stereotype of hard-drinking newspaper men. The heavy self-medicating made sense he writes when you realized their copy editing entailed a lot of "rewriting incomprehensible editorials" and cleaning up copy from the paper's local reporters; a bit like being an English teacher with writing classes and essays to correct, but with worse hours and pay. After two years at the paper, Adams made the switch to full-time freelancing.

Adams writes about the importance of "breaking the frame" — that is, challenging the clichéd narratives that lazy journalists and editors rely on. "The frame in Taiwan was about the uppity island that wanted to 'declare independence' and so spark a disastrous war between China and the United States, which had defense commitments to Taiwan."

The newspaper editors he worked with were "mostly interested in periodic, temperature-taking stories on cross-strait relations (Hot or cold? Moving toward unification or war?). You usually needed a major election on which to hang these stories." Another frame was Taiwan's role in the electronics industry. Adams says the real story was that of "a young democracy going through 'growing pains' and dealing with the legacy of forty years of martial law — and doing it all in the shadow of a giant autocratic neighbor that periodically threatened to blast it to bits. But that story was harder to tell. Editors weren't very interested, and if you pushed that narrative too hard they might suspect that you'd 'gone native.'"

A jitong, *or spirit medium, flagellates himself*
(photograph by J.D. Adams)

Adams' memoir starts in 2010, the year before he called quits on his journalism career, with a description of a trip to two Japanese fertility festivals (vagina and penis festivals) and how his stories went viral. He contrasts this success with the lack of interest in his more serious reporting on how the Japanese workforce was moving from life-time employment to temp work. This was a "useful shorthand" for why he left journalism; but he explains that there were also practical reasons. That year Adams was almost forty and soon to be married. He half-heartedly considered one area of journalism that is more stable and pays better – business journalism – but lacked the interest and aptitude. Continuing freelance journalism was not viable – "one thousand dollars a month wasn't going to feed a family." The advertising-based model for magazines and newspapers was dead. The industry was in carnage, an ongoing bloodletting of profits and jobs.

Adams is not bitter, though – you won't find him as an angry drunk perched on a bar stool, cursing his misfortunes and world's slide into hell. The financial strains and lack of support meant journalism was less glamorous than his early image of the profession, but he's glad he did it: "for much of 2002 through 2011, I had the time of my life." He is relatively upbeat about the future of journalism; partly, that's because he never had a great impression of the classic foreign correspondent, who was too often lazy, uninterested in "breaking the frame," and had little real contact with the place they were supposed to covering. In addition, Adams felt he'd been let down by the coverage he had read of Taiwan. "I learned far more about the island from local media and a handful of well-produced blogs."

The old foreign correspondents have been replaced by low-paid "stringers" like Adams and longtime expats occasionally submitting pieces (which I won't describe as "part-time work," because the financial remuneration makes it more like a hobby). Those in this new generation are often more integrated into the country (usually called "marriage"), have better language skills, and have acquired a deeper knowledge of Taiwan.

There's no better example of the new media making a difference than Taiwan lifer Michael Turton, a former American Peace Corps volunteer in Kenya who followed a friend to Taiwan and ended up staying. His influential blog, "The View from Taiwan," ran from 2005 to 2018, and he continues his political commentary on a number of other websites, including as co-host of an online news program called the Taiwan Report. One of Turton's writing staples are devastating dissections of media coverage of Taiwan from major media organizations that should know better – the likes of CNN, the BBC, Reuters, *Forbes*, and the *Economist*. He highlights factual mistakes, and especially the lazy, inaccurate pro-China framing of cross-strait issues. Common targets include ill-informed references to Taiwan and the PRC having been split by the Chinese Civil War in 1949 (the PRC has never included Taiwan, so a split is an impossibility); journalists repeating CCP talking points and failing to include Taiwanese sources (with a corresponding lack of consideration for the people in Taiwan); and the fallacy of the so-called 1992 Consensus (a term coined by the KMT years after a semi-official meeting between the ROC and PRC at which they supposedly agreed to the "One China principal" but with each side left to their own interpretations – in other words the "consensus" is invented and uselessly vague).

Turton stubbornly refuses to cede the linguistic battlefield: What China seeks is "annexation" and not "reunification;" Taiwanese asserting their country's interests are "pro-Taiwan" rather than "anti-China;" the years of Japanese rule are "Japanese colonial rule" rather than "Japanese occupation," because the latter is faulty history and purposely sets up the KMT to come as liberators and end the occupation. He is relentless in pointing out how the passive voice is used in news stories to hide agency. A typical mainstream news article will have phrasing such as, "Relations have soured between Beijing and Taipei since (insert "democratic election result" or similarly "provocative" action) and talk of "heightened tensions." Turton asks who soured the relations? Who heightened the tensions and is this really the best phrase when the force is coming from one side? Relations sour because Beijing chooses to sour them. But instead, time and again Taiwan is presented as a troublemaker, somehow responsible for heightened tensions when it is China's constant bullying and threats that create the problem.

Through his blog and other writing, Turton has done more than any other contemporary journalist or author in informing people about Taiwan and in shaping the way the country is reported on. In the last ten years I've noticed his reframing of cross-strait issues making a difference in better international coverage of Taiwan.

* * *

Another important figure in the English-language news scene is J. Michael Cole, an analyst at the Canadian Security Intelligence Service (CSIS) in Ottawa and then a deputy news editor and journalist at the *Taipei Times* from 2006 until 2013. He goes into the reasons he quit the newspaper in a self-published 2014 book, *Officially Unofficial: Confessions of a Journalist in Taiwan*, which, while offering some insights into reporting in Taiwan, is awkwardly written in the third person.

Cole's **Black Island** (2015), written the following year and with the personal stuff out of his system, is a better read. It's an exciting, on-the-ground account of the tumultuous awakening of civic activism in 2013–2014. Although the Taiwanese population is admirably nonchalant (that's somewhere between stoic and apathetic) in the face of Chinese pressure, there are naturally upswings and dips in the national mood. During these years, the mood turned dramatically; the people would not quietly resign themselves to the notion that ever-closer Chinese ties were inevitable.

The events described in the book took place during the two-term presidency of Ma Ying-jeou (2008–2016). Hong Kong-born, a golden boy who had been primed for high office from an early age and yet was all too stiff when out mingling with the public, Ma was elected with a mandate to prioritize economic growth. Taiwan rode out the prolonged global financial crisis comparatively well; Ma won reelection comfortably in 2012 (and his party, the KMT, retained control of the legislature). His second term, however, was marked early on by growing public dissatisfaction – there were corruption cases, food-safety scandals, and a lack of economic growth. The devil's bargain of closer ties to China was not producing the promised payoff of higher salaries. And the proposed solution of even greater engagement with China didn't convince a skeptical public. The feeling that Taiwan was moving too close to China too quickly was the main impetus behind protests that coalesced into what would be called the Sunflower Student Movement. Events would come to a head over the Cross-Strait Services Trade Agreement (CSSTA). The CSSTA aimed to liberalize trade in services between China and Taiwan by loosening investment rules in industries such as banking, healthcare, and media, and relaxing visa rules for residency. Following negotiations with China, President Ma tried to hurry the agreement through the legislature without proper review.

Resistance within the KMT made things messy in the legislature, and then DDP resistance held it up. Still, it seemed that Ma would succeed. Student and citizen protesters, however, had other plans, occupying the legislature on March 18, 2014. Some in the

KMT wanted the students forcibly removed. But how to handle the occupiers was the call of the legislative speaker, Wang Jin-pyng, who'd recently feuded with Ma and wasn't about to help him out now. The students could stay.

On March 23 a second occupation – of the Executive Yuan, the seat of the Cabinet – was attempted. Riot police cleared protesters around and in the building. In this case the protestors had over-reached, and the police response was more aggressive than needed. This, however, was an anomaly; during all the turmoil through spring, the police and protesters had handled themselves well – this was the chaos of Taiwanese democracy but also the civility. The crisis ended peacefully; after obtaining certain concessions regarding the passage of the trade pact legislation, the students agreed to leave the legislature and did so on April 10.

In *Black Island*, Cole looks at the growth of grassroots protests against heavy-handed government and corrupt big business interests from late 2012 up to the climax of the occupation of the Legislative Yuan. Cole is full of admiration for the young activists – their organization, perseverance, civility, and bravery. And their success in shining a light on relatively minor injustices – land expropriated here, an illegal construction there – that would not normally have received media attention.

> They have exposed government officials as liars, corporate leaders as thugs, county commissioners as crooks, legislators as self-serving, media moguls as unprincipled, and oftentimes they have brought out the very worst in individuals of authority, forcing them to show their true colors to the electorate.

Cole praises the student protestors' focus on local issues. Good local governance is vital, he says, in standing up to Chinese infiltration;

if a free, democratic Taiwan is to survive, the people will need to get rid of sleazy politicians willing to cut deals.

He trumpets the Sunflower Movement as "an entirely new phenomenon in Taiwan, an awakening from a slumber of defeatism," and the emergence of a civic nationalism which "has finally transcended the 'ethnic' politics that for far too long had kept the nation in a perpetual state of war with itself."

* * *

In 2016 Tsai Ing-wen of the Democratic Progressive Party was elected president, the first woman to achieve this honor. Her resounding victory was a rebuke of the KMT's approach of placating the Chinese Communist Party and pushing further economic integration with China, something that had been, in effect, ransoming the country's future to the CCP. The Ma presidency was, in a roundabout way, extremely valuable for the continued development of Taiwanese identity. By showing that appeasement didn't temper China's belligerence and that the economic payoff was middling, it paved the way for his successor to reduce dependency on China and to look entirely reasonable doing so. If we're looking for big historical analogies, think of Chamberlain's attempts at appeasement allowing for the defiance of Churchill.

In *Convergence or Conflict in the Taiwan Strait: The Illusion of Peace?* (2016), J. Michael Cole explains how the supposed improved relations and reduced tensions between China and Taiwan under Ma's presidency were an illusion. There was movement on economic and cultural matters, but no political gain; China continued its aggressive military build-up and propaganda efforts, still determined to annex Taiwan.

Cole lambasts the Western world for ignoring Taiwan's plight – a free, peaceful democracy being bullied by an authoritarian regime – and for choosing, from greed and cowardice, to side with the aggressor. And worse, many in the West resent Taiwan because, as Cole astutely states, it is "a constant reminder of our double standards.... We know what we're doing is wrong, but we do it nonetheless. And we blame Taiwan for nagging at our conscience."

* * *

World indifference to Taiwan's fate and an increasingly assertive China is a trajectory for war. In 2017 a book burst into the international limelight with newspaper headlines screaming its purported warnings of Chinese intentions to invade Taiwan in 2020. The book in question was ***The Chinese Invasion Threat: Taiwan's Defense and American Strategy in Asia***, by Ian Easton, a researcher at the Project 2049 Institute, an American think tank that focuses on security issues in Central Asia and the Asia-Pacific region.

The assertion that Easton was predicting a Chinese invasion in 2020 was nonsense – the result of so-called journalists writing pieces without reading the book or talking to the easily contactable author. The actual point of the book is that Taiwan is stronger than normally assumed and that China does not have the capacity to successfully invade Taiwan in the near future. And the significance of the year 2020? Unlike the trigger-happy reporters, let's actually look at what was said in the book. The money quote – and the first appearance of the year "2020" in *The Chinese Invasion Threat* – is as follows:

Just prior to the Sunflower Movement, ROC defense officials received intelligence that spooked them so much that they decided to unveil it publically, even at the price of showing President Ma's peace policies were failing. In late 2013, Taiwan's Ministry of National Defense (MND) openly reported that China had developed a plan to invade Taiwan by 2020. They revealed a secret pact had been made in Beijing at the

18th National Congress of the Communist Party, when Mr. Xi Jinping replaced Mr. Hu Jintao as general secretary of the CCP. At this meeting, the new Chinese leadership committed to complete their 2020 Plan for building and deploying a comprehensive operational capability to use force against Taiwan by that year. Instead of peace, the CCP and PLA, four years into cross-Strait détente, still thought it necessary to put down on planning documents the need to invade Taiwan.

So old news from four years earlier, not breaking news; in essence, the CCP wanted to have the capacity by 2020 to take Taiwan by force. It was basically a rededication of a core PLA mission.

Easton first started thinking about the threat of a Chinese invasion in the late summer of 2005, soon after arriving in Taipei to study Mandarin. Strolling down Heping (Peace) Road he heard "the piercing wail of an emergency alert siren.... Armed police officers and soldiers suddenly materialized on the streets around me, seemingly out of nowhere." Traffic halted, motorists and passengers got out of their vehicles and took cover, sidewalks emptied, and an eerie silence fell over the surreal scene. Easton learned it was an annual air-raid drill, and it set him thinking deeply about what lay behind it all. A dozen years later he had written the most detailed work on the invasion threat, drawing on numerous previously unpublished PRC and ROC sources.

There's a lot of daylight between China wanting to invade Taiwan and being able to do so. Apart from Taiwan's well-armed 290,000-strong military, there are considerations of nature. Weather and sea conditions narrow suitable conditions for an invasion force down to about two months: "PLA materials express a belief that there are only two realistic time windows open for invading Taiwan. The first is from late March to the end of April. The second is from late September to the end of October. During these two periods, winds are usually light, and waves low."

Geography also makes it tough to choose a landing area. Easton writes:

> Taiwan's 770-mile-long coastline is remarkably unsuitable for amphibious operations. The number of invasion beaches is shrinking. There are fourteen left. The shores of Taoyuan and Tainan are almost certainly the best options open to PLA generals, but they each have many dangers associated with them. These are heavily populated lowland areas, overlooked by hills. They have each been well studied and well fortified. Taiwan's military has all manner of mines and obstacles piled up in bunkers nearby, ready to deploy on short notice. Mobile tank brigades and massed infantry could overwhelm and obliterate Chinese skirmishers as they approached and landed.

Easton says that negative assessments of Taiwan's ability to resist a Chinese invasion have a faulty starting point in that the invasion will be a surprise. He goes through a range of warning signs that would make detection of a mobilizing invasion force obvious to both Taiwanese spies and electronic surveillance. The author sees the gloomy assessments of Taiwan's defensive strength as not only wrong but dangerous and deliberate: "the Chinese propaganda system has for many years churned out a steady line, arguing that the doom of Taiwan is already sealed and annexation is a simple matter of time."

A passage that exemplifies the fascinating inside information revealed in *The Chinese Invasion Threat* relates to the targeting of Taiwan's nuclear power plants.

One Chinese field manual takes pains to remind the intended readers (PLA officers) not to bomb nuclear power plants, because the radioactive fallout could poison the broader political situation and turn world opinion against China. Another PLA field manual, however, contradicts this guidance, specifically urging attack helicopter pilots to hit Taiwan's nuclear plants. This passage confidently states that air-to-ground missiles would be accurate enough and small enough to only temporarily black out power generators, leaving reactors stable and intact for China to use after Taiwan was conquered.

While I agree with the author's assessment that Taiwan's defensive situation and capabilities are formidable and any invasion attempt would likely be a debacle for China, I believe he is overly optimistic when it comes to Taiwan's will to fight. How would the Taiwanese public react? Would soldiers and their commanders desert? Would the poorly trained reserves muster for battle? Would outrage over civilian deaths – even PLA sources say the inaccuracy of rocket and air force strikes would produce significant collateral damage – awaken the Taiwanese fighting spirit? Or would this generation of only sons not consider the sacrifice worthwhile; after all, a lesson of Taiwan's history – from those resisting Koxinga, the Qing, the Japanese, and later the KMT – was that accepting your new masters was the smartest move for yourself and family. It's hard to know, and I hope Easton is right. Similarly, does America (and Japan to a lesser extent) have the will to fight China? The positive assessments of Taiwan resisting the PRC are based on the assumption of the American cavalry coming to the rescue.

And so we turn to the soft-power war, the need to promote Taiwan's story to the world and also its strategic importance to the region. I believe books have an important role in fighting Taiwan's good fight — not books that are little more than clumsy government propaganda pieces, not political polemics, not even war thrillers, but works that highlight and humanize Taiwan as the peaceful, tolerant civil society it is.

* * *

Two recent travelogues that showcase free and friendly modern Taiwan are *Taiwanese Feet* and *Formosan Moon*. John Groot's ***Taiwanese Feet*** (2020) is a travel account of the Canadian expat's circumnavigation, on foot and in stages, around the island's entire 1,200 kilometers of coastline. It was an epic trip and makes a great frame for a travelogue. Originally, I had planned to take my own long walk – but from north to south through the mountains – and make it the frame of my *Formosan Odyssey: Taiwan, Past and Present*, but the massive 9-21 earthquake of 1999 trashed my plans and I instead wrote a hybrid history/travel account – Taiwan's odyssey rather than my own.

Groot's project was in part "a mid-life crisis, or my little stab at living the life of an adventurer." Inspired by reading about the likes of exploring legend Sir Ranulph Fiennes, Groot's exploits were "far more comfortable, much less dangerous, and involved a lot more beer drinking." The other motivation was to forge a deeper attachment to his adopted home.

Groot came to Taiwan in 2001 at the age of thirty-six, an experienced traveller looking to teach English and explore East Asia. "Like so many others, I fell in love with the place. Despite the congestion and industrialization, there's a lot of physical beauty. Much of the terrain is covered in forested mountains and picturesque farms, and the sea is never far. There's way too much noise, but also a Zen-like calm in the culture, and it's super friendly."

The flip side of the warm welcome that Taiwanese extend to foreigners is the frustration, slowly growing through the years, at always being an outsider; not to family, friends, or colleagues – but certainly to society in general. After Groot had been in Taiwan for five years, he was "looking for some way to break through this barrier." The answer was his walk around Taiwan; it would, he hoped, connect him more deeply to the land and its people.

Groot's trek was undertaken on weekends and other days off, with each stage resuming where he had finished the last. He set off on November 19, 2006, from his home in the old town of Danshui, travelling clockwise — occasionally with company but mostly alone. He arrived back in Danshui on June 7, 2014, after a total of 83 walking days spread out over eight years.

A great strength of a long-distance walking adventure is that it forces slow travel through difficult, unusual, and ugly areas — places we would normally bypass or speed past. In *Taiwanese Feet* the obvious highlights of the walk are along the beautiful, rugged East Coast, with its lush vegetation, sea cliffs, and soaring backdrop of mountains. However, for me, the drudgery of walking along the worst of the ugly west coast held the most interest, because of the novelty of the strange seascapes and the mental challenge Groot faced to keep trudging through such unrewarding territory. Groot's glass-half-filled optimism was much needed as he made his way along the coast of Yunlin County. It was "incredibly boring," with "nothing more than vast areas dominated by aquaculture fields stretching off to the horizon to the right, bounded on the near side by a seawall with a small road next to it." He tried to find merit in the messy shambles of buildings, "the overlay of the region's historical layers" and points of interest, but it's a challenge for even a good-natured traveler.

It was pleasant enough weather, and the somewhat dull countryside at least had the compensation of occasional villages that were bustling with small-town life: markets, religious ceremonies, or folks simply sitting outside and gossiping. The horror of the day, however, was the smell: I must have passed dozens of pig, duck, goose, and chicken farms, all active sources of fresh sewage; and upstream facilities drained into the numerous small rivers and canals that passed under the road! Damn! There were some stinky moments on that walk. I gagged many a time that day.

Such desolation – and the distance from Taipei, meaning expensive, time-consuming trips back and forth from the route – wreaked havoc on his motivation, and he let the project slide for months and months at a time.

Even on his very last day, the scenery was more apocalypse than travel brochure:

There were some graves by the sea, then some grungy beaches with garbage, and lots of industrial installations of one sort or another. On my right, there was the hillside leading up to the Linkou Plateau, which loomed above the Taipei Basin still ahead. The hillside to the right was forested in patches, and had some small roads with mixed farm and industrial land, the smell of burning plastic in the air, stray dogs running around on the roads. There were homesteads with junk piled around, sometimes with an old taxi parked in front.

Despite my perverse quoting of such bleak sections, *Taiwanese Feet* is an enjoyable, fresh look at Taiwan. It also has a happy ending, the author accomplishing both goals of completing a big adventure and feeling more connected to the people and country.

* * *

Another recent travelogue with an excellent frame is **Formosa Moon**, by Joshua Samuel Brown and Stephanie Huffman. The book has the brilliant setup of pairing a Taiwan old-timer with a newbie, and presenting this in parallel, alternating commentary. Veteran travel writer Joshua Samuel Brown is showing his partner, Stephanie Huffman – on her first trip to Asia – around Taiwan before they settle down in Taipei. It's important that she like the place, which adds a bit of edge to the travels. The framework is more than a gimmick designed to look good in a blurb – Brown and Huffman's commentated adventures are an intimate slice of real life with meaningful consequences for the authors. Soon after becoming a couple in Portland, Brown made it clear that he loved Taiwan and planned to return: he and the country came as a package. Four years later after living together, the (unmarried) pair left the United States for Taiwan.

The places visited and the activities engaged in by the forty-something couple reflect their – and especially Huffman's – interests. So on top of the usual attractions like temples and night markets, there's an emphasis on arts and crafts.

Brown writes about Taiwan with wit and affection, which is not always an easy combination – humor, almost by definition, involves some cruelty. Huffman is good-natured, too, and gives a positive spin to her adventures. As readers we're rooting for her to be able to keep up with Brown, a professional traveler on his home turf, which she does indeed do.

After traveling down the beautiful East Coast, they take the ferry from Taitung to Green Island, a notoriously nausea-inducing crossing that lives up to its reputation. Huffman writes: "the next forty-five minutes was a challenge in meditation." Huffman managed both crossings, but Brown loses his breakfast on the return journey … and once again on a trip to the remote aboriginal village of Smangus, where the winding mountain road proves too much for Brown's stomach: "We piled back into the car for more climbing and switchbacks through some of the most beautiful country and on one of the worst roads I'd been on yet in Taiwan. Josh managed to not vomit again, but I knew he wasn't feeling well. He wasn't talking, which is highly unusual."

The two Americans attend a *weiya* for the East Coast National Scenic Area staff. A *weiya* is a company dinner party held before the Chinese New Year vacation, often involving enforced cheesy camaraderie and, horrors of horrors, karaoke. It's a good setting for cultural observations and some caustic asides; but instead we get an unexpectedly moving passage from Brown about his love of Taiwan. Explaining his choice of song, an old Teresa Teng classic called "The Moon Represents My Heart," he writes:

> Once it drew me into its gravity, this strange and alien land I've chosen to call home for long stretches has been the one true constant in my life. Taiwan has granted me a near-constant reprieve from my most feared nemesis, boredom, but at times she's driven me half-mad. Taiwan has been my muse, the source of inspiration for much of my creative output as a writer, while at the same time never quite letting me forget that the language in which I write is not the lingua franca of the place about which I write. I have loved Taiwan for nearly all of my adult life. At times this love has shone as brilliantly as the moon over Kenting during the Mid-Autumn Festival, at others far less brightly, like a crescent moon during the long rainy season in Taipei.... So when I sang it was this love for Taiwan, waxing and waning, but always present, that I felt.

Formosa Moon contains a remarkable fortune-telling episode in which Brown visits a Madame Chen in Tainan, who warns of the couple's financial incompatibility for marriage. What Brown thought would be a light bit of fun and good local color for the book gets rather intense:

> "You two shouldn't get married," proclaimed Madame Chen, which I found quite a blunt statement coming from either a Taiwanese person or a person in the nominally New Age industry. I was taken aback.

Brown presses for clarification, assuming that she's referring to them getting married in the near future.

"No," she said. "Ever. You can stay together, for the rest of your lives even. But you should never make yourselves financially bound to one another. To do so will court disagreement."

Huffman returned to Madame Chen the next day without Brown and on top of repeating the previous warnings the fortune teller added some interesting new predictions.

After that, a bit worn down by being on the road for a month, and with Chinese New Year approaching – a good time to avoid travel – Brown and Huffman took a break from traveling and headed back to Taipei to see an apartment that had become newly available. Thus begins the second part of the book, "Settling In and Further Excursions."

Their home in New Garden City, a green hilly area to the south of Taipei, seems ideal, especially with a nice apartment at a bargain price. They're away from the bustle, pollution, and madness of the city. But not the noise, which has them referring to their Garden Road location as "Dog Lane." Brown writes:

The price was a series of morning wake-up calls in the form of high-pitched yapping from the poodle schnauzers at the end of the street, bellicose barking from the nasty mastiffs three doors down, all echoed by indeterminate dog noises from the dozen or so other canines on Dog Lane. The first dog alarm generally began at dawn before dying down for a while until some other trigger caused one of the dogs to bark, in turn causing all of the dogs to start over again.

They were sometimes quiet during the day, except when they weren't, and largely quieter at night except when one of them caught the scent of a stray or some other animal intruding into the neighborhood, or when someone on the block coughed in their sleep, sounding off the bark alarm yet again.

As I remarked earlier, humor requires an element of suffering. Apart from the noise, the couple – Huffman especially – also found the location too out of the way and the lifestyle isolating. Huffman writes, "Life in New Garden City was becoming increasingly stressful. As the sun rose earlier, so did the canine orchestra. Even with earplugs, we were not getting a full night's sleep and fatigue was setting in."

Rescue came in the form of Huffman's acceptance to a master's program in East Asian studies at National Chengchi University, which necessitated a move into Taipei. The book ends with her accurate observation: "Taiwan is never boring, and if there's one thing I expect, life here will continue to be interesting. The adventure continues."

Formosa Moon is a singular book, a quirky mix of memoir, travelogue, and practical travel information. It's well written, immensely likeable, and informed. I started the book thinking the switching of the text passages between the two authors would get old by the end, but it didn't. Nor was it ever confusing: there are circular portrait icons of Brown and Huffman marking each change of the baton. The pairing of new eyes with an old Taiwan hand works beautifully. Of course, having a good idea and executing it effectively are two different matters. This is where Brown's writing talents come in. He has a good nose for anecdotes, story hooks, segues, and funny phrasing.

Brown came to Taiwan in 1994 to teach English; his *Vignettes of Taiwan* (2006) describes his first decade on the island. That book led to his working on various Lonely Planet travel guides, including the one for Taiwan.

* * *

These last two books show that despite being two decades into the twenty-first century, with travel and publishing (at least self-publishing) easier than ever, the travelogue is not a worn-out genre. Taiwan remains greatly unrepresented; it's virgin territory awaiting willing writers. How about a travel account of a trek along the length of Taiwan's magnificent mountain ranges, or a series of walks retracing historical trails? Or a maritime circumnavigation, visiting not only Taiwan's offshore islands but those of the Philippines and Japan: the gorgeous Batanes Islands in the Bashi Channel, and Yonaguni Island, the westernmost point of Japan? How about Taiwanese-Americans discovering their family roots? A leisurely pilgrimage around Taiwan's Buddhist monasteries? Historical battlefields? Or a look at Taiwan's wildlife woven around a search for the extinct clouded leopard? The possibilities are intoxicating.

And beyond travelogues, the Taiwan bookshelf is crying out for accessible English-language non-fiction works on aborigines (surely each group deserves at least one book on its history and culture), architecture, art, biographies of important Taiwanese, crime, conservation, economics, flora, and an array of other subjects too numerous to mention. There is even greater scope for fiction writers. If I had magic pixie dust, then for my own reading pleasure I would conjure up a noir detective series, historical adventure stories, and several military novels, including a counterfactual one describing the ROC retaking the mainland circa 1960.

THE END

Some Books That Missed Out

Some noteworthy books didn't make the cut for a variety of reasons. For example, I didn't include Tehpen Tsai's informative *Elegy of Sweet Potatoes* because I already had enough 2-28 titles. Likewise, Syd Goldsmith's *Jade Phoenix*, a romance set during the 1970s, missed out because I had sufficient coverage of the Cold War period. I overlooked José E.B. Matteo's two-volume *Spaniards in Taiwan* because I didn't want to get too deep into the historical weeds. Conversely, there were some titles providing a good overview like Denny Roy's *Taiwan: A Political History*, Jonathan Manthorpe's *Forbidden Nation: A History of Taiwan*, and Shelley Rigger's *Why Taiwan Matters: Small Island, Global Powerhouse*, when what I wanted was a narrower focus. I excluded bilingual works, which meant there was no room for Rolf-Peter Willie's *Formosa in Fiction: A Collection of Rather Exotic Tales* or Nick Kembel's *Taiwan in the Eyes of a Foreigner*. I didn't include any of the numerous works on Taiwan's cinema because I will deal with the subject in a planned book on English-language works translated from Chinese. And, of course, there were books that simply didn't interest me. For example, I tried reading Lin Tao's best-selling *Taipei* several times, but failed. *Taiwan in 100 Books* is a work in progress, and I'll be adding both new and overlooked titles in future editions. If I've not included one of your favorite Taiwan books, then I'd be happy to hear from you; write to john@camphorpress.com and tell me why it should be included in the next edition.

About the Author

New Zealander John Ross has spent most of the past thirty years living in and writing about Asia. His extensive travels – undertaken alone and far off the beaten track – include exploration in Papua New Guinea, dispatches from the Karen insurgency in Burma, and searches in the Gobi Desert and Altai Mountains on the trail of an ancient Mongolian myth.

Ross lives in a small town in southern Taiwan with his Taiwanese wife. His books include *Formosan Odyssey* and *You Don't Know China*. When not writing, reading, or lusting over maps, he can be found on the family farm slashing jungle undergrowth (and having a sly drink).

Acknowledgements

Taiwan in 100 Books owes its existence, of course, to all the authors and publishers of the works featured in it. Thank you for your contribution to Taiwan and to readers everywhere. I'm also grateful to Michael Cannings and Mark Swofford for their excellent work on this and my other books.

Bibliography

Aandahl, Loren. *The Taiwan Railway: 1966–1970*. Taipei: Loren Aandahl, 2011.

———. *The Taiwan Railway: 1971–2002*, Taipei: Loren Aandahl, 2012.

Adams, J.D. *Welcome Home, Master: Covering East Asia in the Twilight of Old Media*. Manchester, England: Camphor Press, 2015.

Albright, David, and Andread Stricker. *Taiwan's Former Nuclear Weapons Program: Nuclear Weapons On-Demand*. Washington, D.C.: Institute for Science and International Security, 2018.

Alexander, McGill. *Hostage in Taipei: A True Story of Forgiveness and Hope*. Santa Rosa, CA: Cladach Publishing, 2000.

Alford, William P. *To Steal a Book Is an Elegant Offense: Intellectual Property Law in Chinese Civilization*. Stanford, CA: Stanford University Press, 1995.

Andrade, Tonio. *The Lost Colony: The Untold Story of China's First Great Victory over the West*. Princeton, NJ: Princeton University Press, 2011. Ball, John Dudley. *Dragon Hotel*. New York: Walker Weatherhill, 1969.

Berglund, Ken. *An American Teacher in Taiwan*. Scotts Valley, CA: CreateSpace, 2012.

Bergvelt, Joyce. *Lord of Formosa*. Manchester, England: Camphor Press, 2018.

Caldwell, John C. *China Coast Family*. Chicago, H. Regnery Co., 1953.

———. *Still the Rice Grows Green: Asia in the Aftermath of Geneva and Panmunjom*. Washington, D.C.: Henry Regnery Co., 1955.

Boehm, Lise. (pen name for Elisa Giles) *Playing Providence*. (Vol. 2 of China Coast Tales), Singapore: Kelly and Walsh, 1897.

————. *Formosa: A Tale of the French Blockade of 1884–1885.* (Vol. 6 of China Coast Tales). Shanghai: Kelly and Walsh, 1906.

Brown, Joshua. *Vignettes of Taiwan.* San Francisco: ThingsAsian Press, 2006.

Brown, Joshua Samuel, and Stephanie Huffman. *Formosa Moon.* San Francisco: ThingsAsian Press, 2018.

Caltonhill, Mark. *Private Prayers and Public Parades: Exploring the Religious Life of Taipei.* Taipei: Dept. of Information, Taipei City Government, 2002.

Campbell, William. *Formosa Under the Dutch: Described from Contemporary Records, with Explanatory Notes and a Bibliography of the Island.* London: Kegan Paul, 1903.

————. *Sketches from Formosa.* London, New York: Marshall Brothers, 1915.

Chang Hsiu-jung et al. *The English Factory in Taiwan: 1670–1685.* Taipei: National Taiwan University, 1995.

Clune, Frank. *Flight to Formosa: A Holiday and Fact-finding Tour of Nationalist China's Fortress of Freedom and the Ports of Hong Kong and Macao.* Sydney: Angus and Robertson, 1958.

Charette, Rick. *Reflections on Taipei: Expat Residents Look at Their Second Home.* Taipei: Dept. of Information, Taipei City Government, 2003.

Chin, Ko-lin. *Heijin: Organized Crime, Business, and Politics in Taiwan.* New York: M.E. Sharpe, 2003.

————. *Going Down to the Sea: Chinese Sex Workers Abroad.* Chiang Mai, Thailand: Silkworm Books, 2014.

Cole, J. Michael. *Officially Unofficial: Confessions of a Journalist in Taiwan.* Scotts Valley, CA: CreateSpace, 2014.

————. *Black Island.* Scotts Valley, CA: CreateSpace, 2015.

————. *Convergence or Conflict in the Taiwan Strait: The Illusion of Peace?* London: Routledge, 2016.

Copp, DeWitt S., and Marshall Peck, Jr. *The Odd Day*. New York: Morrow, 1962.

Craft, Stephen G. *American Justice in Taiwan: The 1957 Riots and Cold War Foreign Policy*. Lexington: University Press of Kentucky, 2015.

Crook, Steven. *Keeping Up With the War God: Taiwan, As It Seemed to Me*. Brighton, UK: Yushan, 2001.

———. *Dos and Don'ts in Taiwan*. Bangkok: IGroup Press, 2010.

———. *Taiwan: The Bradt Travel Guide*. Chalfont St. Peter, UK: Bradt Travel Guides Ltd., 2011, 2014, 2019.

Crook, Steven, and Katy Hui-wen Hung. *A Culinary History of Taipei: Beyond Pork and Ponlai*. Lanham, Maryland: Rowman & Littlefield, 2018.

Dalton, John. *Heaven Lake*. New York: Scribner, 2004.

Davidson, James W. *The Island of Formosa, Past and Present*. London; New York: Macmillan; Yokohama: Kelly & Walsh, 1903.

Day, Michael. *Fight for the Tiger: One Man's Battle to Save the Wild Tiger from Extinction*. London: Headline, 1995.

Department of Information, Taipei City Government. *Birdwatcher's Guide to the Taipei Region*. Taipei: Dept. of Information, Taipei City Government, 2004.

Dickson, Lillian. *These My People: Serving Christ among the Mountain People of Taiwan*. Grand Rapids, MI: Zondervan, 1958.

Duffield, Jessie. *Taiwan: A Travel Guide for Vegans*. Hsinchu, Taiwan: Jessie Duffield, 2015.

Easton, Ian. *The Chinese Invasion Threat: Taiwan's Defense and American Strategy in Asia*. Manchester, England: Camphor Press, 2017.

Erway, Cathy. *The Food of Taiwan: Recipes from the Beautiful Island*. Boston: Houghton Mifflin Harcourt, 2015.

Ezell, Scott. *A Far Corner: Life and Art with the Open Circle Tribe*. Lincoln: University of Nebraska Press, 2015.

Flood, James. *see* Spencer, D.J.

Groot, John. *Taiwanese Feet: My Walk Around Taiwan.* Clear Sky Communications , 2020.

Edwards, Jack. *Banzai, You Bastards!* London: Souvenir, 1991.

Fox, Melodie, and Shari Ho. *My Name Is Also Freedom: The Shari Ho Story.* Westminster, CA: Square Tree Publishing, 2018.

Franck, Harry A. *Glimpses of Japan and Formosa.* New York: Century, 1924.

Goedhart, Menno, and Cheryl Robbins. *The Real Taiwan and the Dutch: Traveling Notes from the Netherlands Representative.* Taipei: Taiwan Interminds Publishing, 2010.

Henley, J.W. *Bu San Bu Si: A Taiwan Punk Tale.* Manchester, England: Camphor Press, 2017.

Hong, Keelung, and Stephen O. Murray. *Looking Through Taiwan: American Anthropologists' Collusion with Ethnic Domination.* Lincoln: University of Nebraska Press, 2005.

———. *Taiwanese Culture, Taiwanese Society: A Critical Review of Social Science Research Done on Taiwan.* Lanham, Maryland: University of America Press, 1994.

Hopgood, Mei-ling. *Lucky Girl.* Chapel Hill, NC: Algonquin Books, 2010.

Huang, Marijane. *Beyond Two Worlds: A Taiwanese-American Adoptee's Memoir and Search for Identity.* Bloomington, IN: AuthorHouse, 2017.

Jordan, David K. *Gods, Ghosts, and Ancestors: Folk Religion in a Taiwanese Village.* Berkeley, London: University of California Press, 1972.

Jordan, David K., and David Overmyer. *The Flying Phoenix: Aspects of Chinese Sectarianism in Taiwan.* Princeton, NJ: Princeton University Press, 1986.

Kaser, David. *Book Pirating in Taiwan.* Philadelphia: University of Pennsylvania Press, 1969.

Katz, Paul R. *When Valleys Turned Blood Red: The Ta-pa-ni Incident in Colonial Taiwan.* Honolulu: University of Hawai'i Press, 2005.

Keating, Jerome F. *The Mapping of Taiwan: Desired Economies, Coveted Geographies.* Taipei: SMC Publishing, 2011

Keliher, Macabe. *Out of China, or Yu Yonghe's Tale of Formosa: A History of Seventeenth-century Taiwan.* Taipei: SMC Publishing, 2003.

———. *Small Sea Travel Diaries: Yu Yonghe's Records of Taiwan.* Taipei: SMC Publishing, 2004.

Kerr, George H. *Formosa Betrayed.* Boston: Houghton Mifflin, 1965.

Khortsa, Tsering N. *Searching for Buddha's Tooth: Personal Stories of Tibetan Culture.* Hong Kong: Inkstone Books, 2005. Knapp, Ralf. *Ferns and Fern Allies of Taiwan.* Taipei: KBCC Press & Yuan-Liou Publishing, 2011.

Lederer, William. *A Nation of Sheep.* New York: Norton, 1961.

Lederer, William, and Eugene Burdick. *The Ugly American.* New York: Norton, 1958.

Lin, Ed. *Ghost Month.* New York: Soho Crime, 2014.

———. *Incensed.* New York: Soho Crime, 2016.

———. *99 Ways to Die.* New York: Soho Crime, 2018.

Lin, Francie. *The Foreigner.* New York: Picador, 2008.

Lin, Hsiao-ting. *Accidental State: Chiang Kai-shek, the United States, and the Making of Taiwan.* Cambridge, MA: Harvard University Press, 2016.

Locke, T.C. *Barbarian at the Gate: From the American Suburbs to the Taiwanese Army.* Manchester, England: Camphor Press, 2014.

Lu, Alvin. *The Hell Screens.* New York: Four Walls Eight Windows, 2000.

Mackay, George Leslie. *From Far Formosa: The Island, Its People and Missions.* New York: F.H. Revell, 1896.

Mader, Eric. *A Taipei Mutt*. Taipei: Cheng Shang Publishing House, 2002.

Martinson, Barry. *Song of Orchid Island*. Taipei: Gabriel Press, 2006.

———. *Chingchuan Story*. Taipei: Gabriel Press, 2007.

McGovern, Janet B. Montgomery. *Among the Head-Hunters of Formosa*. London: T. Fisher Unwin, 1922.

Michener, James A. *The Voice of Asia*. New York: Random House, 1951.

Morris, Andrew D. *Colonial Project, National Game: A History of Baseball in Taiwan*. Berkeley, CA: University of California Press, 2010.

Moskowitz, Marc L. *The Haunting Fetus: Abortion, Sexuality, and the Spirit World in Taiwan*. Honolulu: University of Hawai'i Press, 2001.

O'Callaghan, Sean. *The Yellow Slave Trade: A Survey of the Traffic in Women and Children in the East*. London: Blond, 1968.

Patterson, Alan. *Crossing the Red Line: Consequences of Taiwan's Emergence as a Nuclear Proliferant*. Amazon Digital Services, 2018.

Peng Ming-min. *A Taste of Freedom. Memoirs of a Formosan Independence Leader*. New York: Holt, Rinehart and Winston, 1972.

Pickering, William Alexander. *Pioneering in Formosa: Recollections of Adventures Among Mandarins, Wreckers, and Head-hunting Savages*. London, Hurst & Blackett, 1898.

Psalmanazar, George. *An Historical and Geographical Description of Formosa, an Island Subject to the Emperor of Japan*. London:, 1704

———. *Memoirs of ****: Commonly Known as George Psalmanazar: A Reputed Native of Formosa*. London: R. Davis, J. Newbery, L. Davis, and C. Reymers, 1764.

Rea, Dennis. *Live at the Forbidden City: Musical Encounters in China and Taiwan*. Seattle, WA: Blue Ear Books, 2006, 2016.

Reid, Daniel K. *Chinese Herbal Medicine*. Boston: Shambhala, 1983.

———. *Insight Guide: Taiwan*. Singapore: APA Publications, 1984.

———. *The Tao of Health, Sex, and Longevity: A Modern Practical Guide to the Ancient Way*. New York; London: Simon & Schuster, 1989.

———. *Shots from the Hip: Sex, Drugs and the Tao*. Lamplight Books, 2019.

Reid, Daniel K., and R. Ian Lloyd. *Reflections of Taiwan*. Singapore: R. Ian Lloyd Publications, 1987.

Rutter, Owen. *Through Formosa: An Account of Japan's Island Colony*. London: T. F. Unwin, 1923.

Ryan, Shawna Yang. *Green Island*. New York: Alfred A. Knopf, 2016.

Seagrave, Sterling. *The Soong Dynasty*. New York: Harper & Row, 1985.

Shackleton, Allan James. *Formosa Calling*. Upland, CA: Taiwan Publishing Co., 1998.

Shepherd, John Robert. *Statecraft and Political Economy on the Taiwan Frontier, 1600–1800*. Stanford, CA: Stanford University Press, 1993.

Slimming, John. *Green Plums and a Bamboo Horse: A Picture of Formosa*. London: John Murray, 1964.

Smith, Robert W. *Secret Fighting Arts of the World*. Tokyo: Charles E. Tuttle Co.,1963.

———. *Chinese Boxing: Masters and Methods*. Tokyo; New York: Kodansha,1974.

———. *Martial Musings: A Portrayal of Martial Arts in the 20th Century*. Erie, PA: Via Media Pub. Co., 1999.

Sneider, Vern. *A Pail of Oysters*. New York: Putnam, 1953.

Stark, Gilbert Little. *Letters of Gilbert Little Stark, July 23, 1907–March 12, 1908*. Cambridge: Riverside Press, 1908.

Spencer, D.J. (pseudonym of James/Jim Flood) *The Jing Affair*. New York: Funk and Wagnalls, 1965.

Taylor, Jay. *The Generalissimo: Chiang Kai-shek and the Struggle for Modern China*. Cambridge, MA: Belknap Press of Harvard University Press, 2009.

Teng, Emma Jinhuang. *Taiwan's Imagined Geography: Chinese Colonial Travel Writing and Pictures, 1683–1895*. Cambridge MA: Harvard University Press, 2004.

Thornberry, Milo. *Fireproof Moth: A Missionary in Taiwan's White Terror*. Mechanicsburg, PA: Sunbury Press, 2011.

United States Department of Defense. *Pocket Guide to Taiwan*. Washington, D.C.: Office of Armed Forces Information and Education, 1958.

Voigt, Emily. *The Dragon Behind the Glass: A True Story of Power, Obsession, and the World's Most Coveted Fish*. New York: Scribner, 2016.

Ward, Sherry. *Finding Freedom Was Just the Beginning: God's Hand in the Journey*. Westminster, CA: Square Tree Publishing, 2018.

Wolf, Margery. *The House of Lim: A Study of a Chinese Farm Family*. Englewood Cliffs, NJ: Prentice-Hall, 1968.

———. *Women and the Family in Rural Taiwan*. Stanford, CA: Stanford University Press, 1972.

———. *A Thrice-Told Tale: Feminism, Postmodernism, and Ethnographic Responsibility*, Stanford, CA: Stanford University Press, 1992.

Wunderle, Nola. *Lost Daughter: A Daughter's Suffering, a Mother's Unconditional Love, an Extraordinary Story of Hope and Survival*. Labrador, Queensland: Phoenix Rising Press 2013.

Yu, Junwei. *Playing in Isolation: A History of Baseball in Taiwan*. Lincoln: University of Nebraska Press, 2007.

Also by John Grant Ross

Until the early twentieth century, Taiwan was one of the wildest places in Asia. Its coastline was known as a mariners' graveyard, the mountainous interior was the domain of headhunting tribes, while the lowlands were a frontier area where banditry, feuding, and revolts were a way of life. *Formosan Odyssey* captures the rich sweep of history through the eyes of Westerners who visited and lived on the island — from missionaries, adventurers, 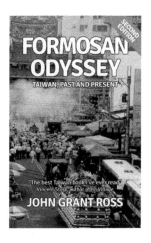 lighthouse keepers, and Second World War PoWs, to students coming to study martial arts. It finishes with the story of Taiwan's economic miracle, the political transition from police state to vibrant democracy, and its continuing stand-off with China.

The author's travels, made around the island in the wake of the devastating 921 earthquake, and his experiences from five years of living in a small town, provide an intimate picture of modern Taiwan.

The island is a storehouse of Chinese and indigenous cultures, a fascinating mix of the new and the traditional, and likewise *Formosan Odyssey* is a smorgasbord of delights that both the general reader and any "old Asia hand" will find informative and amusing.

Find out more at camphorpress.com/books/formosan-odyssey

Lightning Source UK Ltd.
Milton Keynes UK
UKHW020424030720
365940UK00001B/16/J